Fitness Swimming

SECOND EDITION

Emmett Hines

Human Kinetics

Library of Congress Cataloging-In-Publication Data

Hines, Emmett W., 1956-
    Fitness swimming / Emmett Hines. -- 2nd ed.
        p. cm.
    ISBN-13: 978-0-7360-7457-5 (soft cover)
    ISBN-10: 0-7360-7457-0 (soft cover)
    1. Swimming--Training. 2. Physical fitness. I. Title.
    GV837.7.H56 2008
    613.7'16--dc22

                            2008013353
ISBN-10: 0-7360-7457-0
ISBN-13: 978-0-7360-7457-5

This publication is written and published to provide accurate and authoritative information relevant to the subject matter presented. It is published and sold with the understanding that the author and publisher are not engaged in rendering legal, medical, or other professional services by reason of their authorship or publication of this work. If medical or other expert assistance is required, the services of a competent professional person should be sought.

Acquisitions Editor: Tom Heine; **Developmental Editor:** Amanda Eastin-Allen; **Assistant Editor**: Laura Podeschi; **Copyeditor:** Erich Shuler; **Proofreader:** Ann Meyer Byler; **Permission Manager:** Martha Gullo; **Graphic Designer:** Nancy Rasmus; **Graphic Artist:** Kim McFarland; **Cover Designer:** Keith Blomberg; **Photographer (cover):** Julian Finney/Getty Images; **Photographer (interior):** Emmett Hines, unless otherwise noted; **Photo Asset Manager:** Laura Fitch; **Photo Office Assistant:** Jason Allen; **Art Manager:** Kelly Hendren; **Associate Art Manager:** Alan L. Wilborn; **Illustrator:** Gary Hunt, unless otherwise noted. Illustrations on pages 28, 32, 33, and 52 by John Hatton; **Printer:** United Graphics

Human Kinetics books are available at special discounts for bulk purchase. Special editions or book excerpts can also be created to specification. For details, contact the Special Sales Manager at Human Kinetics.

Printed in the United States of America   10   9   8   7   6   5   4   3   2   1

Human Kinetics
Web site: www.HumanKinetics.com

United States: Human Kinetics
P.O. Box 5076
Champaign, IL 61825-5076
800-747-4457
e-mail: humank@hkusa.com

Canada: Human Kinetics
475 Devonshire Road Unit 100
Windsor, ON N8Y 2L5
800-465-7301 (in Canada only)
e-mail: info@hkcanada.com

Europe: Human Kinetics
107 Bradford Road, Stanningley
Leeds LS28 6AT, United Kingdom
+44 (0) 113 255 5665
e-mail: hk@hkeurope.com

Australia: Human Kinetics
57A Price Avenue
Lower Mitcham, South Australia 5062
08 8372 0999
e-mail: info@hkaustralia.com

New Zealand: Human Kinetics
Division of Sports Distributors NZ Ltd.
P.O. Box 300 226 Albany
North Shore City
Auckland
0064 9 448 1207
e-mail: info@humankinetics.co.nz

*This book is dedicated to John—my little brother,
a big friend, and a guy I admire greatly. I love ya, man.*

CONTENTS

PART IV
Training Over the Long Haul

PREFACE

It has been 10 years since I wrote the original *Fitness Swimming*. I've been quite pleased with the results of that endeavor. As I write this, that first edition is selling out the last bits of its third English-language printing. It has been translated into, and has been published in, Spanish, French, Chinese, and Turkish. College instructors have adopted *Fitness Swimming* as a textbook for a number of swimming and coaching courses. Swim coaches have built programs around the techniques and training principles espoused therein. Most satisfying of all, I've heard from hundreds of readers since the book's original release. I am indebted to everyone who has taken the time to tell me what they liked about the book and, more to the point, what they'd like to see changed or added if a second edition were ever considered.

The profession of coaching swimming is in its infancy. Martial arts masters have evolved their discipline over 10,000 years or so. The handful of decades in which the words *swimming* and *coach* have been uttered in close succession are a comparative blink of an eye. Methods of producing highly effective swimmers are evolving rapidly. Throughout the 25 years I've coached adults, I have maintained that if at any point I were to look back 5 years and realize that I was still teaching the same things in the same way, it would be time to find another line of work. So far, so good.

That statement, however, paints the original *Fitness Swimming* into a bit of a corner. You see, from the moment the first edition was published, my words on the page have remained both public and static, while what I teach my real-life athletes and how I teach it to them have changed. So, after a decade, a *Fitness Swimming* upgrade is due. In the following pages, you will find my current understanding of how swimming works—and of how best to improve your swimming. While the basic concepts in the original *Fitness Swimming* are the same, the *way* I express and apply them has changed—by a great deal, in some cases. I've expanded my discussions of many technique and training topics, added a number of new drills, and included 60 new practices—all to help you swim as effectively as possible, improve your conditioning, and enjoy the journey. Stay wet and swim smart.

ACKNOWLEDGMENTS

Swimming is both an individual sport and a team sport. A team's success depends on the performances of its individual swimmers. Those swimmers, in turn, rely on the team—i.e., swimmers, coaches, managers, and others—for training, facilities, instruction, motivation, inspiration, and everything else that helps them prepare for, and rise to, the competitive occasion. Neither do coaches work in a vacuum. I thank and acknowledge the following people in no discernable order, each of whom has helped, supported, or inspired me along the way (so far):

Coach Bill Boomer, who goes his own way and who unselfishly allows others to follow him and to look over his shoulder from time to time; Coach Mike Collins, who is a constant inspiration and role model; Coach Phil Hansel, who let me hang around and learn from him; Dr. Joel Bloom, for inspiring me to make a career of teaching; Coach Clay Evans, for demonstrating how to turn Masters coaching into a profession; Coach Max Zeller, for helping to spread the art of talent development around the world; Coach Dick Bower, for the cruise interval concept; Coach Terry Laughlin, who makes it all make sense; Dr. Ken Forster, for being a friend and co-conspirator; Coach Scott Rabalais, for his kind words, friendship, and example; Coach Glenn Mills, for his cutting-edge instruction and video imagery; Coach Richard Quick, for pushing the performance envelope through technique; author Phil Whitten, for his friendship and inspiration; astronaut Dr. Scott Parazynski, for testing some of my swimming theories in microgravity.

I must especially acknowledge the swimmers of H_2Ouston Swims for motivating me, for trusting me to use them as guinea pigs, and for being receptive to new ideas.

My wife, children, and parents are due loud and public acclaim for being patient and for continuing to put up with me while I try to save the world (or at least the swimming part of it).

PART I

Preparing to Swim

Swimming is one of the most popular of all fitness activities. It can be pleasurable, allowing for the physical expression of fluidity and grace as well as of power, speed, and stamina. Swimming conditions the cardiorespiratory system and it tones and strengthens the body. As such, it can be an excellent tool for improving and maintaining lifelong fitness.

Improperly done, though, swimming can be an exhausting and excruciating struggle that makes you feel like you are almost drowning. It is estimated that fewer than two percent of Americans who call themselves swimmers are able to swim more than 500 yards without stopping. It is technique, not physical conditioning, that limits most swimmers. Their technique causes them to waste so much energy that they fatigue quickly and must stop long before they receive any aerobic benefit. For these people, swimming is more of a survival skill than a fitness tool.

Perhaps you can swim for extended periods but you still have room for improvement. Perhaps you currently swim for fitness, or to train for a triathlon or for Masters competition, or perhaps just for the pleasure of being in the water. Regardless, chances are that you envy certain swimmers who are faster, more efficient, or simply look more like real swimmers.

Swimming is a technique-limited sport. It is more like golf in this respect than running or cycling. As with golf, almost anyone who is willing to spend enough time and effort practicing can learn and maintain the skills necessary for fluid, graceful swimming. The fitness payoff for such practice can be enormous. Few other activities offer a full-body workout that people can fully participate in even when they are well beyond the age at which participation in other sports is unthinkable.

Few swimmers, however, reach the fluid, graceful stage without following the plan of a coach, an instructor, a video, a book, or a combination thereof. My hope is that this book will serve as a kind of road map that will start or keep you on course to a lifelong, pleasurable, and beneficial relationship with the water.

The information in the first three chapters lays the groundwork for your training. Chapter 1 introduces you to swimming as a lifelong sport and covers the benefits of making a habit of swimming. Chapter 2 helps you choose the proper swimming equipment to fit your needs and offers suggestions on finding the best places to swim. Chapter 3 defines what swimming fitness is and helps you determine your current swimming skill and conditioning level. The information in these chapters will help you identify where you are starting, give you ideas for where you might want to go, and ensure you have what you need to start the journey.

CHAPTER 1

Lifetime Swimming

Swimming—there is no other truly lifelong sport. Babies are born with a natural affinity for water and its womblike feeling of security. Beginning with a baby's first bathtub experiences, there are numerous opportunities to develop a relationship with the water. From six months, parent-and-tot programs teach parents how to make their children's formative experiences with water safe, comfortable, and encouraging. Real swimming lessons begin as early as age three. In many areas of the country, children start racing in summer swim leagues as early as age five. Kids can stay involved in swimming through programs such as community summer leagues and USA Swimming's (USAS) age-group teams, then move on to high school swimming and then to college varsity and intramural swimming. United States Masters Swimming (USMS) is an extension of age-group swimming that offers organized training and competition for swimmers of all abilities age 18 or older. Masters competitions range from small local meets with a couple dozen swimmers lasting just a couple hours all the way up to international meets that draw thousands of competitors together for a week or more. Senior Olympics offers popular, though more limited, competitive opportunities for swimmers of all abilities age 50 and over. Of course, YMCA classes and community lap-swim classes are always an option. Many adults continue swimming literally until the day they die. It is common to see people in their 60s, 70s, or 80s swimming laps in lanes next to 20- or 30-year-old swimmers. In 1993, USMS amended its competition rules to add age groups for swimmers 100 years of age and up!

In this chapter we'll explore where you might fit into the broad spectrum of adult swimmers. Next we'll talk about the variety of benefits you can derive from claiming your rightful place among the chronically wet. Finally, I'll dispel the common myths that sometimes give an otherwise would-be swimmer pause.

Categories of Swimmers

Swimming is enjoyed by more Americans than any other sport. Certainly some of the 60 million Americans who indicate on questionnaires that they participate in swimming are referring to one week last summer when they waded knee-deep in the ocean and got their beach-baggies wet. Yet, if you visit a lap pool in the morning, during lunch, or after work and see the numerous fitness swimmers vying for lane space, you'll quickly come to appreciate that a large percentage of those 60 million Americans are, in fact, regular, serious swimmers. Chances are, if you ever immerse yourself farther than knee-deep into water, you fall into one of the following categories:

Novice Swimmer   You can swim one or two lengths of the pool without stopping. You use the crawl stroke or breaststroke, and you wouldn't drown if you were to fall into the deep end. In fact, you could swim a couple hundred yards if your life depended on it, but you probably have never swum more than 500 yards in one day.

Lap Swimmer   You swim a mile or more on a good day. You swim your last few lengths pretty fast so that you feel good and tired, or you time a couple of 50s if the pace clock is on. You swim freestyle well and maybe one more stroke well enough to do in public. We commonly refer to this largest segment of the fitness-swimming public as lap swimmers. Every day, millions of people head to a nearby pool to swim an hour or so of solitary laps.

Former Competitor   You have some competitive background—USAS, Amateur Athletic Union (AAU), high school, or college. You swim (or swam) all four competitive strokes. Although you rarely swim more than 1,000 yards, you are usually good for a couple of races at pool parties.

Competitor   You're a participating triathlete or a Masters swimmer. You compete often or occasionally. You work out regularly and swim 1,500 to 5,000 yards on a workout day. You do drills and interval work and probably swim with others whose ability is similar to yours or you belong to a Masters swim club.

Whichever group you are in, you can use this book to increase your involvement in swimming, whether for fitness or competition. If you're a novice swimmer, you will learn how the water affects your body and how you can use physical principles to make swimming easier. You will also learn how to use swimming as a fitness tool. If you're a lap swimmer, you will learn what it takes to look and move like an accomplished swimmer, using more efficient positions and motions. You will discover new ways to focus your training time so that it's more productive.

If you're a former competitive swimmer, you will find new information about swimming technique and conditioning that was not available during your earlier swimming years. As an active competitor, you will learn cutting-edge information about technique and training that you might have caught only snippets of from magazine articles, coaches, or training partners. This book will also give you ideas for using pool time efficiently when training on your own, whether at home or on the road.

No matter what level you are starting at with *Fitness Swimming*, you have a wide-open opportunity for improvement. By faithfully following a skill-building program and a progressive structure of workouts, you can develop your abilities far beyond what you might initially think possible. Even novice swimmers can improve to the point where they can experience the thrill of international competition or gain a lifelong fitness tool if they're willing to work hard and follow a proven plan.

Benefits of Swimming

Swimming is widely recognized by health and fitness professionals as a nearly perfect activity for improving aerobic fitness, flexibility, body strength, muscle tone, and coordination. Wear and tear on the body is an almost universal problem with any activity more strenuous than channel surfing. Swimming has the distinction of being the sport lowest in wear and tear, particularly if you use proper technique.

Coaches and trainers in virtually every sport acknowledge the efficacy of water exercise in various forms as an adjunct to their athletes' training. Whether it's a professional boxer using the natural resistance of water to make his punches more powerful, an Olympic 100-meter runner using water running to augment her sprint training, or a professional football or basketball player using water exercise as part of a physical therapy regimen, athletes in all sports are coming to water to improve their primary sports.

Swimming, quite simply, is the supreme form of water exercise. Challenging to the mind and the body, uplifting to the spirit and the flesh, swimming is a fascinating sport that can grab you, hold you, and keep you healthy for the rest of your life. "There are two things in existence that nobody thinks are bad for you—swimming and yogurt," says Leonard Goodman in the *Wall Street Journal*.

Aerobic Conditioning

If you canvas the ranks of fitness swimmers, you will find that a nearly universal goal is to improve aerobic fitness. Exercise intended to improve aerobic fitness affects two different yet related systems—the cardiorespiratory system and the muscular system—each of which has different conditioning components.

Any exercise that raises your heart rate higher than 120 beats per minute for longer than 20 minutes improves the cardiorespiratory system. The cardiorespiratory system is the well-known system of heart, lungs, and blood vessels that takes oxygen from the air you breathe into your lungs and transports it to the individual muscle cells where it will be used. Oxygen enters the lungs, diffuses through the capillary walls, and then enters your red blood cells.

Through a maze of various-sized blood vessels, the heart pumps these red blood cells, which are carrying their precious cargo of oxygen, to the capillaries that surround the muscle cells and fibers. Here, the transition from the cardiorespiratory system to the muscular system takes place.

Once the cardiorespiratory system delivers the red blood cells to a muscle cell, the oxygen diffuses across the muscle cell membrane and into the cell, where it helps produce energy for muscle contractions. The term *aerobic metabolism* identifies a complex set of chemical interactions that use fat, carbohydrate, and oxygen to produce energy for exercise. Aerobic conditioning causes a variety of adaptations within the muscle cell that improve the cell's ability to perform work for extended periods. Swimming properly involves a greater percentage of your body's muscle mass in aerobic exercise than any other popular activity. Cross-country skiing is the only other sport vying for this position.

Aerobic conditioning of any specific muscle occurs only when an exercise causes that particular muscle to contract repeatedly and consistently throughout the workout. It is no wonder that runners or cyclists who take up swimming find that, despite their excellent cardiorespiratory conditioning, swimming a few laps leaves them fatigued. They have spent time aerobically conditioning the sport-specific muscles of the legs but have done little or no conditioning of the upper body.

© Icon Sports Media

Swimming is a great way to attain a healthy body composition and maintain flexibility.

Muscular Strength Although swimming does not build huge, rippling muscles, even moderate-intensity distance swimming is excellent for improving strength and tone in several muscles, especially in the torso, shoulder, and arm. More experienced swimmers use high-intensity interval and sprint training to increase overall body strength. One of swimming's advantages is in developing functional strength throughout the large ranges of motion inherent in the sport.

Flexibility Improving flexibility may be one of the greatest benefits of swimming. It is an important factor that allows people to participate fully in swimming well past ages where they must discontinue participation in other sports. Because of the positions and large ranges of motion that swimmers ask the body to move through when making proper strokes, virtually all people who swim regularly become more flexible.

Body Composition   Much has been said over the years about whether swimming is a good way to get leaner. As with any form of exercise, the intensity with which you approach the sport determines, to a large extent, the results. You need only look at the evenly-toned, long-muscled bodies of swimmers mounting the blocks at any swimming competition to know that intense swim training can produce a body a person would be proud to wear almost nothing on. By the same token, there are plenty of people who go to the pool and just piddle around, applying the bare minimum of effort to slowly move from one end to the other. Those people are likely to complain that swimming does nothing for them. If they were to put the same amount of effort into running, cycling, or any other sport, those people would most likely have the same complaint.

Common Swimming Myths

Here are a few prominent myths about swimming that I must dispel.

- *Swimming in cold water causes your body to store fat.* There is a phenomenon called the cold-water immersion response that tends to spare body fat for insulation. As soon as you begin exercising at an intensity great enough to elevate your core temperature, however, this becomes a moot point. Most swimming pools are kept at 78 degrees or warmer, plenty warm to allow all but the thinnest people to elevate core temperature. In fact, if a pool is too warm, a swimmer can become overheated, which decreases work capacity and fat metabolism. Swimming in cool water allows greater exercise volume and intensity than does any exercise that is performed in air that is too hot. Even English Channel swimmers experience significant fat loss during their 55 °F (13 °C) ordeal. By far, intensity and duration most greatly influence fat metabolism.

- *Swimming is performed in a prone position, which means that your heart rates during training will be lower than in other sports. You therefore don't get as much of a workout.* Just being in the water reduces the amount of work that the heart must do to circulate your blood, because it no longer must pump against the force of gravity. While this does reduce your resting pulse rate, it has no influence over how hard you can push yourself. Regardless of training intensity and duration, the workout you can get in swimming is no less effective than if you invested the same intensity and time in another sport.

- *Swimming makes you hungry.* Okay, you got me. It is true that most swimmers tend to be hungry after workouts. The same is true in nearly every sport. But the timing of after-exercise hunger is more directly related to body temperature than to the type of exercise. You are less likely to be hungry when your core temperature is far above normal resting levels. Runners and cyclists generally have elevated body temperatures for longer periods after their workouts, postponing hunger. Swimmers, on the other hand, generally spend enough time in cool water after intense training to lower their body temperature enough that hunger seems more directly linked to the workout.

So now are you convinced? Swimming *will* be your next life challenge and passion. Now you need a swimsuit and a few other goodies and you're off to find a swimmin' hole!

CHAPTER 2

Getting Equipped

An appealing thing about swimming is that it requires very little equipment. Yet, for those who like to own every conceivable bit of paraphernalia that could be used in a sport, a variety of optional equipment is available. To follow the drills and workouts presented in this book, you'll need a bit more than the minimum. This chapter explains all the equipment you'll need and gives some hints about making the right selections when options exist. In addition, you'll learn about where it is best to put all your new stuff to use.

Essential Equipment

For less than the cost of a cheap date, you can have all the necessities for full participation in the sport—swimsuit, goggles, cap, towel, and water bottle. With this minimal outfit, you can get a workout or even compete in any suitable body of water. And when it's time to travel, you can take comfort in knowing that, with towels and water available everywhere, your suit, goggles, and cap are all you need in order to swim anywhere in the world. As you search for variety and shortened learning curves, you'll probably end up with more than the bare essentials, but this minimum configuration will come in handy.

Swimsuit

Of all the pieces of equipment you'll need, your suit is the most important. There are, in general, five types of suits in the swimsuit universe—competition suits (what *you* are looking for), high-performance suits (what competitors wear for important competitions), fashion suits (what you see in *Sports Illustrated*), casual swimwear (what cool people wear at the beach), and monstrosities (what my grandmother wears at the beach).

The term *competition suit* doesn't mean that the suit should be used only for competition. It is a term that describes a variety of suits that offer a minimum of drag in the water. If you swim laps, this is important. The key is to wear a suit that is comfortable but that snugly fits your body, leaving no loose fabric to flap around in the water.

Two common workout-suit materials are Lycra and polyester. If you stick with major brands, you'll get a 128-grade Lycra fabric that is more resistant to chlorine and mold than cheaper Lycra suits—well worth the extra expense. Lycra suits will stretch one full size within your first few sessions in the pool. If in doubt, buy one that is a bit small rather than too big. Polyester, on the other hand, will not stretch with use, so how it fits in the store is how it will continue to fit. It will last longer in chlorinated water than Lycra will, but many people find that it is not as comfortable. Not all suit styles are available in polyester. If you swim daily, get at least two suits. Putting on a cold, wet suit, especially first thing in the morning, is about as much fun as watching a cat cough up a fur ball.

For women, choosing a suit only begins with the size printed on the tag. Because swimming involves so much range of motion of the arms and shoulders, the way the back and strap configuration fits you will influence the way you move. Try on suits of various styles and manufacturers, making sure to stretch yourself into a full streamline position and to move your arms through swimming motions in order to see if the suit will hamper your movement.

It is particularly important to not get too big a suit. A suit that is not snug enough will catch large amounts of water and act as a drag chute. In general, if the shoulder straps can stretch higher than your ears, the suit might be too big. Women have the option of a one-piece workout suit (figure 2.1) or a two-piece workout bikini.

For men, for the most part, a suit is a suit is a suit. Once you decide which size fits you best, you will likely be happy with any suit from any of the major manufacturers. Some guys just can't bring themselves to wear skimpy little racing suits. Several manufacturers offer a line of fuller-cut suits with 4- or 5-inch (10 or 13 cm) side panels instead of the standard 3-inch (8 cm) side panels. Jammer suits (figure 2.1) that snugly cover the thighs are gaining popularity for workout swimming. Briefs (figure 2.2) are still the most popular style for workout swimming, however.

Figure 2.1 Women's one-piece workout suit and men's Jammers.

If none of these will suffice and you just have to have a pair of beach baggies, do yourself a favor and sew the pockets shut so that they don't balloon up like drag chutes as you plod down the lane.

Women's top-quality suits in the latest prints usually cost $50 to $75 U.S., and men's suits cost about $35 to $45, depending on style. In many swim shops you'll find a rack of discontinued prints of the same high-quality suits for as little as half the price of the latest prints. Additionally, now performance suits are made from high-tech materials that, according to the manufacturers' claims, offer less resistance to water flow than your skin does. Different styles of these suits cover different amounts of the body, up to full-body suits that cover all but the head, hands, and feet. Many competitors wear these for high-level competition. Because they cost anywhere from $150 to $500 or more and can be worn only a few times, these suits are not for workout swimming. But who knows—if you follow the advice in this book, you might one day need one!

Figure 2.2   Men's briefs.

Goggles

Goggles maintain a small pocket of air directly in front of the eyes, and they have a transparent lens that allows for nearly normal vision. They also protect swimmers' eyes from the discomfort of chlorine exposure.

Modern materials and a growing swimming population that is willing to part with its cash have spawned an abundance of inexpensive, compact, lightweight, comfortable goggle styles. Only a few of those styles, however, are likely to be right for you. Aside from your swimsuit, there is nothing within your control that will more greatly affect your comfort and appreciation for swimming than the right pair of goggles. Here are a few things to consider when choosing your perfect pair of goggles.

Shape   The two basic shapes for goggles are what I refer to as "sort of round" and "more oval." If you find one pair of oval goggles that works well for you, then most likely any goggle that works well for you will be more oval in shape. The same kind of thinking also applies if you find that a pair of sort-of-round goggles works well.

Nosepieces   Most goggle styles come with an adjustable nosepiece that is made of plastic, silicone, or string, which, once properly adjusted, will seldom, if ever, need readjustment. Some models have nonadjustable, molded nosepieces that are part of the frame. These are fine if you have average nose and eye placement.

Straps   A good-fitting pair of goggles will stick to your face without the strap. They stay on simply because of a bit of suction and a good seal. Nevertheless, the strap keeps your goggles in place while swimming. A wide, light-colored strap that allows plenty of space to write your name on it is a plus in case you lose your goggles. A double or split strap may stay in place better than a single strap because the forces are spread around more parts of the head.

Strap Adjustment   One of the things you can judge about a pair of goggles before you reach the checkout counter is whether the strap and buckle system allows for easy adjustment. Swimmers with arthritis or any other dexterity-limiting condition should pay particular attention to this. It doesn't get any easier to adjust the goggles when you're poolside.

Gaskets   The gasket is the soft material around the goggle's eyecup that fills the voids at the goggle-to-face union. There are several types to choose from: foam, silicone, polyvinyl, or none. For simplicity, ease of care, and length of service, "none" tops the list. Popular Swedish-style goggles have no gasket, allowing for the most streamlined, face-hugging fit. If, however, your face doesn't have the same contours as the goggle, you will be happier with a gasketed goggle. Solid silicone or polyvinyl gaskets make a good seal if the goggle is the correct shape for your face, and they offer excellent resistance to microbial growth. Foam gaskets, although more forgiving in making a leakproof seal, are prone to grow low-order life-forms if not properly maintained.

Lens Color   Goggle lenses come in a variety of colors and shades. If you plan to swim outdoors in daylight, you should stick with darker goggles that have UV protection.

Antifog Properties   Goggles fog up when moisture in the warm air trapped in the eyecup condenses on the inside surface of the goggle, which has been cooled by the surrounding water. Many goggles on the market tout antifog properties. In addition, antifog sprays or liquids are available. You can make your own by mixing equal parts baby shampoo and water. I have yet to encounter, through experience or anecdote, any better antifog system than good ol' swimmer's spit. A thin coating of saliva on the inside of the eyecup keeps it from fogging for a good portion of your workout. Alternatively, a few drops of pool water in the eyecup, just enough to roll around freely, works a bit like windshield wipers for a long swim.

People who wear glasses or contacts need not swim blind. Many contact-lens wearers are afraid to wear their lenses with goggles. You are less likely to lose lenses while swimming, however, than you are while taking them out and putting them back in. You will be much happier if you keep your lenses in while swimming because you'll be able to see. If you wear glasses, check with your optometrist about prescription goggles or prescription inserts for your favorite goggles. There are also off-the-rack corrective-lens goggles available through swim shops and Web sites. You likely can find a pair that allows you to read a pace clock from across the pool.

Price has nothing to do with which goggle is right for a given swimmer. Your goggles could easily be the least expensive item in your swimming bag—or they could just as easily be the most expensive. Most swimmers are able to find a comfortable, leak-free fit in the low end of the price range. Yet many a swimmer doggedly applies the "whatever it takes" attitude to fussing with an expensive pair of goggles, trying in vain to coax perfection from them. After spending $30-plus on a pair of the latest high-tech goggles, some people are loath to abandon their investment for a pair of $5 goggles that they know will fit better. Once you find your perfect goggle, buy several pairs. Murphy has a law. I don't recall the exact wording, but it has something to do with the availability, at any point in the future, of the only goggle style that fits *your* face.

Swimming Cap

For anyone whose hair is more than a few inches long, a swimming cap is a necessity. Caps are one size fits all and serve multiple purposes, including keeping your hair out of your eyes, nose, and mouth; affording less water resistance than hair; keeping your hair from absorbing too much chlorine; coordinating with your swimming ensemble; and proclaiming your affiliation.

The three common materials for caps are latex, silicone, and Lycra. Latex caps are the most popular and the least expensive, and they fit most swimmers. Silicone caps are more expensive and they last longer (unless they get even a slight tear, in which case they are instant history). Silicone caps are harder to keep in place, and they work well for fewer swimmers. Lycra caps are the least popular and most expensive. They look funky and they don't protect your hair at all. I'm not sure why there is a market for them.

Regardless of what kind of cap you use, dry it thoroughly after each use. Dust it lightly with baby powder before you store it. Avoid leaving it wadded up in the bottom of your bag or in a hot car. Carry several, in case one becomes damaged.

Water Bottle

Despite being immersed in cool water, your body still perspires when you swim, and you are constantly blowing off water vapor as you breathe. Replenishing that water is vital to a safe and productive workout. Drink before you get thirsty and drink more than you think you need. You will want a container with a cap on it that will keep out water that could be splashed into the container from the pool. If you train outdoors in the hot sun, you will want an insulated water bottle, or you can freeze a half-full liter-size water bottle overnight. Just before you head to the pool, fill the bottle the rest of the way with water, which will provide you with cold water throughout your workout. Even if it is just an old milk jug full of tap water, bring this precious elixir of life to the pool with you.

Supplemental Equipment

For the person who doesn't feel complete until he is surrounded by equipment and gadgets, there are plenty of additional products available to complement the basics. The drill progressions and workouts in this book call for the use of several more pieces of equipment than just the essentials. Some offer fitness benefits, others help you master skills more quickly, and others will help keep you motivated, organized, and on track. The following equipment will add variety, utility, and a bit of fun to your training.

Training Fins   If you follow the workouts in this book, you will want at least one pair of training fins. Fins extend your feet and legs, making your kick faster and more efficient. They help increase ankle flexibility and leg strength, and they also activate more muscle mass, all of which will shorten the learning curve for many of the skills you'll be working on. Plus, you'll find that the extra speed they provide when you swim is simply lots of fun.

Most fins are made of natural rubber and give good service for several years if properly cared for. Some are made of silicone, which lasts longer than rubber. Others are made of a nearly indestructible high-density, heat-treated polyurethane that will last forever. You might want two pairs of fins: a pair of short training fins (with a blade length of 1 or 2 inches, or 2.5 or 5 cm) and a pair of normal-size training fins (with a blade that is roughly the same length as your foot). Avoid rigid fins, blades that are more than one-and-a-half times wider than your foot, and blades that are longer than your foot, because any of these will be detrimental to your technique. Also avoid fins that float quickly to the top of the pool or that sink quickly. Ideally, your fins should be almost neutrally buoyant. Unless you have *very* flexible ankles (a very small percentage of adults do, and runners almost never do), opt for the most flexible fins you can find.

Training Snorkel   If you follow the workouts in this book, you will want a training snorkel. This type of snorkel is designed specifically for swim training. It mounts in the center of your forehead and curves over the top of your head to allow for a proper head position. For several of the drills, many of the skills, and much of the swimming described herein, a proper snorkel will remove the distraction of turning to breathe so that you can concentrate on other aspects of your technique. If you are not used to snorkels, understand that it takes a while to get comfortable with one, but it is well worth the effort. Two models are offered by Finis (www.finisinc.com). One is called the Swimmer's Snorkel (figure 2.3), which is the best choice for most swimmers, and one is called the Freestyle Snorkel, which is a bit harder to use but promotes further skill refinement in more skilled swimmers.

Heart-Rate Monitor   Electronic heart-rate monitors for swimming are becoming more popular. A monitor with a watch-style display and a sensor that straps around the chest is the only accurate way to get heart-rate readings for swimming. Heart-rate monitors work very well for women because they are worn under the suit and they stay in place well. Some men, however, find a heart-rate monitor uncomfortable for extended use because it must be tight enough to not slip down the body when pushing off from the wall. If you follow the workouts in this book, a heart-rate monitor is strongly recommended. See chapter 6 for details on using a monitor in your training.

Figure 2.3 The Swimmer's Snorkel.

Pace Clock or Training Watch

Most workouts are organized in an interval-training format that requires a visible timing device. If the pool you frequent does not have a pace clock, you will want to provide a timing device. The ideal device is a portable 15-inch (38 cm) analog pace clock with a sweeping second hand and minute hand. The face is numbered from 5 to 60 in 5-second jumps, with small tick marks for each second in between. A more portable solution is a personal pace clock or timer that is designed to sit at the end of your lane, either on the deck or in the gutter. This can be a workable option for people who have a hard time seeing a pace clock at a distance. Yet another alternative is a sports watch with a timer. Look for one with multiple stopwatch functions, including lap-split memory with countdown and count-up interval timers. Some heart-rate monitors include sports-timer functions in the watch portion of their system. Two drawbacks to using a watch-type timer are that you can't see it without stopping your swim, and that recording lap splits requires reaching over with your other hand to press a button, which is awkward at best. It is difficult, however, to beat the portability of a watch.

Tempo Beeper   These small electronic-pacing devices slide under your cap or attach to your goggle strap. You set a specific beep tempo to match your stroke to, and then bone conduction transmits the tones to your inner ear. Tempo Trainer and Wetronome are common tempo beepers for swimming.

Waterproof Notebook   A poolside notebook allows you to keep track of times, jot down training notes, and record those "Aha!" moments (and maybe even capture a phone number or two) without getting out of the water. Look for Wet Notes and Wet Log waterproof notebooks. In a pinch, you can cut Tyvek envelopes into sheets and then use a pencil to write on them poolside.

Equipment Bags   So you took this book to the local swim shop and said, "I'll have one of each, two of some." You now have a pile of stuff to schlep back and forth. Invest your last couple of sawbucks in two good swim bags. First, get a nylon-mesh drawstring bag for wet pool toys (fins, snorkel, and the like). Then get a conventional workout bag for the usual locker-room stuff. It should have one or two external mesh pockets for damp suits and goggles and a waterproof compartment for wet towels. A waterproof bottom also comes in handy around constantly wet pool decks.

Though you'll see swimmers use other items at the pool, they aren't necessary for improving your swimming. In fact, some of them could indeed be detrimental. Until you have mastered the skills and workouts in this book, stay away from pull buoys, kickboards, hand paddles, wrist weights, swimming gloves, and the like. My bet is that once you have mastered the *Fitness Swimming* program, you'll find that you have no need or desire to use them.

Where to Swim

Where do you go to put all your new stuff to best use? As with any activity, the environment affects your enjoyment of swimming, influencing how often you participate in it and how long you stick with it. Sometimes you have little choice over where you swim. If there's only one swimming hole available and only one hour of the day for lap swimming, then you have to make due. Usually, though, you will have a variety of swimming options from which to choose. Swimming in different pools, at different times of day, with different people, sometimes in open water—all these things tend to make for a fulfilling swimming experience. Always be on the lookout for a swimming experience that's different from your normal routine.

Pool Swimming

Most lap pools in the United States are either 25 yards or 25 meters in length and are referred to as short-course pools. In many hotel, motel, and fitness facilities, space limits a pool's size to 20 yards in length, sometimes even to 15 yards. Long-course pools have 50-meter lanes (this is the length of an Olympic-size pool), and most are either 25 yards or 25 meters wide so that, during certain periods or seasons, the lane lines can be installed across the pool to allow for short-course swimming.

The only requirements for a lap pool are clean, clear water that is at least a meter deep and wave-quelling lane markers, which are tightly stretched cables with 3- to 5-inch (8 to 13 cm) diameter floats and discs that run the length of the pool. They define and control the space for swimming laps and absorb most surface waves. Ideally, you'll find a pool that has a section with deep water—there are a couple of drills you will learn that will require it.

78 to 82 degrees Fahrenheit (25.5 to 27.8 degrees Celsius) is considered an optimal temperature range for lap swimming. 78 degrees will likely seem cold at first, but once you have been moving for a while, it'll feel fine. A strenuous workout in water over 82 degrees can get uncomfortably warm, and in water over 85 degrees Fahrenheit (29.4 degrees Celsius), you can risk overheating. On the other end of the spectrum, most people can adapt over time to temperatures in the high 60s Fahrenheit (upper teens to low 20s Celsius) as long as they continue working hard enough to maintain body temperature. Temperature in indoor pools is usually controlled within a degree or two. Outdoor pool temperatures are affected more by the weather, but in some parts of the country, outdoor pools operate year-round. They are heated with gas, solar, or geothermal systems in the winter and they are cooled by aeration or geothermal systems in the summer.

Swimmers commonly complain about chlorine, which tenaciously attaches itself to the skin and hair. Consistent exposure can also make hair feel and act like straw. Your skin and hair absorb water, mostly when you first get wet. If you take a shower, so that tap water is absorbed first, it tends to block out pool water, which typically has 2 to 10 times as much chlorine as tap water. A cap will help even more, especially if you rub a dab of conditioner into your wet hair first.

Lap-Swimming Etiquette

Whether swimming as part of a group workout or just by yourself during a crowded lap-swim session, you are likely to share lane space with others from time to time. Everyone's water time is more enjoyable when everyone knows and lives by the basic rules of swimming etiquette. You don't want to be charged with antisocial behavior while nearly naked.

Read the Signs   Your pool may have signs with the local guidelines for swimming etiquette, lane speed, circle patterns, use of equipment, and the like. If so, follow the posted rules.

Equipment   Neatly stack any personal equipment at the pool's edge in order to leave room for other swimmers' equipment and to minimize tripping hazards. Mark your personal equipment to avoid confusion.

Fragrances, Hair Products, Skin Products   A small percentage of people are adversely sensitive to the fragrances in various hair and skin products. Deep breathing during exercise and nasal irritation from chlorine in the water tend to make a larger percentage of swimmers ultrasensitive during workouts. Fragrant hair and skin products rinse off in the pool and become concentrated at the surface, right under people's noses. Even fragrance-free products end up in the pool—and thus in other swimmers' ears, eyes, noses, and mouths. Please, take a shower before you hit the water.

Lap-Swimming Etiquette, *continued*

Oral Hygiene   You will be breathing heavily near other heavy breathers. Avoid embarrassment and make your presence a joy to others by brushing your teeth and using mouthwash just before hitting the water.

Sports Drinks and Coffee   A crowded lane usually has a number of beverage bottles at the end of it on the deck. Be sure to mark yours plainly to avoid midworkout confusion. Coffee is never an appropriate pool-edge beverage, even with a lid on your cup. It has a strong odor that easily wafts across several lanes. Many people find the odor unpleasant (or downright nauseating) when breathing deeply. (As for coffee breath, see the previous paragraph.)

Selecting and Entering a Lane   Never dive into a lane that has people swimming in it. Find a lane where swimmers of your speed are doing their laps and communicate with them so that they know that you are about to join them. If they are swimming nonstop, slip feet-first into the right-hand corner of the lane and stay there long enough for everyone to cycle through the lane and to see that a new swimmer is about to join the fray. Then begin swimming at the same speed as the rest of the people in that lane.

Circle Pattern   Three or more swimmers in a lane must swim in a circle pattern in order to avoid head-on collisions—each swimmer stays to the right of the lane. Each swimmer should leave at least a five-second gap between himself or herself and the next swimmer. If you stop for any reason, it is your responsibility to stay out of the way of everyone who is still swimming.

Drafting   Just as in cycling, swimming close behind somebody allows you to benefit from the effort of that swimmer. It may be tempting to tuck in behind someone and let that swimmer do most of the work, but it is considered bad form and can lead to ugly locker-room gossip.

Passing and Getting Passed   Even in well-matched lanes, passing or getting passed is sometimes unavoidable when circle swimming. In general, the person doing the passing should move to the center of the lane, speed up, and finish the pass quickly. The slower swimmer should anticipate being passed, stay close to the lane rope, slow down a bit, and let the faster swimmer pass quickly. Stopping briefly in the corner to allow a faster swimmer to turn and take the lead is okay. A tap on your foot means someone wants to pass you—act accordingly. If you are frequently passing people or being passed, you probably belong in another lane.

At the Wall   Regardless of how many swimmers are using a lane, it is everyone's responsibility to keep clear the center third of the wall for other swimmers who are either turning or finishing. When you stop at the wall, move quickly to a corner of the lane.

Do Unto Others   Treat your lane partners with respect and expect the same from them. Even a crowded lane can be a joy when everyone has this attitude.

When the Party's Over   As soon as you've finished your workout, leave the lane and let someone else use it.

Open-Water Swimming

Many swimmers eschew the black line for a more natural setting. Virtually anywhere you can find clean water warmer than 55 degrees Fahrenheit (12.8 degrees Celsius), you will find open-water swimming enthusiasts. Experts agree that you should always swim in a properly supervised open-water swimming area. You can easily get into trouble if you swim on your own, especially if you are swimming in an unfamiliar area or in conditions you aren't used to. Properly supervised, open-water swimming is a great way to log many unfettered miles, and it gives the sport a whole new feel. Try an ocean, lake, or quarry swim sometime. This is where true distance swimming takes place—everything else is just practice.

CHAPTER 3

Assessing Your Swimming Fitness

You have rendered unto Caesar in return for a full bag of swim goodies, and you have located a near-perfect swimming hole. There remains one task to complete before you launch yourself into the blue and start stroking with abandon. You must get a feel for your current level of swimming fitness. This chapter defines what swimming fitness is and describes two types of swimming tests that, in combination, will pinpoint your level of swimming fitness.

Defining Swimming Fitness

My operating definition of fitness for swimming is as follows: Fitness is the ability to express the technique you have developed over whatever time you choose, at whatever intensity you choose. Fitness is specific to the task at hand. A person may have a high level of fitness for distance running or for cycling yet be completely unfit for swimming. A person might be fit for swimming long distances yet be unfit for sprinting one length of the pool.

The terms *health* and *fitness* are often used in the same breath, as if they were inseparable. Although it is true that if you have a high level of fitness, you have a greater likelihood of being healthy, the converse is not necessarily true. You can be healthy in the sense of being illness and injury free, yet be completely unprepared for any prolonged or intense physical exertion. Before you start your swimming training program, check with your physician to be sure that you can handle the added stress of exercise at a variety of intensities.

If you are in good health and already exercise vigorously on a regular basis, you can probably handle 45-minute (or longer) swim-training sessions at a moderate pace with relatively short rest periods. If you exercise only occasionally or only at moderate levels, you may need to take longer rest breaks during a training session. If you are a NEBAB (never ever been athletic before), you may need to take frequent, longer breaks and swim or drill more slowly. Beginning a new physical activity when you are at a low fitness level can be frustrating if your expectations are too high. You should count your initial trips to the pool as major accomplishments even if you get tired easily or feel pooped. Moving from relative inactivity into a fitness activity is a big change that takes a while for your body to get used to. Keep after it. The lower your initial fitness level, the greater your rewards will be in the near future.

Testing Swim Fitness

Highly effective swimming is considered to be roughly 70 percent technique and only about 30 percent conditioning. A person may have a high fitness level for a variety of sports, but if he lacks effective swimming technique, he will be unable to swim very far or very fast. His ineffective stroke wastes most of the energy he puts into the effort and produces minimal forward motion. On the other hand, consider the former elite-level competitive swimmer who has been sedentary for 10 years and is now in poor condition. Though he doesn't have much energy to spare, he'll likely be able to swim farther and faster than many people who are in better shape, because the excellent technique habits he ingrained long ago still allow him to take long, smooth, effective strokes that are highly propulsive and waste little energy.

For a swimming training program to be enjoyable and productive, the training regimen must enhance both elements of swimming effectiveness— technique and conditioning. I encourage you to think of this book as a detailed roadmap leading to highly effective swimming—swimming that combines the efficiency of great technique and the fitness and energy reserves of great conditioning. Before a map can help you get anywhere, you must locate the "You are HERE" mark. The two swimming tests described here will mark your starting point on the road to highly effective swimming. They will precisely test, in two ways, the effectiveness of your current swimming. And as you engage in the *Fitness Swimming* program, these tests will be used from time to time to mark your progress along that road. The improvements you chart after each test will help motivate you to continue. It's time to get your new swimming suit wet. Your entrance exam is about to begin.

T-20 Swim

The idea of the T-20 swim test is to see how far you can swim in 20 minutes. This test is an excellent practical indicator of your swimming ability and is an ideal way to assess both your technique and conditioning levels at the same time.

1. Swim any stroke or combination of strokes as far as possible in 20 minutes. You must count your laps. (A lap in a pool is two lengths, which means, as on a running track, returning to where you started. In a 25-yard pool, one lap is 50 yards; in a 50-meter pool, one lap is 100 meters.) Strive for an even pace throughout the swim. Do not speed up in the last two

minutes of the swim. During the swim, if you need to stop and rest for short periods, you may do so. The clock keeps ticking, however, and these rest periods are part of your elapsed time.

2. At the end of the swim, finish the lap you are on when 20:00 ticks by. Note your elapsed time when you complete that lap. This means you will have an elapsed time that is a bit *over* 20:00. (For example, near the end of the swim, you arrive at the wall and the pace clock shows that you have been swimming for 19:40. You need to swim one more lap. When you complete that lap, the clock shows 20:30. Now you are finished.)

3. Upon completing the swim, take your immediate heart rate (IHR) reading. If you have a heart-rate monitor, use the reading that appears immediately after you finish swimming. Otherwise, take a manual heart rate (more about heart rates and how to take them is included in part II).

Once you complete your swim, record in your waterproof notebook three pieces of information, as shown in the following example. Note that these figures provide a sample of possible outcomes for the T-20 test and are not a guideline for you to shoot for.

Number of yards (or meters) you swam	*1,250*
Your IHR after the swim	*150*
Elapsed time of the swim	*20:32*

Once you have recorded the information, swim or tread water easily for at least five minutes in order to cool down.

After your swim, you will look up and record your T-20 cruise pace—your average pace per 100 yards (or meters) during the swim (refer to page 206). This is the fastest pace you can swim for an extended time, and it indicates your combined swimming fitness and ability level (in the above example, it would be 1:38.4). Later you will learn to use your cruise pace to determine training speeds and intervals during some of the practices in the workout section of the book.

You can repeat the T-20 swim test often, perhaps once per week. There are three ways to note an improvement in your T-20 performance: if you swim at a faster average pace (T-20 Cruise Pace Per 100 Chart in appendix A), if you swim the same pace but show a lower IHR, or if you have a lower average stroke count (as you read this book and start doing some practices, you will become aware of how many strokes you take to swim a length of the pool). Over the long haul, the best way to make the largest improvements in your T-20 swims is to focus your efforts on technique and efficiency.

After you have swum a few T-20s, you will feel confident enough to do T-30 swims. The concept and execution are the same as with the T-20, except that you swim for 30 minutes instead of 20 minutes. Use the T-30 chart in appendix B to chart your progress in the T-30 tests. See page 202 for a blank chart that

Be sure to take your heart rate immediately after finishing the T-20 swim test.

you can photocopy and then use to keep track of your T-20 and T-30 swim performances, which will allow you to easily see your progress over time.

Swimming Golf

Swimming golf is more a test of technical ability than conditioning, and it can be used as a benchmark to indicate technique improvement over a period of time. The rules are as follows:

1. Swim 50 yards (or meters), counting the total number of strokes you take—count once for each hand as it enters the water. (If you are in a short-course pool and you take 21 strokes on the first length followed by 22 strokes coming back, your total is 43.)

2. At the end of the swim, note your elapsed swim time in seconds. (Let's say the swim took 47 seconds.)

3. Add the number of strokes to the number of seconds. The total is your score for that swim. (Add the 43 strokes to the 47 seconds for a total of 90.)

4. Take as much rest as you want, and repeat from number 1, this time attempting to get a lower score—hence the name "swimming golf."

5. Do this four times and average your scores. This is your par the next time you include a swimming golf set in your workout. (Say your scores are 90, 89, 89, 88. Your average, or new par, is 89.)

Over 50 yards, better swimmers take fewer strokes in less time than less-accomplished swimmers. In a typical Masters group, 50-yard freestyle golf scores can easily range from the high 40s to more than 100. Start lowering your scores by lowering your stroke count. Once you get comfortable with a lower stroke count, try to increase stroke tempo (how often you take strokes) without adding any strokes. Every time you hit a new, lower score, you have become a better swimmer.

If you swim with others, swimming golf allows people of different abilities to compete head to head. Two experienced swimming golfers can take turns swimming 50s and then compare their score for each swim to their personal par, keeping score over several 50s. Jotting down numbers in your waterproof notebook between swims makes it easy to keep track of your scores. You can photocopy the blank Swimming Golf (SGolf) Performances chart, found on page 203, in order to to keep track of your swimming-golf performances so that you can easily see your progress over time.

PART II

Swimming the Right Way

Let's face it: The human body wasn't designed for swimming. Human beings were not intended to leap headlong into a river and chase after their dinner. God gave the greatest of the apes the power of reason and thus the fly rod came to be. If a person should fall into that river, the instinct to lift his head toward the heavens, thrash about wildly, and scrabble his hairy carcass back onto the shore would serve immediate survival needs well enough. The advance of civilization, however, has allowed those of us at the top of the food chain to spend our idle time tinkering with nature. As such, we have made modest progress in the area of aquatic travel.

By far, the most popular swimming stroke is the *freestyle* stroke. In competitive swimming, there are four regulation strokes—butterfly, backstroke, breaststroke, and freestyle. The first three have very specific and constraining rules that govern how you perform the strokes. In contrast, according to the rules, a freestyle event may be swum in any manner the swimmer chooses as long as she or he completes the distance without using the bottom or sides of the pool or the lane ropes for propulsion.

Most swimmers choose some variation of the crawl stroke for freestyle events. This is because, when swum properly, the crawl is the fastest, most efficient method of moving through the water. Thus, the term *freestyle* has become the standard term for the crawl. In addition to being the fastest stroke, freestyle is the easiest to learn and is therefore the overwhelming favorite of fitness swimmers. I concentrate entirely on refining and training the freestyle stroke in this book. Nevertheless, many of the concepts, fundamentals, and drills that I describe and build into the workouts in this book also apply to one or more of the other three strokes.

Running and, to a large extent, cycling involve relatively simple and instinctive patterns and ranges of motion. Athletes have found that in both sports, speed, endurance, and technique all improve dramatically by simply training more or harder. This is why most running and cycling training regimens concentrate chiefly on conditioning rather than on technique. Swimming is an entirely different animal. It involves a complex set of repetitive, rhythmic motions. The level of coordination required to execute fluid, efficient swimming strokes is almost beyond comprehension. And because swimming motions and positions are by no means natural, we find that "just doing it" isn't enough to improve technique.

When we watch athletes perform, our eyes, and thus our attention, are naturally drawn to where we see the largest motions—a pitcher's throwing arm, a golfer's arms and club, a karate master's arms and legs. As a result, we tend to describe and then learn these sports using the appendages as a starting point. Yet in each of these sports, the most critical actions and postures begin in, and radiate from, the body's core. Without mastery of central-line posture, balance, and coordination of the appendages relative to the core, the pitcher tosses cream puffs, the golfer slices short into the weeds, and the karateka winds up on the mat. Similarly with swimming, we tend to focus almost entirely on the motions of the arms and, to a lesser degree, the legs. Thus, most self-taught swimmers tend to swim by focusing on just their arms and legs. They yank their arms backward through the water with the hope that this will move them forward; they rely on their kick to push them forward like a motorboat and to haul their torso along like cargo. The result is usually an effort-filled struggle down the lane rather than a flow of graceful strokes.

Part II employs an inside-out approach to teaching highly effective swimming. In chapter 4, you'll learn how to use your core muscles to organize your critical body masses into a water-worthy vessel. Next, you'll learn and master fully-supported aquatic balance in a variety of positions and through a variety of motions. You'll learn how to drive the fundamental motions of freestyle swimming with the largest muscles in the body. Chapter 5 introduces full-stroke swimming and provides drills for building your stroke. This approach lays down a foundation of concepts and skills, then builds on that foundation in a logical sequence of manageable steps.

Carefully practicing the skills of swimming allows you to continually improve, while conditioning becomes a by-product of the effort spent practicing those skills. In contrast, mindlessly plodding back and forth between the end walls is like trying to improve your tennis game by simply running back and forth between the baselines of the court. You know intuitively that in order to become an excellent tennis player, you need to practice backhand drills, forehand drills, shot-placement drills, serving drills, and then to use those skills as you play the game. So too with swimming.

My conditioning program is built around practicing drills and exercises that become increasingly complex with each chapter but that condition the muscles and ranges of motion that are required for repeating those skills over long distances. Each drill has one or more feedback tools that will help you determine whether you are doing the drill correctly.

In this part of the book, I also use numerous focus points, each of which distills a complex concept down to a few words. Pay special attention to these points, because I refer to them repeatedly throughout the text and workouts. The concepts will be important not only throughout the rest of the book but for as long as you continue swimming.

CHAPTER 4

Posture and Balance

It is important to understand how the human body interacts with the water. This involves understanding the nature of the medium through which you are moving and understanding how to orient and control your body to maximize the beneficial effects of water while minimizing its detrimental effects. This chapter covers various types of resistance to aquatic motion and how posture and balance can help you avoid much of that resistance. Then it details a variety of drills and focus points that will help you improve your posture and balance skills. Subsequent chapters teach you effective stroke technique. Before diving in, let's explore the alien aquatic environment and how we relate to it.

Resistance to Aquatic Motion

Most of a swimmer's energy is used to overcome resistance. Even world-class swimmers spend more than 90 percent of their swimming energy overcoming resistance, and less than 10 percent translates into forward motion. For less accomplished swimmers, as little as 2 percent of expended effort yields forward progress. Much of your swimming improvement will come from learning how to combat (or, more accurately, *avoid*) several types of resistance. To do this, though, you need to understand more about resistance and about the general strategies you'll employ to minimize its effects.

External Resistance

Because water is roughly 800 times denser than air, it offers strong resistance to a body moving through it. There are three major types of resistance, or drag, acting on a swimmer: form drag, wave drag, and surface drag. Form drag is the resistance that results from the shape of an object moving through the water (figure 4.1*a*). Reducing the front surface area that meets the oncoming water reduces form drag (figure 4.1*b*). This means always keeping the body balanced as close to horizontal as possible, as well as keeping it long and narrow, while swimming. It also means eliminating unnecessary motions. If you are perfectly streamlined, any motion you make increases form drag, so avoid any movement other than the minimum necessary to propel yourself. Just as a boat builder shapes long, tapered hulls instead of flat, square hulls for a racing boat, you want to taper the form and profile of your body for traveling through the water—and you want to maintain that form as you swim. A swimmer who understands and applies the concepts of balance and streamlining can dramatically reduce form drag.

Wave drag is the result of creating a wake. For the body to move forward through the surface of the water, it must move water out of the way. This creates a wave that travels away from the body. Cutting a wider path through the surface means that the water must be pushed further and faster to get it out of the way, which creates a bigger wave. The bigger the wave, the more energy the swimmer gives away to the water. In freestyle, you try to cut a narrow path through the surface by maximizing the time you spend on the sides of your body rather than flat on the belly.

Surface drag is the resistance caused by the frictional force of a moving body in water. You can reduce surface drag not through technique but through preparation and equipment. Properly fitting swimsuits and swimming caps help achieve this result. For competition, shaving body hair and wearing special high-tech, low-drag swimsuits are common practices.

Use your senses to give you feedback about places on your body where you are fighting the water. Listen for splashing or kerplunking sounds and try to eliminate them. Try to make smooth, flowing movements, instead of bulldozing movements, with every part of your body. Look for large or numerous bubbles in the water around you. They are a sure sign that you are causing turbulence.

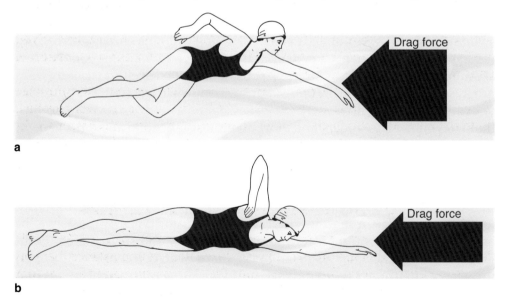

Figure 4.1   The largest source of resistance in swimming is form drag *(a)*. Reducing the front surface area that meets the oncoming water *(b)* can dramatically reduce form drag.

The technique work presented in this book will help you reduce or eliminate these drag indicators and thereby stop wasting energy.

Internal Resistance

Drag is not the only type of resistance with which a swimmer contends. There are three kinds of internal resistance as well: passive resistance, active resistance, and inertia. Passive resistance is caused by the soft connective tissues that surround joints and restrict a swimmer's range of motion (ROM). Effective swimmers move through, or stretch to, the ends of their ranges of motion, where connective tissues begin to oppose and limit further motion.

Active resistance occurs when muscles work against each other. When first learning new skills, or when improving established skills, your neuromuscular system fires many more muscle fibers than are necessary to complete the desired actions. Many of these extra fibers work antagonistically against each other—a bit like a bunch of guys trying to push one car in several different directions. In addition, some people are, by nature or disposition, tenser than others. The person who is always wound up like a tight spring, bouncing and vibrating with just-waiting-to-be-unleashed energy, will have lots of muscle fibers working against others.

Inertia is the tendency for a body at rest on the couch to remain at rest on the couch—instead of grabbing the swim bag and heading to the pool. 'Nuff said.

The internal resistance of unwanted muscle tension or of poor range of motion will be reduced as you refine your stroke technique to avoid ineffective ranges of motion and improve your flexibility by regularly stretching into effective ranges. As you get better at performing skills in a relaxed and fluid manner, the neuromuscular system will fire fewer unnecessary muscle fibers, thus reducing the amount of energy lost to active muscular resistance. If you are like most athletes who undertake a planned program, the anticipation of improving will do wonders for overcoming couch inertia.

The drills and training approach in this book will help you to minimize resistance of all kinds in your swimming. The less resistance you work against, the more efficient you will be. You will have greater control over your workout, look more proficient as a swimmer, have more fun, and feel better about doing it all again.

Aquatic Posture and Balance

Human beings have evolved to function effectively on land in an upright position. Early in childhood, you learned land-based posture and balance that you have subsequently used throughout your life. The posture and balance that serve you well on land, however, do not serve you nearly as well in the water. You understand that balance is essential on land—you simply *never* choose to do anything on land without first getting balanced. Yet most swimmers swim with poor posture and balance, because the skills needed for good posture and balance in the aquatic environment are neither instinctive nor intuitive. In the water, just as on land, poor posture and poor balance will prevent you from correctly performing other swimming skills. This section teaches you what effective aquatic posture and balance are and how to achieve them.

Posture

I liken a swimming human being to a kayak. A kayak is an efficient design for an aquatic vessel. It takes little effort to make it move forward, and once it is moving, it wants to keep moving. Now imagine cutting that kayak into three pieces—front, center, and rear—then tying them back together loosely with bungee cords. It is clear that you'd have a much less effective kayak—less stable, tougher to paddle, and positively impossible to maneuver.

A swimming human being is also an aquatic vessel. In learning to shape and control that vessel, a swimmer must focus on three bodily sections—the head, thorax, and hips. Without good posture, each of these sections will move somewhat independently of the others, despite the structures and tissues—the spinal column, muscles, tendons, ligaments, fascia—connecting them, somewhat like a three-piece, bungee-connected kayak. But when the three sections are drawn into a straight and tightly connected line, the human body behaves more like a solid kayak.

You can get a feel for good aquatic posture by standing with your back against a wall. If your hair is bunched at the back of your head (a bun, a ponytail, or just a tangle of hair stuffed into your swim cap), first let it down. Place your heels a few inches away from the wall. Your butt, shoulder blades, and head should touch the wall. When you are relaxed, your lumbar spine forms an arch (the small of your back), which does not touch the wall (figure 4.2*a*). Now decrease or eliminate this arch by contracting your lower abdominal muscles to draw your navel toward your spine. This will tilt your pelvis, as if tucking your tail under. You want to do this entirely with abdominal muscles without involving your gluteal muscles. Then use your upper abdominal muscles to tuck in your lower ribs (figure 4.2*b*). While holding this abdominal tension, tuck your chin in a bit and try to bring the back of your neck closer to the wall. This should lengthen your neckline, pushing the top of your head a bit higher. The idea is to align your three sections (head, thorax, and hips) in a tight line from the floor of your pelvis, up your spine, and through the top of your head (figure 4.2*c*).

Your body parts are now organized so that you are taller than you have been in a long time. Note what muscles you are using to hold this tight, straight, tall position, and resist the urge to schlump back down to normal height. While continuing to hold this posture, step away from the wall and try walking around, maintaining your full height. Experiment with breathing fully. Experiment with first extending one, then both arms overhead. Experiment with turning your head as far as possible to each side without letting the crown of

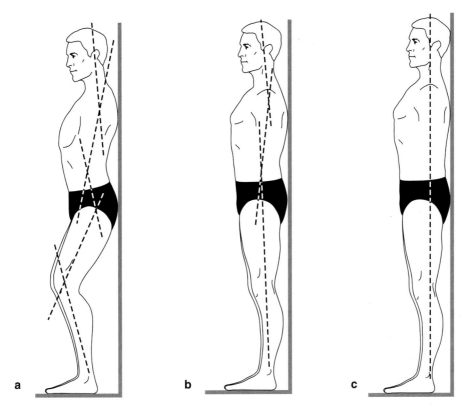

Figure 4.2 The tight line of a well-organized swimming posture creates a far more effective aquatic vessel than the disorganized, relaxed line of a schlumpy swimming posture. *(a)* Schlumpy posture with body sections out of alignment, *(b)* good land-based posture with body sections somewhat aligned, *(c)* well-organized, aquatic tight-line posture with all three body sections fully aligned.

your head move off your spine line. At first, you will find that keeping your body parts organized in a tight line while walking and breathing is a complex task, but keep practicing—it will get easier. Learning to properly organize your three sections in the water and to maintain that posture as you swim at various intensities also takes time. Luckily, acquiring and keeping a tight line is one of the few aquatic skills you can practice effectively on land. In addition, Pilates training can greatly enhance your understanding of how to effectively link your core and extremities, and it can help you strengthen and condition the muscles that maintain excellent posture while swimming.

FOCUS POINT ➤ Tight Line

Throughout this book, we'll keep reinforcing the fact that swimming tall with a tight line, rather than swimming schlumpy, allows you to slip faster and farther through the water with less energy. And the muscular tension used to keep your line tight will allow your balancing and propelling mechanisms to work together (rather than against each other, as they will when you allow yourself to revert to a schlumpy posture).

Balance

Aquatic balance is dependent on aquatic posture. In general, a balanced position for the freestyle stroke is one in which the head, thorax, hips, and legs are all in one line, parallel to the surface of the water. This position allows for minimal frontal resistance, the strongest of the resistance forces a swimmer encounters.

Many swimmers understand the need to have their whole body parallel to the surface, but they go about it the wrong way—by using a strong kick to lift the hips and legs up to the surface. Kicking uses a tremendous amount of energy. Great swimmers use a different approach that requires much less energy to achieve and maintain this balanced position. It starts with maintaining a tight line of good aquatic posture but adds keeping the head in line and pressing the buoy (chest).

Your head, weighing 10 pounds or so, and its position have a great influence on the balance of your body in the water. The crown of your head needs to be in line with your spine, and your nose needs to be pointed straight toward the bottom of the pool when not breathing (figure 4.3a). Lifting or tilting your head off this line puts a large downward force on your hips, causing them to sink (figure 4.3b). (You can easily feel this by lying facedown on the ground,

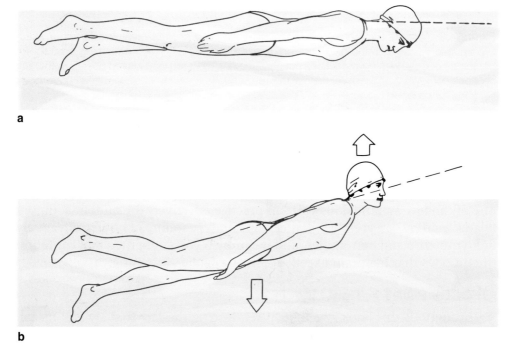

a

b

Figure 4.3 Aquatic balance, dotted line depicting the spine line. *(a)* Keeping the crown of your head in line with your spine will help you stay balanced. *(b)* Lifting your head off the spine line, even a little bit, will immediately and dramatically drive your hips toward the bottom of the pool, destroying balance.

hands at your sides, and lifting your head up off the ground. You will feel your hips press toward the ground.) If your posture is organized tall, your head will be in the right position. But the instinct to lift your head to look forward will remain strong until you have developed an even stronger habit of keeping the crown of your head on your spine line. When balanced, whether on your belly, side, or back, only about one-quarter to one-third of your head will be exposed above the surface. The rest will be under water.

Pressing your buoy will also help keep you balanced. Your lungs are a buoy that tends to float the upper body. By contrast, your center of mass, which is located near your navel, tends to sink your hips and legs (figure 4.4a). Imagine a kickboard placed on the water's surface. If you press one end of the kickboard toward the bottom, the other end rises. Similarly, if you are holding a tight line, then leaning on your buoy to press it toward the bottom raises the hips (figure 4.4b). The greater the force you lean on your buoy with, the greater the buoyant force the water exerts in response. The muscular tension used to hold a tight line transmits the buoyant forces from your buoy to all other points along your spine line. As you press your buoy, you should feel your entire body tilting slightly downhill, fully supported by the water.

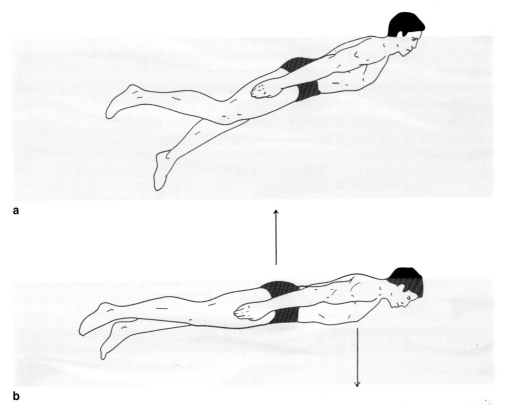

a

b

Figure 4.4   Pressing the buoy. *(a)* Even if your posture is good, without sufficient buoy pressure, your body's center of gravity will sink below the surface, taking your legs with it. *(b)* Leaning on your buoy (chest) will raise your hips and legs toward the surface.

FOCUS POINT ➤ Buoy Pressure

As you practice the drills and swim the workouts in this book, you always should seek to have enough buoy pressure to be completely supported by the water. If there is too little buoy pressure, you will be forced to work with either your arms or legs for artificial support.

Static Posture and Balance Drills

Following are a series of skill drills that teach your body correct posture and balance in a variety of positions. You will practice the correct motions that will eventually be part of an efficient freestyle stroke. You will want to spend some time on each of these drills before you begin doing full workouts. I have included some ways to experiment with the drills that will help you learn more about your relationship with the water.

Do all these drills with easy kicking. You are encouraged to wear fins as you practice any drill until you master it, especially if you make very little forward progress with easy kicking. Many swimmers find that, in addition to a pair of full-size fins, having a pair of short fins provides a stepping stone on the way to mastering some of the drills. Ideally, you will eventually master all the drills with bare feet. Some people, however, especially those with a strong running background, have poor enough ankle flexibility that they will likely never get much direct propulsion of the motorboat-pushing-you-forward variety. That's not a large problem, because our paradigm does not rely on the kick for this sort of propulsion when swimming. But some of the drills do use kicking as the sole or primary source of propulsion. For these drills, if you get little or no propulsion from your kick, you may be best served by always using either short or full-size fins.

Learning to stand up and to be in balance is a prerequisite to learning to walk. Similarly, learning to establish a tight line and to stay balanced while simply kicking is a prerequisite to highly effective swimming. The static posture and balance drills in this chapter will teach your body what it feels like to have good aquatic posture and to be balanced in several static positions where the only motion you'll make is gentle kicking. Dynamic posture and balance drills will help you learn how to maintain good aquatic posture and balance while performing simple movements other than just kicking.

Vertical Kicking (VK)

Most adult swimmers waste a great deal of energy on kicking. They tend to use the kick for the wrong reasons, which encourages incorrect leg motions, such as bicycle kicking or kicking mainly from the knees. Vertical kicking will help teach you effective kicking motions while it conditions precisely the right muscles. As you are learning this drill, use full-size training fins.

As the name indicates, this is a kicking drill in a vertical position. Go to a deep section of the pool where your feet cannot touch the bottom. Place one hand on top of the other on your chest and start kicking. The goal is to keep your head above the surface, with the water just below your chin and with your nose pointed straight forward (figure 4.5). Check your aquatic posture— tall and tight, just as you practiced while walking on land. Keep your hips directly under your shoulders; do not lean forward or backward.

The standard kick used for freestyle swimming, and for this drill, is called flutter kicking. The word *kick* refers to the action of driving your leg forward from behind your body plane to an equidistant point in front of your body plane—like kicking a ball. As one leg kicks, the other leg recovers—that is, the recovering leg moves from in front of your body plane to behind your body plane, thus putting it in the correct position to kick. The legs alternate their opposing kick and recovery motions in a continuous rhythm. Each kick should come predominantly from your hips, allowing the knee to yield slightly to the pressure of the water as the leg kicks forward. There should be no knee bend *at all* on the recovery portion of the kick cycle.

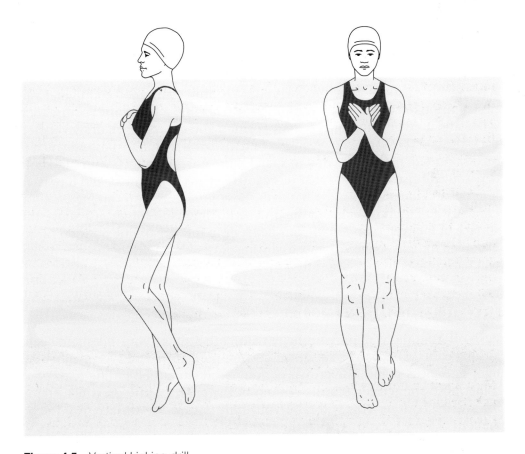

Figure 4.5 Vertical kicking drill.

Kick mainly from the hips and keep your ankles loose. A small, fast kick is better than a larger, slower kick. Kick in this manner for 15 seconds and then rest (hold the lane rope or side of the pool). Start with small doses of this drill, perhaps just a few repetitions of 15 seconds, followed by 15 seconds or more of rest. After you gain confidence, add more and longer repetitions with less rest.

Though it is physically demanding, vertical kicking is an excellent drill to do early in your training. Survival instincts will quickly tell your neuromuscular system which motions are most effective for keeping your blowhole dry. Once you master VK with full-size fins, particularly the tight-line part, you can try short fins. Eventually, you should work toward doing VK with bare feet. In moving to bare feet, you may find that holding a small, floating object (a pull-buoy works well) against your chest will give you enough extra buoyancy to allow you to avoid tilting your head back to keep your blowhole dry. Be careful not to lean on the float; instead, hang from it.

Feedback Tools

- If your nose is pointed anywhere but straight forward, horizontal to the surface, then you have tilted your head off your tight line.
- If you find yourself bobbing up and down a bit with each kick, then your kicks are too large—keep the kicks compact.

Experiment a Bit

After you have spent some time with the VK drill, using good abdominal and neck tension to keep a tight line, purposely relax into a schlumpy posture for a while and note how this affects your position and efforts. Then draw yourself back into good posture. You will likely find that with schlumpy posture you feel less supported, perhaps having to spend more energy to keep your blowhole dry. You will also likely find that reorganizing your head, torso, and hips back into tall aquatic posture quickly solves those problems. You can increase the difficulty and training value of the drill by holding your hands just above the surface of the water, on top of your head, or in full streamline position (arms extended straight above your head) during the kicking. Each of these positions will require you to kick faster to keep your head above the water.

Front Balance (FB)

Push off from the wall on your belly with both arms at your sides and begin kicking easily. Check to be sure your posture is organized tall—remember the tight-line focus point. The crown of your head should be in line with your spine, nose pointed toward the bottom of the pool. Lightly press your buoy toward the bottom. This will raise your hips toward the surface. Adjust the amount of buoy pressure so that the cheeks of your butt just break the surface. Don't make the mistake of pushing your face, instead of your buoy, toward the bottom—you may need to consciously tuck your chin a bit and draw your face away from the bottom to maintain your tall posture. When you need to take a breath, lift your head straight up in front and get a breath of air, then put your head down so that the crown is in line with your spine. Press your buoy again and make sure to re-flatten your lower back, making yourself as tall as possible. Each time you lift your head, your hips and legs sink rapidly toward the bottom. As soon as you return to good posture and press your buoy, you regain balance.

Stepping-Stone to FB

Using a training snorkel for this drill eliminates the distraction of lifting your head to take a breath, thus allowing you to focus completely on the basic skills of tight-line posture and balance. If you are new to snorkel use, plan on spending a half hour or so getting used to breathing with your face in the water and learning to purge the snorkel by exhaling forcefully (which you may need to do after pushing off the wall at the beginning of each length).

Feedback Tools

- When your posture is correct and you are in balance, the back quarter of your head and most of your backside (including your shoulder blades and the cheeks of your butt) will be exposed to the air, and your heels will just break the surface as you kick.

- In your nose-down position, you should see the hairballs and Band-Aids that are directly under your face, not the ones you will soon cruise over.

- If water enters the training snorkel as you do the drill, it usually indicates that you have buried your head (which means that you've pushed your face toward the bottom of the pool instead of keeping your head in tight-line posture) or that you have buried your whole front end by putting too much pressure on your buoy.

Experiment a Bit

After you have spent some time with the FB drill using good tight-line posture, purposely relax into a schlumpy posture for a half length or so and note how this affects your position and efforts. You will likely find that with schlumpy posture you slow down, feel less supported, have trouble regaining balance after breaths, and spend more energy. Reorganizing your head, torso, and hips back into good, tall, aquatic posture should quickly solve those problems.

Back Balance (BB)

Push off from the wall on your back with both arms at your sides, head aligned with your spine, and nose pointed up and breathing freely. Begin kicking easily. Lightly press your buoy (lean on a spot between your shoulder blades) toward the bottom. Check for the tight line of good aquatic posture. This may feel different when you're on your back than it did when you were on your belly. You may notice a tendency to tilt your head back and to arch your back—both motions will work against balance. Using abdominal tension to flatten your lower back and extending your neck and bodyline may seem counterintuitive until you have practiced them a few times.

Feedback Tools

- When you are in balance, note that only about one quarter of your head (i.e., just your face) will be exposed above the water's surface. Your ears should be underwater. The waterline around your head should be at the tip of your chin, at the crest of your forehead, and equally on both sides of your goggles.
- Your pelvis should be at, or within an inch of, the surface.
- Your knees and toes should barely break the surface of the water as you kick.

Experiment a Bit

After you have spent some time with the BB drill using good aquatic posture, experiment as you did with the FB drill—purposely relax into a schlumpy posture and note the effects. Then draw yourself back into a tight line. You will likely experience the same problems with schlumpy posture as you did in the FB drill, as well as the benefits of regaining good, tall posture.

Side-Glide Nose-Down (SGND)

As mentioned before, the water offers less resistance when you cut a narrower path through it. This means that you want to swim freestyle as much on your side as possible and avoid spending time on your belly. The foundation of an efficient freestyle stroke is a series of alternating right and left side-lying glides, connected by snappy rotations of the body from one side position to the other. This drill will get you balanced and comfortable on your sides.

SGND is best done with a training snorkel, which allows you to swim complete lengths of the pool without worrying about turning your head to breathe. Push off from the wall while turned on your side, with your lower arm extended generally toward the far end of the pool, but at a slight downward angle. Begin kicking easily. Press your other arm firmly against your side. Point your nose straight down. Lean on your buoy (the side of your chest or armpit). Maintain a tight line of good aquatic posture. Stay in this side-glide position (figure 4.6) for the length of the pool. Do this drill on both sides of your body.

As with the other balance drills, establishing correct aquatic posture in this drill may require some experimentation, but the fundamental point of drawing yourself into as tall a posture as possible still applies.

Feedback Tools

- When you are balanced on your side, you will be able to feel a strip of flesh exposed to the air all the way down your arm from your shoulder to your wrist. Putting a bit more pressure on your buoy by leaning in on your armpit will help expose more of your arm to the air. That strip of flesh is an indicator of the position of your hips. If your arm is firmly pressed to your side and your wrist is dry, then your hips are right at the surface.
- Your extended arm should feel weightless at all times.
- Note that when your posture is correct and you are balanced, your head should be in almost exactly the same position as in the front-balance drill—nose pointed straight down and just the back of your head exposed to the air.
- If water enters the snorkel as you do the drill, it usually means that you have buried your head (which means that you've pushed your face toward the bottom of the pool instead of keeping it in tight-line posture and simply leaning on your buoy) or that you have buried your whole front end (by putting too much pressure on your buoy).

Experiment a Bit

After you have spent some time with the SGND drill with a tight line, experiment as you did with the previous drills—purposely relax into a schlumpy posture for a few yards, then draw yourself back into good posture. As before, note the effects, both positive and negative, of each of these postures. Also experiment with the amount of buoy pressure you need to use in order to feel fully supported by the water. You will likely find that when you relax the posture tension in your core, the sensation of support is elusive or nonexistent.

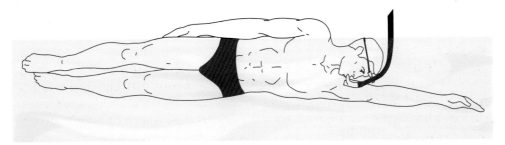

Figure 4.6 Side-glide nose-down drill.

Side-Glide Nose-Up (SGNU)

Just as important as side-lying nose-down balance is side-lying nose-up balance. This drill builds on the skills you learned in SGND and will get you balanced and comfortable on your sides while your blowhole is exposed. But you should practice SGND until you are balanced and very comfortable with it before trying SGNU.

Eschew the snorkel this time. Push off in SGND position. As soon as you are balanced, turn just your head until your nose points straight up and you can breathe freely (figure 4.7). Nothing else should change when you turn your head. Don't roll onto your back. Don't lift your head as you turn it—even the slightest lift will undo your balance. Check for good aquatic posture. Stay in this side-lying nose-up position for the length of the pool. Do this drill on both sides of your body.

If you are losing your balance as soon as you turn your head to breathe, try the following strategy: Starting in SGND position, make sure that your lungs are full of air when you turn your head to take your nose out of the water. Do not exhale immediately; instead, hold your breath in the nose-up position while you mentally check your feedback tools. Once you are satisfied that you are well balanced, exhale slowly and begin breathing normally.

Feedback Tools

- Use the same feedback tools you would use for SGND, except that when you are balanced, your head should be in almost exactly the same position as in the back-balance drill—ears under the water, nose pointed straight up, and water line at the tip of the chin and crest of the forehead.

Figure 4.7 Side-glide nose-up drill.

Experiment a Bit

After you have spent some time with the SGNU drill with a tight line, experiment as you did with the previous drills—alternate between tight-schlumpy-tight, noting the effects, both positive and negative, of each of these postures. Also experiment with varying the amount of buoy pressure you need to feel fully supported by the water. As before, relaxing your posture tension may erase the sensation of support.

FOCUS POINT ➤ Downward Angle Arm Extension

In the side-glide drill descriptions, I indicated that the extended arm should be at a slight downward angle. This is a departure from the conventional wisdom of extending the lead arm straight toward the far end of the pool. Most adult swimmers have range of motion issues in their shoulders that affect the choice of the arm extension position. Several considerations strongly favor having the extended arm at a downward angle, both in this drill and throughout most of your freestyle endeavors. They are as follows:

- **Avoiding injury.** Extending the arm horizontally toward the far end of the pool (or at any upward angle) can pinch the shoulder tendons between the upper-arm bone and the shoulder socket. Doing this thousands of times per day is a cause of chronic pain for a large number of swimmers. But extending the arm at even a small degree of downward angle greatly reduces the risk of an impingement.

- **Mechanical advantage.** A shoulder joint at or near the end of its ROM has poor mechanical advantage (in other words, you exert lots of muscular force but get very little work done). Extending your arm at a bit of a downward angle keeps the shoulder away from the end of its ROM, increasing mechanical advantage during the first part of the stroke.

- **Skiing uphill.** As the swimmer glides forward through the water, an arm extended at any degree of upward angle will mean that the onrush of water will hit the bottom surface of the hand and arm, which will tend to raise them. Due to the long lever of the extended arm, this will lift the upper body (and drop the hips)—a bit like skiing uphill. Alternatively, extending the arm at a bit of a downward angle will help your hips hug the surface.

- **Energy use.** Choosing an extension line near the end of your shoulder ROM (horizontal or upward angle) requires lots of extra internal tension to maintain the position. Choosing a bit of a downward angle greatly decreases the internal tension (and, consequently, the energy) required.

- **Fatigue-induced hip drop.** While the extra internal tension required by a horizontal or upward angle extension is sustainable for short durations, for longer durations it soon results in fatigue stress. The usual response is to release some core body tension and break out of the balanced stream-line position by letting the hips drop. This relieves some of shoulder stress but greatly increases total frontal resistance. If you had to choose between having a spindly little hand a bit out of streamline below the rest of the body or your big ol' hips dragging deep, which would be your preference?

It is often hard to judge your arm extension angle yourself. Have a swim partner give you feedback about your extended arm position. Then experiment with various amounts of downward angle in your arm extension line while monitoring how much tension is required in and around your shoulder to support the position. What you are looking for is just enough downward angle to allow you to maintain good aquatic posture and to keep your hips glued to the surface.

Dynamic Posture and Balance Drills

Side Glide With Breathing (SGB)

This drill is an alternation between the SGND and SGNU drills. Start as you would for the SGNU drill. With good posture and balance, take several breaths in the nose-up position, turn your head so that your nose points toward the bottom of the pool, and exhale a little bit of air underwater. Then turn your head back to the nose-up position. Take several breaths in this position before turning your head to exhale again underwater. The only thing you move in this drill, besides your legs, is your head. The body should stay in a balanced, side-glide position throughout the drill. As you practice this drill, work toward exhaling more air each time you are nose down and try to take fewer breaths each time you turn your head to the nose-up position until you can exhale normally underwater and until you can take just a single breath when nose up. Do this drill on both sides of your body.

Feedback Tools

- When your nose points up, your head should be in the same position as in the SGNU drill—ears under the water. When your nose points toward the bottom, just the back of your head is exposed to the air. The idea is to rotate your head as if it were on a skewer (one that runs through your spine and up through your crown) without bending the skewer.

- Feel for that dry strip of flesh all the way down your side arm, from your shoulder to your wrist, at all times during this drill. Many swimmers tend to lift the head a bit when turning to the nose-up position. This causes the hips to drop. You'll feel the water line creep up your side arm toward your shoulder, indicating that you have lost your balance. You may need to press your side and the back of your head slightly toward the bottom of the pool in order to avoid lifting it as you rotate it to the nose-up position.

- Another common tendency with this drill is to lean on the extended arm, pressing it toward the bottom of the pool as the head turns for a breath. This is an attempt to artificially support a slightly lifted head. The cure is to support yourself by leaning on your buoy more and by keeping the extended arm at a slightly downward angle. This arm should feel weightless throughout the drill.

Experiment a Bit

As with each of the other drills so far, it is helpful to spend time consciously shifting back and forth between holding a tight-line posture and relaxing into a schlumpy posture. Becoming aware of how the two different postures affect your swimming will help motivate you to make a habit of good posture.

FOCUS POINT ➤ Risky Breathing

To take a breath, the uneducated swimmer instinctively lifts his head to a position where he is absolutely sure he'll get nothing but air, with no risk of swallowing water. This causes the hips and legs to sink—maybe a little, maybe a lot. A 2-inch (5 cm) vertical lift of the head can cause a 4- to 6-inch (10 to 15 cm) drop of the hips, which shows up as an 8- to 12-inch (20 to 30 cm) drop of the feet—enough to nearly double form drag. Sensing this problem, the uneducated swimmer then uses extra kicking to support his hips and legs near the surface. The process becomes a struggle that wastes a *lot* of energy.

You, on the other hand, must be risky about how low you keep your head when going for air—risky enough that you might take in some water. Hint: If you *never ever* take in water, then you are not being risky enough. Rotate your head far enough that your nose is pointed more skyward than sideways. The closer you come to a nose-straight-up position, the deeper your head can be when you take a breath. If you create a habit of going for a risky-deep head position every time you breathe, you will decrease the amount of energy you waste in extra support kicking. You goal is zero head-lift, zero torso-lift, and zero extra-energy consumption.

Balanced-Body Rolling (BBR)

This drill is best done with a training snorkel. Push off from the wall in the same position you used for the FB drill—on your belly and with both arms at your sides, nose pointed toward the bottom of the pool—and begin kicking easily. Keep a tight line and keep enough pressure on your buoy to stay balanced. Once you are balanced, roll onto your side. Keep your nose pointed straight down and keep your hands at your sides. If you keep a tight line and keep pressure on your buoy as you roll, you will already be in a balanced position when you reach your side. Stay balanced while on your side. With your arms at your sides, you'll likely need a bit more buoy pressure to be balanced than when you had one arm extended in front. After you are well balanced, roll again to your front, keeping a tight line and pressure on your buoy as you roll. Do this drill rolling in both directions.

Feedback Tools

- As you roll from the front position to the side position, you should feel the strip of flesh from your shoulder to your wrist become exposed to the air all at once without having to adjust your balance.
- As you roll back to the front position, you should feel the cheeks of your butt become exposed to the air without having to adjust your balance.
- To stay balanced, you may find that you need to keep a bit more pressure on your buoy when you are on your side than when you are on your front.

Experiment a Bit

Again, spend time consciously shifting back and forth between holding a tight-line posture and relaxing into a schlumpy posture. If you do enough of this, you will begin to set up an automatic feedback cycle that will set off alarm bells in your head whenever you begin to break out of good posture.

FOCUS POINT ➤ Red Dot

In many swimming drills and in full-stroke swimming, it can be helpful to imagine a 2-inch (5 cm) red dot in the center of the top of your head that you keep underwater at all times. A person watching you from a vantage point under the water as you swim toward him should not be able to see that red dot move up, down, or side to side as your body rotates or as you take strokes. They would only see the dot rotate as you turn your head to breathe. This focus point combines the three head-related ideas discussed thus far: the neck tension of aquatic posture, keeping your nose pointed toward the bottom of the pool when not breathing, and the zero head-lift of risky breathing.

Vertical Kick With Rotation (VKR)

Freestyle swimming is powered by rhythmic rotations of the body around its long axis. The VKR drill teaches you how to initiate full-body rotations and how to alternate them in a rhythmic fashion.

The VKR drill starts like the standard VK drill—in deep water with your hands on your chest, elbows tucked in at your sides, and a tight-line posture. After you have established a comfortable vertical-flutter-kick rhythm, use one of your kicks to rotate your body roughly a quarter turn to the right and then continue flutter kicking in this new position. After a handful of flutter kicks, use one of your kicks to make a quarter turn back toward the left where you started. The kicks you use to rotate yourself—one kick to turn you to the right and, later, one kick to turn you to the left—are called rotation kicks.

With a rotation kick, kicking your right leg forward drives your right hip backward (Newton's equal and opposite reaction). Simultaneously, the left leg recovers backward, which drives the left hip forward (Newton again). Left hip forward and right hip back equals turning your hips to the right. To rotate your hips to your *right*, kick your *right* leg as you recover the left leg. To rotate your hips to your *left*, kick your *left* leg as you recover the right. It sounds simple, but it takes some real awareness and focus to grasp. It does not take an extra-hard or extra-large kick to rotate. Simply release your hips and *let* them rotate that quarter turn, then hold them in place as you continue to flutter kick. Each time your hips rotate, allow the top part of your body to take a ride along with your hips (which will happen automatically if you are holding a tight line). You may be tempted to try to help the rotation by throwing your shoulders around as you kick. Don't. Throwing your shoulders doesn't help. Not at all. Not even for you. Just take my word for it.

Once you are comfortable with making occasional rotations, add rhythm to the rotations. You'll use what is called a six-beat rotation pattern, which is simply two flutter kicks (F) followed by one rotation kick (R), which turns you to the right, followed by two flutter kicks and another rotation kick that turns you back to the left, where you started. That's a total of six kick beats to complete a cycle of two rotations (F F R F F R), after which a new cycle starts without breaking rhythm (. . . F F R F F R F F R F F R F F R . . .). It helps to count these beats out loud, one for each foot as it kicks forward. Continue this six-beat rotation pattern while keeping your head still, nose pointed straight forward—just let your body rotate under your stationary head.

Even if you have mastered standard VK without fins, I strongly encourage you to use fins when you are first learning VKR. Fins will allow you to slow the tempo of your kick. This allows distinct awareness of each beat, making it easier to pinpoint which kicks should be flutter kicks and which should be rotation kicks. Fins will also improve the feedback you get about which muscles you are using to drive each rotation. Once you master VKR with full-size fins, you can try short fins and, eventually, bare feet. In moving to bare feet, you may find that hanging from a small floating object held against your chest is helpful, as it was with VK.

Feedback Tools

- Each time you rotate your hips, you should be aware that your shoulders rotate at exactly the same time as, and exactly as far as, your hips. Your tight-line posture instantly transmits the rotation of your hips along your spine, allowing the action of your legs to drive the rotation of the entire upper body as a single unit. If you find that your shoulders lag behind your hips or that they don't turn as far as your hips, you have lost your tight line. If you find your hips lagging behind your shoulders, then you are trying to help the rotation by throwing your shoulders ahead of your hips (which, surprisingly, works to hinder hip rotation instead of helping it).

- Check to see if, in preparation for a rotation kick, you are bending your knee on the recovering leg to bring that foot a bit farther back for a bigger or more forceful kick to drive the rotation. It is important not to try to help the rotation by doing this—it simply moves the rotation fulcrum from your hips to your knees, effectively cutting your lever length in half and making your effort much less effective.

Experiment a Bit

After you are comfortable with an easy six-beat rotation pattern, experiment with increasing the tempo. If you maintain the six-beat pattern, a faster kick tempo will result in a faster rotation tempo. With faster rotations, you may find that you need a bit more tension on your tight line to keep the upper body rotating as a separate unit. And, as usual, be sure to experiment with schlumpy vs. tight-line postures.

Long-Axis Rotations (LAR)

This drill takes the long-axis rotation skills you just learned in the VKR drill and puts them to use in a horizontal position, where you will add your balance skills to the mix. Once you are comfortable with VKR, you can transition to LAR by slowly leaning forward and allowing your hips and legs to rise to the surface. Keep a tight line as you transition to a horizontal position, and keep the same six-beat rotation pattern going. Press your buoy to the balance point and be sure your nose is pointed straight down. Once you are horizontal, extend your arms forward toward the end of the pool. Your flutter kicks will propel you gently along while your rotation kicks will result in quarter turns that swing your navel from pointing roughly 45 degrees to the right to pointing roughly 45 degrees to the left. Do not try to rotate all the way to the side-glide position. Once you are comfortable with the six-beat rotation pattern in a horizontal position, you may begin by pushing off from the wall instead of by starting from VKR.

When it is time to grab a breath, turn your head as you rotate and allow the elbow on the breathing side to slide back to your chest while the fingers on that hand remain pointed toward the end of the pool (figure 4.8). This gets the arm out of the way of your head without taking a stroke and without pushing down on the water. As you rotate back, extend that arm back out in front of you. You may want to go a bit beyond the 45-degree mark when rotating to the air to avoid lifting your head (remember the red dot and risky-breathing focus points). It is important to have at least three, and preferably five, rotations between breaths—at least until you are able to take a breath with no effect on your balance and no change in your rotation rhythm.

Use of a training snorkel can greatly shorten the learning cycle for the basic skills of LAR by eliminating the distraction of having to turn your head to breathe. Continued use of the snorkel is valuable for further refinement when long segments of LAR are called for in the workouts, but you'll still need to know how to take a breath when the snorkel is not convenient. If you have no deep water in which to use VKR as a starting point, it is still possible to learn the LAR drill by starting from a wall push-off. Just plan on it taking a bit longer to accomplish.

Figure 4.8   Breathing position for the long-axis rotations drill.

Feedback Tools

- Use your butt for feedback about balance—at all times you should have one butt cheek or the other exposed to the air. Doing so indicates that you are keeping your hips glued to the surface.

- You should be aware that each rotation happens with and because of a single kick beat, rather than two or three beats.

- Matching your rotation tempo to a tempo beeper (or to a familiar tune with a distinctive beat in your head) can help you determine whether you are changing the tempo of your rotations. The goal is to set and keep an uninterrupted rotation tempo throughout the drill (even when breathing).

- Be aware of whether you are using a bigger or more forceful kick to drive the rotation. All the kicks should be the same size and force.

- Use the red dot and risky-breathing focus points to help you stay aware of whether you are lifting your head for air.

Experiment a Bit

After you become comfortable with easy LAR, try a variety of different kicking tempos, from very slow to very fast, always with the goal of making the hips and thorax rotate as a single unit. Try doing LAR on your back and on your sides. Also, supplement the usual tight-schlumpy-tight posture-switching experiment with a similar balance experiment: occasionally release buoy pressure to become unbalanced and see how this affects rotation, stability, and forward progress.

CHAPTER 5

Stroke Integration and Turns

If you are comfortable in the water and have spent enough time with the drills in the previous chapter to feel confident about your posture and balance skills, you are ready to add a few stroke skills to your repertoire. This chapter describes how an effective swimming machine (soon to be you) works, and I introduce an easy-to-incorporate concept used by many world-class swimmers called front-quadrant swimming. Several stroke-integration drills will help you assemble your swimming machine and incorporate front-quadrant swimming. These drills help you put together the discreet skills you learned in the posture and balance drills, integrating arm strokes to create a coordinated set of motions that propels you easily down the pool. After you've spent some time with the drills, the whole stroke cycle is covered again, offering some fine-tuning tips that will help improve your drills and bridge the gap between drilling and swimming. Finally, you will learn about the two most effective ways to turn when you come to a wall.

As you follow and practice the drills in the order presented in this and later chapters, you will progressively build a new freestyle stroke from scratch. For a while, when you swim rather than practice drills, you will tend to revert to whatever stroke style you had before you read this book. The more comfortable and relaxed you become with these skills and drills, though, the easier they will be to incorporate into your everyday swimming. The workouts in subsequent chapters are built around progressively practicing the drills while first mixing in small and later larger amounts of full-stroke swimming.

Your Swimming Machine

Earlier I mentioned that freestyle swimming is a series of alternating side-glides connected by propulsive strokes. Rotating correctly, with good initiation and properly connected arms, allows the swimmer to involve much more muscle mass and power than when he is rotating incorrectly or with improperly connected arms or when simply swimming flat. Before I can explain how this works, let's introduce a bit of terminology. I divide a single-arm stroke cycle into three parts—the stroke, the recovery, and the entry and extension.

1. The stroke is the propulsive underwater action of moving the hand from the fully extended position in front of the body to the finish position somewhere by your thigh. The stroke starts as the body begins to rotate from one side-lying position, and it ends as the body finishes rotating to the other side-lying position.

2. The recovery is the non-propulsive action of taking the arm out of the water from the spot by your thigh and carrying it through the air to a point where the hand is even with or just past the top of the head. The body stays on its side while the arm recovers—no rotation at all, just gliding—and the other arm simply remains extended out front at a bit of a downward angle, helping keep the body long throughout the recovery.

3. The entry and extension is the movement of the arm and hand from the point just past the top of the head to full extension. The entry starts as the body begins to rotate from one side-lying position and ends as the body finishes rotating to the other side-lying position. To an observer, it should appear that body rotation is the reason that the arm enters the water and then extends in front of the body. You should feel as if the arm is de-spooling off the rotating body rather than as if the hand is stabbing forward from the shoulder. From here, go back to step 1, the stroke, to start a new stroke cycle.

Note that your arm motions alternate with each core body rotation. With one rotation, the right arm is engaged in 1 above while the left arm is engaged in 3, and vice versa on the next rotation—which brings us back to the topic of how you create those rotations and how you connect your strokes to them.

In the previous chapter, you learned and practiced leg-driven core-rotation skills in the VKR and LAR drills. In swimming, you want to use these leg-driven core rotations as the main engine of propulsion and to allow the shoulders, arms, and hands to act more as transmissions than engines, distributing the work among many muscle groups. How can rotating around the long axis of the body (rotating the hips and shoulders in a plane at right angles to your intended motion) propel you toward the far wall? To answer that, think of your body as a swimming machine—much as your car is a driving machine.

The car has an engine, which produces rotational forces by way of its crankshaft. Your swimming machine's engine encompasses your legs and core lower-torso muscles. Used properly, they initiate the rotations of your hips, spine, and shoulders.

The car's transmission and differential transmit the rotation of the crankshaft to the tires. In your swimming machine, muscles of the back, shoulders, and arms act as the transmission and differential. They do this by supporting and stabilizing the upper arm, forearm, and hand in order to direct the core's rotational forces through them to the water.

What began as rotational force from the engine is finally applied to the road through the tires to produce linear motion. The tires grip a spot on the road so that the applied force becomes propulsion. Because your swimming machine is an aquatic craft, you have paddles—your arms and hands—instead of tires. The large surface area of your arm-plus-hand paddle, in a sense, holds onto a spot in the water so that the force of core body rotation produces linear propulsion.

For your car to work properly, all three components must work together—the engine turns the crankshaft, the transmission is engaged, and the tires grip the road. If any one of the components is not operating properly, the vehicle will come to a halt—so too with your swimming machine.

Imagine that your swimming machine is in motion, gliding on your right side just as the hand on your recovering left arm has passed your head. Your right arm is extended out front. You can see this position in figure 5.4b on page 53. Kick your right leg to initiate rotation (the engine) of your entire body around your tight line (the crankshaft). As your body begins to rotate, you engage your back, shoulder, and arm muscles (the transmission) by rotating your upper arm to get your forearm and hand (the paddle) moving toward vertical and as far out in front as possible without dropping your elbow (figure 5.4c, page 53). This action firms the entire muscular path from the spine to the hand. At this point, early in your rotation, your transmission is fully engaged. Once the forearm and hand are at a 45-degree angle toward vertical, the paddle has established a traction spot to hold onto. Maintain traction by keeping your paddle as vertical as possible and glued to that spot as your body rotates past it (figure 5.4d, page 53). If you drop your elbow or simply use your arm and shoulder muscles to yank your hand backward in the water, you'll be slipping water—the same as spinning your wheels in your car. Keep your transmission engaged as your core body rotation continues by applying only enough shoulder and arm force to finish the stroke at the same moment that core body rotation finishes.

Leg-driven body rotation makes your swimming more powerful and fluid, reduces local muscle fatigue, and has great fitness benefits. You involve as much as five times more muscle mass as you would when using primarily arm and shoulder muscles to do the work. This greatly increases the amount of fat that is burned during the few hours following a high-intensity workout.

Front-Quadrant Swimming

Now that you're acquainted with how the stroking arm is connected and timed to the rotation engine, you need to understand how the recovering arm and stroking arm are connected. The shape of any vessel in the water, including your swimming machine, and the ratios of length, width, and depth determine the amount of wave drag that that vessel has at any given speed. This is why racing boats of all kinds are long and sleek. The implication for your swimming machine is that drag and the power required to overcome it are significantly reduced when the body stays as long as possible throughout each stroke cycle. Imagine a sailing event in which two evenly matched racing boats and crews are pitted against one another. Also imagine that once every second, one of the boats morphs into a tugboat shape for half a second, then morphs back into a racing-boat shape. You would bet on the other boat because it keeps its long, sleek shape.

Now imagine a 6-foot-tall (almost 2 m) person who, when stretched to full streamline position, becomes an 8-foot-long (2.4 m) vessel in the water. We'll call this his racing-boat shape (figure 5.1).

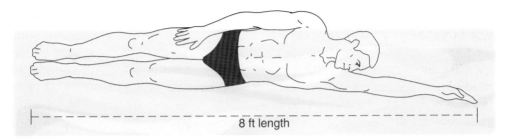

Figure 5.1   Long, streamlined racing-boat shape.

Say that he begins his recovery and his stroke at the same time and that his recovering arm and pulling arm are therefore passing the shoulders at about the same time. He has shortened his vessel back to 6 feet. We will call this his tugboat shape (figure 5.2). This swimmer alternately morphs from the 8-foot racing-boat shape to the 6-foot tugboat shape and back with every stroke he swims.

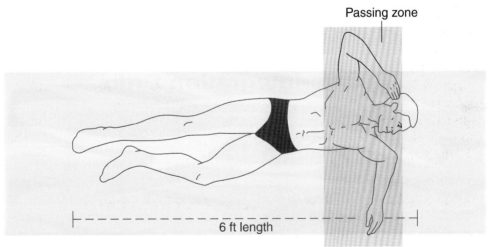

Figure 5.2   Shorter tugboat shape with stroking hand and recovering hand passing each other near the shoulders.

The woman in the next lane (same height, same racing-boat shape) has learned a technique called front-quadrant swimming. In the following figure, you can see that instead of starting her recovery and pull together, she stays on her side with her lead arm extended until her recovering hand has passed her head. The large circle shows that the woman's recovering arm is about to enter the water while her stroking hand is still in the front quadrant. Another way of thinking about this is by imagining that her passing zone—the area where the recovering hand, which is moving forward, passes the stroking hand, which is moving backward—is in front of her head (figure 5.3). In this way, she maintains her streamlined, side-lying position and most of its length for nearly the entire stroke cycle. Keeping her vessel long throughout each stroke cycle reduces wave drag dramatically and allows the arm stroke and core rotation to begin together. The stroke-integration drills will teach you to keep your swimming machine long and to properly time your arm motions.

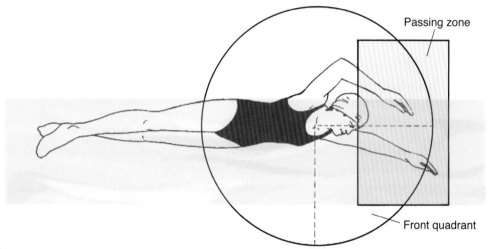

Figure 5.3   Front-quadrant swimming. This swimmer is still in a long, streamlined racing-boat shape. Her stroking hand will pass her recovering hand in front of her head.

Stroke-Integration Drills

So how do you integrate all these concepts—swimming on your sides, using leg-driven body rotation as your primary source of propulsion, and front-quadrant swimming—into normal swimming? You will use several stroke-integration drills. Before you begin learning these drills, however, you already should have become comfortable with all the posture and balance drills. And you should continue practicing them even as you add the more complex drills that follow.

As you practice these drills, notice that when you breathe without a snorkel, you will be taking roughly half your breaths to one side of your body and half to the other side. It is important to breathe well to either side of your body. This idea applies to all of the drills and to full-stroke swimming as well.

Side-Glide Single Strokes (SGSS)

This drill, best learned with a snorkel, introduces the skill of taking a single stroke to turn from a side-glide position on one side of your body to a side-glide position on the other side. Start by pushing off from the wall. Begin kicking easily in a side-glide nose-down position (figure 5.4a). Check your posture

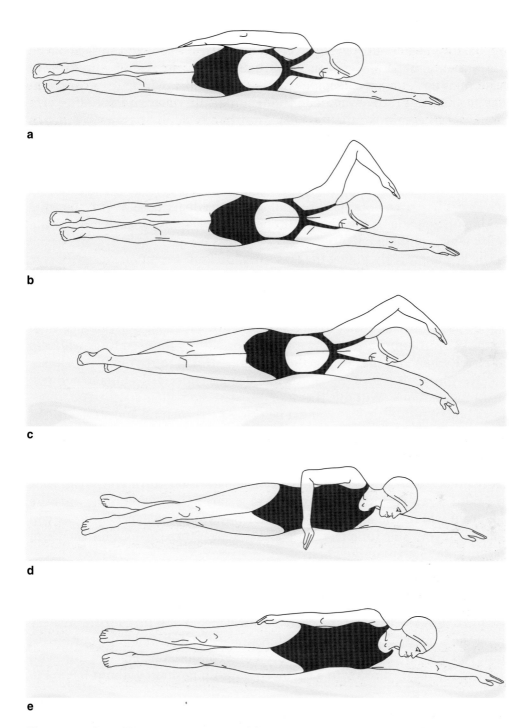

Figure 5.4 Side-glide single strokes drill. *(a)* Begin in a balanced, side-glide nose-down position. *(b)* Your recovering arm just passes your head. *(c)* As core rotation begins, your recovering hand pierces the surface as your other arm begins the stroke. Your hands pass each other in the passing zone. *(d)* Rotation and stroke continue as your other arm reaches full extension in front of your body. *(e)* Body rotation finishes just as your arm stroke finishes at the thigh. With your nose still pointed down, you are now side-gliding on your other side.

and balance feedback tools. Recover your side arm above the surface of the water. As that hand passes your head (figure 5.4b), use one of your kicks to begin rotating your body, keeping your nose pointed down. As your core rotation begins, your recovering hand should enter the water and the other arm should begin the stroke (figure 5.4c). Your hands should pass each other in the passing zone. Continue the stroke (figure 5.4d) while rotating toward the other side-glide position. You want your rotation to reach the other side-glide position just as the arm stroke finishes at your thigh. You should now be in a side-glide nose-down position (figure 5.4e). Take a few breaths as you continue to kick easily. Check your posture and balance feedback tools as you continue kicking on your side a little longer. Repeat these actions for each arm for the entire length of the pool.

The key to properly timing the arm's motion with a rotation kick is to have your hand enter the water just as the leg on the *opposite* side kicks forward (the downbeat of the kick). Alternatively, you can focus on your hand entering the water just as the leg on the *same* side recovers backward (the upbeat of the kick). It will be easier to pair a hand entry with a kick on one side than on the other. Getting a feel now for either or both of these pairings will help you later when you start connecting multiple strokes to rhythmic rotations.

Once you've mastered this drill while using a snorkel, it's time to add real breathing motions. Without the snorkel, start side-gliding with your nose down and begin the drill as you did before. As the rotation and stroke begin, however, allow your head to turn with your body instead of remaining nose-down. You will end up in a side-glide nose-up position at the end of the stroke instead of in a nose-down position. Take a few breaths as you continue to kick easily. Check your posture and balance feedback tools. Turn your head back to a nose-down position. You are now in a starting position on the opposite side from where you started. Check your posture and balance again as you remain on your side for a few more kicks. Repeat these actions for each arm for the entire length of the pool.

Despite the work you did in the SGB drill, you may still tend to lift your head or upper body as your body rotates to the nose-up position. Turning your head separately makes this situation even worse. Instead, proactively use the red-dot focus point to keep your head low as you turn for air. Also try using the strategy that you used to start the SGNU drill, holding your breath until you are sure that you are balanced and comfortable. Practice until you consistently rotate directly to a balanced nose-up position without having to readjust or "settle."

Be patient with the SGSS drill. Your brain and body may want to rush into the next stroke right away. Resist this temptation. Instead, each time you get to the next side-glide position, pause long enough to assess, correct, and plan ahead by doing the following:

- Assess the position you finished the rotation in—posture, balance, lead arm angle—and how you got there. By the time you start the SGSS drill, you should have done enough side-gliding and spent enough time checking each of the feedback tools to know whether you have finished with an impeccable, horizontal tight line.

- Correct any flaws in your posture, balance, or position.
- Plan ahead for the next repetition. Decide whether you need to make any changes, and mentally rehearse your next step before continuing.

As you improve at the SGSS drill, you will gain confidence in your ability to maintain your posture and balance as you rotate, seldom or never needing to make corrections after assessing your performance.

Stepping-Stone to SGSS

If you find it difficult to stay in balance with your lead arm and your passing zone in front of your head, try the following: Instead of rotating completely from one side to the other, stop halfway, when you are flat on your front, with both arms extended in front of you. Continue kicking in this position for several seconds until you are sure that you are balanced. Then continue the rotation and stroke to your other side.

Feedback Tools

- You already know, and should use, all the feedback tools for your side-glide positions.
- Keep pressure on your buoy as you rotate so that your hips stay at the surface throughout the rotation to your other side. If your butt does not remain at the surface of the water as you rotate and if you are not able to feel your flank (or the dry strip of flesh on the side arm all the way to your wrist) exposed just as you get to the side-glide position, then you have either (1) lost your tight line, (2) lost buoy pressure, or (3) lifted your head. A lifted head is the most likely culprit, and it will almost certainly cause you to lose your buoy pressure and your tight line.
- When you are not using a snorkel, check that your head and body rotate as a single unit rather than head first or body first. Think, *Head and hips move together.*

Experiment a Bit

With practice, you will gradually spend less time in each side-glide position checking your balance and posture. You can then experiment by performing some of the repeats without turning your head to breathe, remaining nose down. Common breathing patterns include breathing every second repeat or every third repeat. Of course, experimenting with shifting between schlumpy and tight-line postures should be a habit by now.

The SGSS drill is a great tool for learning a variety of concepts and skills that you'll eventually apply to other drills and to full-stroke swimming. Each of these concepts and skills will, in turn, refine your execution of the SGSS drill. Before moving on to the next drill, spend some time working on each of the following focus points, one at a time, in the SGSS drill.

FOCUS POINT ➤ Pierce (Not Push) Down to Extension

It is important *how* you extend your arm at a downward angle in the water. As you begin to rotate, your fingertips should pierce the surface of the water and then continue along a straight line, at a slight downward angle, until your arm is fully extended. You also want your forearm to slide through the same small hole that your hand did. A common error is to extend the arm straight forward, either just above or just below the surface, and to then push the hand and arm down to the desired angle. This puts unnecessary stress on the shoulder, forces your front end up and your hips down, and wastes energy.

FOCUS POINT ➤ The Glove

Most novice and intermediate swimmers are rear-quadrant swimmers. To make the change to front-quadrant swimming, it is useful to sometimes exaggerate the arm timing a bit. Imagine that the extended hand has a loose-fitting glove on it. Leave it extended as you begin to rotate and as the other hand pierces the surface of the water forward and down toward the top of the extended hand. As soon as the fingertips slip under the cuff of the glove, the palm of the glove opens, allowing the extended arm to start stroking while the recovering hand continues to slide forward fully into the glove. The idea is to transfer the imaginary glove from hand to hand out in front at the extension point. Note that this is an exaggerated movement for instructive purposes only, and that when swimming normally, the two hands will not actually touch. You will, however, want the recovering hand to almost catch up to the extended hand before the extended arm begins the next stroke—hence, the passing-zone concept.

FOCUS POINT ➤ Wide Tracking

The glove focus point gives you a good feeling for where your arms should be longitudinally, but it has each hand entering and extending along a line directly in front of your head—as if you were moving along a monorail. What you want at any time you are *not* using the glove focus point is for each hand to enter and extend directly in front of its own shoulder—as if you were moving along a standard two-rail track with rails roughly shoulder-width apart. Taking wide tracking a step further, you want the general lines of the strokes to be shoulder-width apart as well.

FOCUS POINT ➤ Patches and Cheeks

Good balance means keeping a horizontal position at all times with your hips right at the surface. When swimming or when doing any drill that involves body rotation, focus on keeping a patch of skin on one hip or thigh just below your suit, or one or both butt cheeks, exposed to the air at all times—especially when breathing. A combination of tight-line posture and sufficient buoy pressure is required. Lifting the head or using a hand to push down on the water in front of the body will quickly sink the hips.

Three Strokes & Glide (3S&G)

Once you have worked enough with the focus points in the SGSS drill to feel comfortable and confident with them, it is time to take more strokes. This new drill will get you much closer to swimming. As the name suggests, it means to take three strokes and then glide. Though it sounds simple, to get it right, you should learn it in several steps:

1. Using your training snorkel, start by pushing off on your right side and kicking in the side-glide position, nose down. As soon as you are in a tight line and in balance, recover the trailing (left) arm over the water, and rotate and stroke onto your left side as you did in the SGSS drill. Immediately begin to recover the trailing (right) arm; then, as it passes your head, rotate onto your right side while taking the second stroke. As soon as you are on your right side, recover the trailing (left) arm. As it passes your head, rotate again while taking your third stroke onto the left side. When you are fully on your side, stop all action except kicking. Spend as much time as you need in the side-glide position to assess and correct your posture and balance and to plan for any changes that might improve the next set of three strokes. Note that you are now gliding on the left side of your body, opposite the side you started on.

   Go through another set of three strokes (which will return you to your original side-glide position on your right side). Again assess, correct, and plan ahead. Repeat for the length of the pool. Each cycle of three strokes is done in a continuous swimming rhythm. Expanding upon the hand-entry-to-kick coordination from the SGSS drill, you now want to *rhythmically* execute that coordination with successive hand entries in each three-stroke cycle. Practice this step until you can complete each set of three strokes with good posture and balance and without having to adjust anything.

2. The second step in the learning progression is similar to the first step. But instead of using the snorkel and keeping your nose down, you will now rotate your head to breathe on the third stroke of each set of strokes. Start the drill as you did before, but as you begin the third stroke, let your head turn with your body just as it did in the SGSS drill. As you finish that stroke and reach your side-glide position, your nose will be up. Assess and correct your posture and balance. Take a breath (or several, if needed) and turn your head back to the nose-down position, assess and correct your posture and balance again, and plan ahead for the next cycle. Repeat for the length of the pool. Practice this step until

you can complete each set of three strokes fully balanced, in the side-glide nose-up position, and without having to adjust anything.

3. The final step in learning 3S&G is to take your breath on the second stroke of each set of strokes and to do the glide portion between each set of three strokes in a nose-down position. As before, assess and correct posture and balance and plan ahead during the glide before you continue with the next set of three strokes. The goal of this step is to take that breath by letting your head rotate with your body to a nose-up position, then to inhale, and then to let your head rotate with your body back to a nose–down position, all without disrupting the rhythm of strokes and without losing your posture or balance. If after a couple of sets of three strokes you find that you need more air, you may turn your head to take an additional breath or two during the glide phase (but only after you have assessed and corrected your posture and balance).

Feedback Tools

- Each time you rotate and stroke, you should be aware of your navel pointing directly toward the sidewall, just as it does when you are in side-glide position.

- Each time you take a stroke, be sure to swap hands out in front of your body, perhaps using the glove focus point from time to time.

- As you reach the side-glide position at the end of the third stroke of each set, you should feel the dry strip of flesh along your trailing arm. If not, you have either lifted your head up, let pressure off your buoy, lost your tight line, or some combination thereof.

- Make any necessary corrections and stay in the side-glide position long enough to think through any changes you will need to make on the next set of three strokes.

Experiment a Bit

If you carefully follow the progression I've laid out, mastering each step before moving on to the next, you will end up with a drill that is close to full-stroke swimming but that provides opportunities to assess, correct, and plan ahead. As you improve at the 3S&G drill, you can take more strokes in each set of strokes, effectively turning the drill into a 5S&G or 7S&G drill in which you will take two or more breaths during each set of strokes. Only increase the number of strokes once you are able to maintain posture, balance, and rhythm while taking breaths and only once you are able to enter each glide phase with a fully balanced tight line that needs no correction.

Fine-Tuning Your Stroke

You have likely noticed that the concepts and drills presented so far each build on prior information. You are constructing both a skill base and a knowledge base, and you are only partially done. Fundamental skills are the foundation on which refinements and more complex skills can be built. This sections details the entire stroke cycle—stroke, recovery, and entry and extension—and offers refinements and additions to what has already been discussed. In subsequent chapters, there will be even more. Why don't I just explain it all at once and *then* send you to the pool? Because experience gained in another complex endeavor is instructive here—that is, detailed instructions for juggling chainsaws while riding a unicycle on a high wire are not germane until sometime *after* you can juggle tennis balls while standing on terra firma. In other words, too much information too soon gets in the way of learning.

Propulsive Arm Stroke

It's time to explain more fully what the hand and arm do during the underwater propulsive part of the stroke. Simply put, your paddle (that is, your hand and forearm) should be vertical to the pool bottom as far out in front of your body as possible and should be kept vertical for as much of the stroke as possible. This is often referred to as swimming with a high-elbow stroke. It sounds simple, but as usual, there are details to clarify.

The stroke begins with what is called the catch—the spot where you first get a propulsive grip on the water. To get a feel for the catch, place an empty beer keg (or similarly sized round container) on its side on a low table. Bend forward and extend your arm in front of you at a bit of a downward angle, placing your hand lightly on top of the keg. Now step forward, keeping your hand on the same spot on the keg so that the keg rolls forward. As the keg rolls, curve your hand and arm over it, lifting your elbow slightly to avoid leaning on or otherwise exerting any downward force on the keg. Continue rolling the keg until your hand is on the far side of the keg and the inside of your elbow and upper arm are touching the top of the keg (remember, no leaning). To reach this position, you had to flare your armpit and contract your back muscles, which engaged a line of muscular tension across your back, through your shoulder, and to your paddle. I call this your paddle linkage. You will recall that the muscular tension of your tight-line posture firmly connects your head, torso, and hips into a kayaklike shape. In the same manner, this new line of muscular tension firmly connects your paddle to your tight line. Now you have an idea of what the beginning of the stroke—that is, the catch—will feel like.

Try it in the pool with an imaginary keg that is just deep enough in the water that as you side glide with your arm extended at a downward angle, your hand rests just on top of the keg (figure 5.5a). As you glide forward, curve your arm over the keg, rolling it forward (figure 5.5b). It should feel as though you are running your elbow forward over your hand (figures 5.5b and c), not pulling your hand back or down. As you reach over the keg, consciously flare your armpit and feel your back muscles connect your paddle to your tight line— engage your paddle linkage. Avoid applying downward pressure—don't sink your imaginary keg.

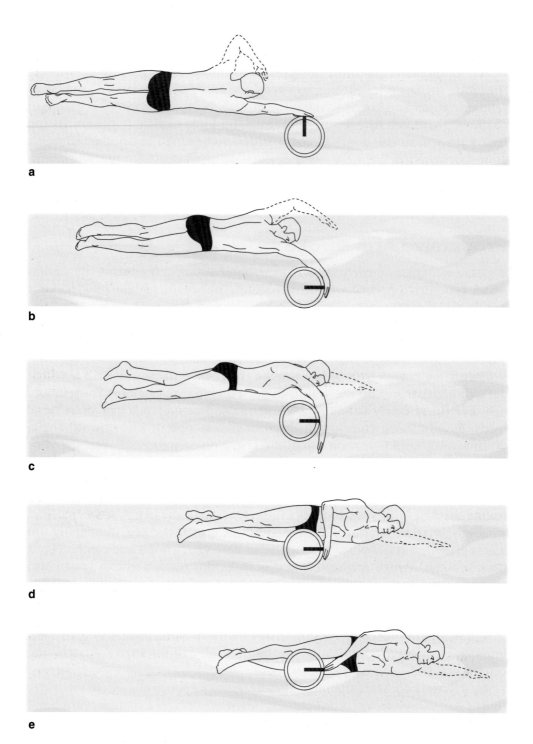

Figure 5.5 Over-the-keg stroke. *(a)* Glide forward on your side. *(b, c)* Reach over the keg as far as you can, putting your paddle in as vertical a position and as far in front of you as possible. *(c, d)* Continue to keep the paddle vertical for as much of the stroke as possible. *(e)* Finish levering past the keg. Note that the keg remains in place throughout the series of drawings, and you move past it rather than yanking it backward.

Depending on your shoulder's flexibility, when you reach your arm over the keg, you are either just about to initiate your next rotation (more flexible shoulders), or you have just begun your rotation (less flexible shoulders). In either case, the typical action is to drop the elbow and to use arm and shoulder muscles to yank the hand backward through the water. Don't. Instead, keep your armpit flared, use mainly your arm and shoulder muscles to keep your paddle vertical through as much of the stroke as possible (figures 5.5c and d), and use your paddle linkage to transmit core rotation to your paddle (figure 5.5e). The sensation should be more like levering past the keg, with as much as 75 percent of the work coming from the back and core rotation and as little as 25 percent coming from the arms and shoulders.

FOCUS POINT ➤ Downward Angle Arm Extension (expanded)

An effective catch eludes most swimmers because they extend the arm either horizontally or at a bit of an upward angle. For most swimmers, unless the arm is extended at a bit of a downward angle, there is not enough room between the ball of the upper-arm bone and the roof of the shoulder to allow for an effective high-elbow catch. Instead, the swimmer will do little more than push down on the water at the beginning of the stroke, which will not propel him forward. Extending the arm at a bit of a downward angle allows greater range of motion as the swimmer attempts to achieve an effective catch.

FOCUS POINT ➤ Over-the-Keg Stroke

Reach over an imaginary keg as far out in front of the body as possible to make a high-elbow catch at the beginning of your stroke. Then use your core rotation, transmitted through the muscular tension of your tight line and paddle linkage, to lever past the keg.

FOCUS POINT ➤ Snappy Hips

Want to put more power in your stroke? Think *snappy hips*. In the car analogy, the faster the engine turns the crankshaft, the faster the wheels turn. Similarly, the faster you rotate your hips from one side to the other, the faster your body rotates forward past that imaginary keg. Use your long-axis rotation skills to drive a faster rotation of your hips. Your tight-line posture and paddle linkage will transmit that extra speed through your paddle to the water, which will produce a more propulsive stroke.

FOCUS POINT ➤ Finish Your Strokes

A common error is to not finish your strokes. While standing up straight, reach down with both arms and touch your thighs. This is roughly where you want to finish each stroke when you are practicing drills or when swimming at easy or moderate paces. When swimming or drilling, occasionally brush your thumb against your thigh as you complete a stroke in order to see where you are finishing your strokes. Do this on both sides, as it is common for them to be different. Correcting strokes that are even a few inches short will let you travel noticeably farther with each stroke and thus take fewer strokes.

Safe and Efficient Recovery and Entry

In swimming, even the motions you make in the air are important. They affect how you move in the water in much the same way that a kayaker's arm motions above the water affect the kayak in the water. Correcting how your arm comes out of the water, moves forward, and reenters the water can increase the effectiveness of your technique. The following focus points are offered in order from the beginning of your recovery to the end of your entry.

FOCUS POINT ➤ Marionette Recovery

The recovery starts from where the stroke and rotation have finished—you are on your side, with your hand just below the surface by your thigh (or, in some drills, resting on your thigh). Imagine that you are a marionette. Your puppeteer has a single string attached—to the elbow on your recovering arm. Your puppeteer lifts your arm out of the water by pulling up on that string. Your elbow rises while your forearm and hand hang down, relaxed from the elbow, with the fingertips near the water's surface (perhaps even dragging through the surface) and close to the body (figure 5.6a). As the elbow travels toward the front end of your vessel, the hand follows a nearly straight line forward, never straying far from the body or the water's surface (figure 5.6b).

FOCUS POINT ➤ Neutral Shoulder

A common recovery mistake is to allow, or force, the elbow to move behind the plane that divides the body between the front (navel) side and back (butt) side. This causes the head of the upper-arm bone to bind against the back and top of the shoulder socket—a no-win bone-on-bone conflict. Over the course of thousands (or millions) of repetitions, this motion will almost certainly cause an injury. But in the marionette recovery, you want to keep the shoulder roughly in the center of its front-to-rear range of motion. This keeps the elbow in front of the body plane and allows the shoulder to stay high and relaxed throughout the recovery (figures 5.6a and b).

FOCUS POINT ➤ Laser-Beam Rotation Trigger

I have talked about rotating the body from one side-glide position to the other, but not much about *when* to rotate. The secret to timing your rotation is in the recovery. Imagine a laser beam stretching across your lane at the front edge of your head, a few inches above the water's surface. As your puppeteer moves your elbow, forearm, and hand forward, nothing else about your body position should change (i.e., you stay on your side and you

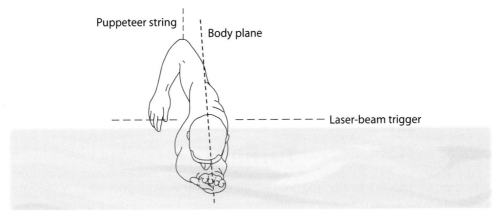

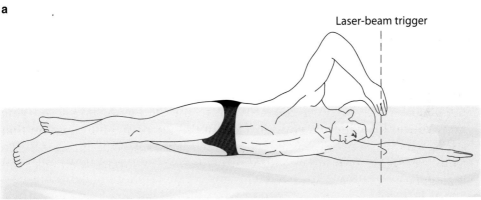

Figure 5.6 Marionette recovery with fingertips dragging through the surface. *(a)* Head-on view. Note the side-glide position and the high elbow in front of the body plane. *(b)* Side view. The recovering hand is passing through the laser-beam rotation-trigger point at the top of the head.

keep the other arm fully extended). When the recovering hand crosses the laser beam, this is the trigger to begin rotating your body (in the side view of the marionette recovery figure, the recovering hand is just crossing this imaginary laser beam). As your legs drive your core rotation, the recovering hand continues moving forward toward the entry point. Using this mental image will result in a nearly perfect front-quadrant stroke.

FOCUS POINT ➤ Sliding-Board Entry

Your legs are not alone in driving your core body rotation. Their job is to *initiate* the rotation, and another mechanism helps complete the rotation. Lifting your arm and shoulder out of the water during the recovery stores energy (potential energy) in the form of a lifted mass that is poised to fall again (kinetic energy). As your hand passes through the imaginary laser beam and you begin the next core body rotation with your legs, you release that stored energy by allowing your arm and shoulder to fall toward the water. You guide its descent—as if the hand were zipping down a sliding board so that it pierces the surface of the water at a downward angle toward your extension point. The kinetic energy of this falling and extending mass adds to the energy of your core body rotation and is thus transmitted to the stroking arm through your tight line and paddle linkage. The muscles that you use along that side of your body to aggressively enter and extend further add to the power and snappiness of your rotation.

Turning

Whether swimming or drilling, once you get to the wall, you need to do one of two things: (1) turn or (2) get out. Assuming that you opt for the former, there are a few considerations. What you want with any turn is a rapid change of direction in a minimum amount of time, without losing speed, and while conserving energy.

You can choose to do a flip turn—that somersault-looking thing that fast swimmers do when they swim freestyle—or you can do an open turn, the turn commonly used for breaststroke and butterfly. The open turn allows you to take a breath at the wall but the flip turn does not. For just a lap or two, this is not a big deal. But for distances of 200 yards or more, this difference adds up. Flip turns are more complex and take much longer to learn than open turns. Virtually everyone who swims laps, however, wants a high-quality flip turn as part of their swimming arsenal. Following are descriptions of lightning-fast, low-cost turns of both varieties and of what should happen following either.

Open Turns

To execute an open turn, as you near the end of the pool, take your last stroke aggressively into your balanced side-glide position, with one arm extended in front of you, your trailing arm just at the surface of the water, and your navel facing the sidewall. (Throughout the turn and push-off, your navel should face the sidewall.) Continue kicking as you finish this last stroke and until your extended hand touches the wall. Allow the wall arm to bend as your momentum moves your body toward the wall (figure 5.7a). Avoid grabbing the gutter, since pulling yourself up breaks the momentum of the turn and wastes energy. Draw your legs up tightly under you and let the momentum of your body swing your hips toward the wall as you push your upper torso away from the wall with your arm (figure 5.7b). Leave your trailing arm near the surface rather than moving it with your hips. Your body will pivot around a point in your midsection.

As the wall arm pushes off the wall, your torso is straight and your legs are tucked in tight under you as you swing them toward the wall. Your wall arm swings over your head as your body continues to pivot around a point in your midsection. At this instant, no part of your body is touching the wall (figure 5.7c). While your upper torso pivots down into the water, you want the top arm to meet the trailing arm below the surface of the water at the instant your

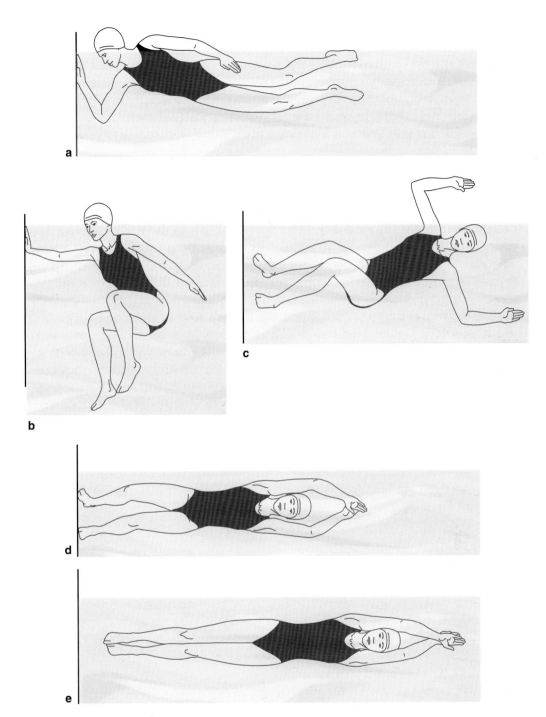

Figure 5.7 A good open turn allows you to take a breath while still turning lightning fast. *(a)* Accelerate your last stroke into the side-glide position. As your extended hand touches the wall, allow the arm to bend without grabbing the gutter. *(b)* Draw your legs up tightly under you. Momentum swings your hips toward the wall as you push away from it, while your body pivots around a point at your midsection. *(c)* Swing your arm straight over your head as your pivot continues. No part of your body is touching the wall. *(d)* Your top arm meets the trailing arm below the surface as your feet make contact with the wall and you begin leaping away. *(e)* Snap into javelin position as you leave the wall on your side.

feet—just the toes and balls, you should not be flat footed—contact the wall at shoulder's width *as* you are leaping into a fully streamlined glide position (figure 5.7*d*). Don't plant your feet or crouch any more deeply before leaping off the wall. Your goal is to have your feet in contact with the wall for no longer than a bouncing golf ball would stay on the ground (figure 5.7*e*).

Flip Turns

Once you have mastered the open turn, and only then, you might want to try the flip turn. Approach the wall by accelerating your last two strokes, finishing each at your thighs (figure 5.8*a*). More speed going into the wall makes for an easier turn. Execute a strong, quick pike, as if doing a toe-touch sit-up (figures 5.8*b* and *c*). Don't let your hands or elbows move out to the sides. Keep them in close to your line of travel throughout the turn. Your upper body should be three-quarters of the way through the turn as the hips and legs continue gliding toward the wall at the surface (figure 5.8*c*). Pick up your heels by quickly bending at the knees (figures 5.8*d* and *e*). This is the only large muscular movement needed to get your legs over the top of the water—momentum does the rest (figures 5.8*e* and *f*). Trying to throw your legs over the surface just pushes the upper body deep into the water. By allowing momentum to swing your legs over, your upper body will remain parallel with the surface of the water.

As you make contact with the wall, your feet should be at shoulder width or wider and your knees should be bent almost to 90 degrees. Your feet should hit the wall *as* your push-off begins (figures 5.8*f* and *g*). Do not plant your feet or, worse, crouch deeper before your push-off. Your feet should hit the wall *because* you are leaping away from it, not *before* you leap. Think *flip-push* instead of *flip-plant-push*.

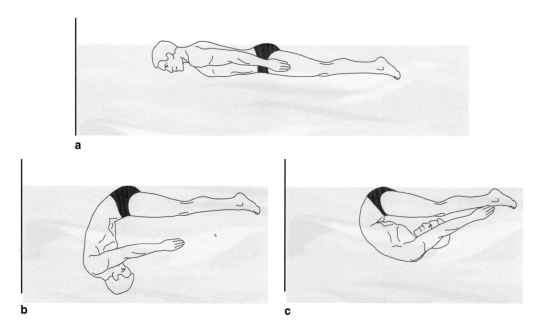

a

b   c

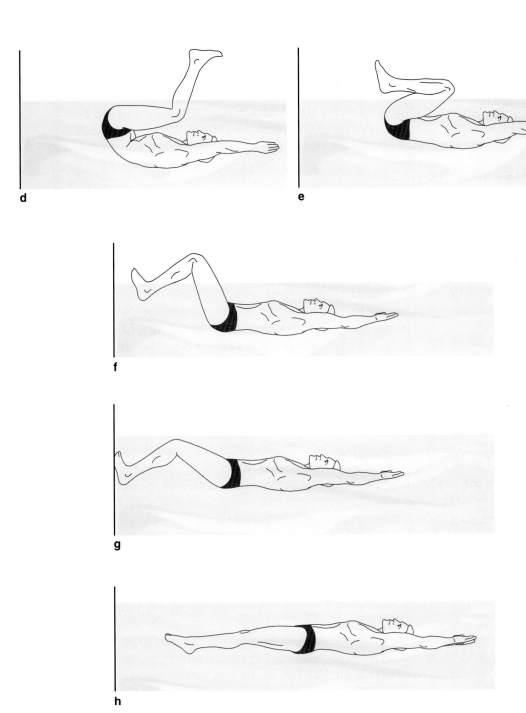

Figure 5.8 A quick, compact flip turn is considered by many to be the defining skill of a real swimmer. *(a)* Accelerate the last two strokes before the wall, finishing each at your thighs. Your nose is pointed straight down. *(b)* Begin a strong, quick pike, keeping your hands and elbows in close to your line of travel. *(b, c)* Your upper body moves most of the way through the turn while your hips and legs glide toward the wall at the water's surface. *(d, e)* Pick up your heels by quickly bending at the knees, as if trying to kick yourself in the butt. *(e, f)* Momentum carries your legs over the surface of the water and your upper body remains nearly parallel with it. *(g)* Feet touch the wall with knees bent *as* your push-off begins. Your feet should be shoulder width apart or wider. *(h)* Snap into javelin position as you leave the wall on your back.

Note from the diagrams that you should enter the turn on your belly and leave on your back (figure 5.8*h*). Twisting onto your side or twisting back to your belly before pushing off slows the turn. Leap off the wall on your back under the water's surface, *then* twist your body slightly so that you corkscrew through the water and end up on your side, gliding away from the wall.

After the Turn

Regardless of which turn you use, when you leave the wall, you will be traveling underwater faster than you can swim on the surface. Because there is less resistance below the surface than at the surface, this first 5 to 9 yards (4.6 to 8.2 meters) of each length (20 to 30 percent of a short-course swimming pool) becomes an opportunity to capitalize on faster-than-swimming glide speed with little or no energy expense—free speed.

During your push-off, snap into a fully streamlined position—tight-line posture, hand on top of hand, top thumb locked around the edge of the other hand, one wrist directly on top of the other wrist, ears squeezed firmly between your upper arms, legs together, and toes pointed. Think *javelin*. As your toes leave the wall, you should already be in javelin position (except that your legs will come together just after the toes leave the wall). An extra fraction of a second to get there will squander a large percentage of your faster-than-swimming glide speed. The push-off should happen 12 to 18 inches (about 30 to 45 cm) below the surface in order to avoid gliding through the waves and surface turbulence that have followed you to the wall.

Pushing off too hard can result in overshooting a streamlined javelin position, arching the back at full extension instead. Start with slow push-offs and focus on hitting a tight-line posture and a streamlined position as your feet leave the wall. As you hone your ability to snap into the javelin position, gradually increase your push-off oomph for more speed and distance.

During your glide, buoyancy should bring you to the surface. Trying to steer yourself to the surface will cause you to lose momentum quickly. Kicking or climbing to the surface costs muscle energy. Allowing buoyancy to lift you to the surface is free. Depending on personal buoyancy, your push-off may need to be either horizontal or angled slightly downward. Adjusting the amount of air in your lungs will alter your ascent rate (less air = slower rise toward the surface). You want to reach the surface just as the first stroking arm breaks the surface as recovery begins. The goal is to begin your first stroke just as your faster-than-swimming glide slows to swimming speed. Taking your first stroke too soon will slow you prematurely. Glide too long and your first strokes will have to accelerate you back to swimming speed.

Begin a compact, rapid kick before you take your first stroke. How early in your streamlined glide you begin that kick depends on the quality of your kick. If you have a fast, compact kick that adds substantially to the distance you travel at faster-than-swimming speed, then it may be useful to start it as soon as your feet leave the wall (realizing that there is a tradeoff here, because even an excellent kick costs a lot of energy). If your kick is weak, it may actually slow you down. Simply gliding with your toes pointed until just before your first stroke may be your best choice. Experiment with both options.

As you learn to stay under the water longer, your body will cry out for air, urging you to cut short your faster-than-swimming glide. You may tend to lift your head or otherwise contort yourself out of streamline to get that first breath of air. Breathing every other stroke (instead of every third or fourth stroke) while swimming will allow you to hold your breath on turns long enough to capitalize on your faster-than-swimming glide. Practicing long glides consistently will help you resist the urge to surface early yet still allow you to get an adequate first breath as you begin to swim.

PART III

Swimming Workouts

A swimming workout is not just about diving in and churning the water as hard as possible until they close the pool (though some people approach it that way). In our paradigm, a workout, and the conditioning that results from it, is a by-product of learning and practicing the skills of highly effective swimming (hence I use the words *workout* and *practice* interchangeably). A well-planned workout involves activities intended to teach or refine a variety of skills and to practice those skills at a variety of planned intensities. This part will help you plan your workouts. Chapter 6 explains various exercise intensities as well as some ways to measure and control your exertion level. It also explains workout training zones and how they relate to the six levels of workouts that follow. In addition, the chapter discusses effective warm-ups and cool-downs. Chapters 7 through 12 include the six workout levels, each of which contains 10 skill-building and conditioning workouts.

Workout Format

In order to fit each workout onto a single, easy-to-photocopy page, we use shorthand notation for most of the workout instructions. Each workout-level chapter includes detailed instructions on how to read the workout notation. As you move from level to level, new and sometimes more complex notation is added.

Because most workout pools in the United States are short-course pools (25 yards or 25 meters long), all workouts are written for short-course pools and can be used in 20-yard pools. With some commonsense adaptations, they can also be used in 50-meter pools.

Before starting a workout, read through the entire workout, as well as the notes, in order to make sure you understand what the instructions call for—you don't want to be chest-deep in the water and need to look up a drill description or a workout notation in the book. Begin each workout with the warm-up and move immediately from one activity to the next. Take no more than 15 to 20 seconds after completing one line of the workout to begin the next line. Skipping any portion of the practice can greatly alter the training effect of the entire workout.

On page 223, you will find a legend showing the abbreviation and full name of each drill used in the book, as well as the page where the drill description appears. You'll also find each of the focus points summarized beginning on page 220. You may want to put photocopies of these in water-tight sandwich bags to keep at the poolside for easy reference.

Choosing a Training Level

Because level 1 workouts consist primarily of posture, balance, and swimming-skill drills, these practices are excellent for isolating skills and refining technique, or for a warm-up before intense workouts. Regardless of your swimming background, I encourage you to start with level 1 and to work through all the practices in the order presented. Skilled swimmers may find that they can breeze through more than one of these practices in a single pool session. Less-skilled swimmers might do just one practice per pool session and, in fact, may need to repeat a practice a couple of times before moving to the next one.

In any exercise regimen, there is a certain excitement, anticipation, and eagerness over moving to the next level. For long-term success, however, it is necessary to be fully prepared for each step up. In each of the levels 1 through 4, be sure to complete every practice before moving up to the next level. I encourage you to make at least two full passes through the level before moving on to the next one. You should be able to complete all the practices in a level without straying out of the target heart-rate range any longer than brief periods. You should also feel confident with the skill drills and focus points presented in your current level before moving up to the next level. If not, you may want to review and practice the areas you are not confident with. When a skill eludes you, often the problem is that you have not mastered an earlier skill. If you find that you are struggling to complete workouts as you progress through a level, then backtrack, either returning to the beginning of the level or even, perhaps, to an earlier level.

If you are an accomplished swimmer who is chomping at the bit to get to the hard work, I strongly suggest that you still progress through the workouts in levels 1 through 4 in the order in which they are presented. If you decide to skip over any levels, however, be sure to at least read through them in order to familiarize yourself with the terminology and training concepts presented in each section.

Every workout level will repeatedly revisit the most fundamental skills. As the practices progress through a level, you will notice a logical pattern of increasingly difficult skills. This repeated cycling through all the skill levels is a cornerstone of long-term stroke development.

Charting Progress

Before you began your exercise program, you completed the T-20 swim (page 21) and kept records of your performance. Each time you cycle through a set of practices in a level, repeat the T-20 swim and compare your new results with previous ones.

As you complete each level, you should see improvement in distance, speed, IHR (or average heart rate for the last half of the swim), average stroke count, RPE, or a combination of these. Eventually you will feel confident about moving up to T-30 swims. By the time you have completed level 4, you should be doing T-30s instead of T-20 swims.

Ability vs. Conditioning

In swimming, as with any sport, ability is a combination of technique and conditioning. In general terms, we can define ability as the intersection of three measureable factors: How fast do you swim? For how long can you swim? How much energy do you use while you swim?

It is common to confuse conditioning with ability or to discount the importance of technique, so ability and conditioning become synonymous in many athletes' eyes. For sports that use motions we are naturally suited for, such as running, or for motions that are easily constrained or controlled, such as those in cycling, it is easy to blur the distinction between conditioning and ability. Technique in these sports is a much smaller component of overall ability than is conditioning. In sports such as golf, tennis, or the martial arts, however, technique is a much larger component of ability than conditioning.

Swimming falls into this latter category. Ability in swimming is 70 to 90 percent technique and only 10 to 30 percent conditioning. In addition to providing you a great conditioning workout, the practices in this book strongly emphasize improving your technical ability. In levels 1 and 2, 60 to 90 percent of each practice is skill drills that isolate specific, critical aspects of freestyle swimming. The remaining 10 to 40 percent are short swims (one or two lengths) with a specific concept or skill to focus on. As you move through the levels, there will be more emphasis on swimming. Levels 3 and 4 include 40 to 70 percent drills, and levels 5 and 6 include 20 to 50 percent drills.

Continuing Technique Education

As you move through the levels, you will continue to learn, build, and refine your technique. New skills, drills, concepts, and focus points are introduced along the way as your experience, confidence, and competence grow. But even as you encounter and master new material, don't assume that you can dispense with the foundational drills you've already learned. These drills show up in practices at every level in the following chapters. In fact, throughout your swimming career, the drills in this book will continue to be beneficial for expanding and refining your skill base.

Cavorting

A special feature of levels 2 and up is cavorting, where playful activities are incorporated into the workouts. Ever notice that kids in a swimming pool behave differently than adults do? They jump, they bob, they do flips, they do cannonballs, they sit on the bottom, and they make up silly games. In other words, they play. They are always learning about their environment and are always expanding their comfort zone within that environment. Because of this constant *unintentional* physical learning, kids are more capable of *intentionally* grasping and executing new skills when the opportunity presents itself. Adults tend to repeat patterns of behavior during every visit to the pool—same number of laps, same strokes, same pace, same equipment, same lane, same thoughts, same, same, same. Adults find a comfort zone and stay well within it. Very little learning takes place when one never does anything new or different.

I challenge you to do something different in the water every day—perhaps something that you've never done before, perhaps something silly. Play! Cavort! You will become more comfortable and relaxed in the water. You will have more confidence in your ability to learn and execute new skills. You will learn these skills more rapidly. In the long run, you will be a better swimmer and you'll have more fun.

Toward this end, I have included a number of cavorts in the workouts. Some may seem entirely unrelated to swimming; some may seem antithetical to effective swimming; others may simply be an interesting variation on a drill or skill that you have been working on. Don't feel limited by what I suggest or how often I suggest it. If the cavort I suggest is not workable in your situation, make up something different. Cavorting is also a great way to warm up or cool down. If you are so stodgy and grown up that you simply can't bring yourself to play or cavort, then think of it as practicing improvised aquatic skills instead. You can always pretend that you aren't having any fun doing it.

CHAPTER 6

Workout Intensity

Much of the conditioning methodology in this book involves regularly monitoring your exercise intensity and adjusting your effort level in order to keep your overall exercise intensities within specified ranges. There are a number of ways to judge training intensity while exercising, but not all are easily applicable to swimming. This chapter presents two methods that you can use separately or in tandem in order to gauge and control your exercise intensity: ratings of perceived exertion and measured heart rate. I also explain how to apply those numbers to the workouts in this book for maximum benefit. Finally, I explain how to prepare for your exertions and how to cool down afterward.

Perceived Exertion

Developed and updated by Dr. Gunnar Borg, the rating of perceived exertion (RPE) scale allows you to assign numbers to how you feel during exercise. By monitoring how hard you are working, you can adjust the intensity of the activity to a prescribed level on the scale. Through the practice of monitoring how your body feels, it will become easier to know when to adjust your intensity. For example, a swimmer who intends to exercise at a moderate intensity would aim for a Borg scale level of somewhat hard (12 to 14). If partway into the swim her muscle fatigue and breathing are very light (9 on the Borg scale), then she should swim faster. But if she finds that her exertion is extremely hard (19 on the Borg scale), she should slow down in order to move into the moderate-intensity range.

You will often see the acronym RPE in the practices described in the following chapters. Each practice will include a target RPE range for the workout. During each practice, you will be asked several times to rate your exertion level. You should use the Borg RPE scale to assess your exertion level *while you are still exercising* rather than after you stop.

Borg's RPE Scale Instructions

While exercising, we want you to rate your perception of exertion, i.e. how heavy and strenuous the exercise feels to you. The perception of exertion depends mainly on the strain and fatigue in your muscles and on your feeling of breathlessness or aches in the chest.

Look at this rating scale; we want you to use this scale from 6 to 20, where 6 means "no exertion at all" and 20 means "maximal exertion."

6	No exertion at all
7	Extremely light
8	
9	Very light
10	
11	Light
12	
13	Somewhat hard
14	
15	Hard (heavy)
16	
17	Very hard
18	
19	Extremely hard
20	Maximal exertion

9 corresponds to "very light" exercise. For a normal, healthy person it is like walking slowly at his or her own pace for some minutes.

13 on the scale is "somewhat hard" exercise, but it still feels OK to continue.

17 "very" hard is very strenuous. A healthy person can still go on, but he or she must really push him- or herself. It feels very heavy and the person is very tired.

19 on the scale is an extremely strenuous exercise level. For most people this is the most strenuous exercise they have ever experienced.

Try to appraise your feeling of exertion as honestly as possible, without thinking about what the actual physical load is. Don't underestimate it, but don't overestimate it either. It's your own feeling of effort and exertion that's important, not how it compares to other people's. What other people think is not important either. Look at the scale and the expressions and then give a number.

Measured Heart Rates

Heart rates are generally expressed as a number of beats per minute (bpm) and, if accurately taken, can precisely assess exercise intensity. You can monitor your heart rate either manually or electronically. In general, you will take your heart rate immediately upon completion of a lap. As soon as exertion ceases, your heart rate begins to drop. The better your aerobic conditioning, the faster it drops. You want to take your heart rate before it drops significantly. An electronic heart-rate monitor (HRM) is the much-preferred method of taking your heart rate. It is immediate and very accurate, and it requires little conscious thought and no refined skill.

A manual (or palpated) heart rate (taken by placing your fingers on an artery in your neck or wrist and then counting the beats) is much less accurate than an electronic reading for two reasons: Counting is difficult because the beats are rapid, you are tired, and your breathing is labored; and because your heart rate is dropping while you find and count your pulse, even an accurate count will be lower than the actual immediate heart rate. Only care and repetition can help with the former. We try to minimize the latter error by keeping the counting period short—0.10 of a minute, or 6 seconds—then multiplying by 10. But even a short count results in a calculated heart rate that is anywhere from 10 to 30 beats per minute lower than your actual heart rate. To offset this phenomenon, you can add 2 to the count before multiplying by 10. Even with this adjustment, the result is, at best, an estimate of your exercise heart rate rather than an accurate measurement.

How to Take a Manual Heart Rate

Use two fingers to locate your carotid artery, which is just below the hinge point of your jaw—an inch or so below your earlobe—and feel your pulse. Use the smallest amount of pressure that allows you to feel the beats. Some people can more easily find their pulse on the inside surface of their wrist, closer to the thumb than the pinkie. For 6 seconds, count the number of beats you feel. As you watch a clock, count one on the first beat after any convenient mark on the clock, then continue counting beats until the sixth second ticks by. If a beat falls on the 6-second mark, include it in your count. (For example, you finish swimming a particular distance, and when you look up, the second hand is on the 37-second mark. You locate your pulse by the 39-second mark. You begin counting on the first beat you feel after the 40-second mark. Start with one. Count all beats up to and including the 46-second mark.) Let's say you count 14 beats and you add your adjustment of 2 to get 16. Multiply that number by 10, and you have your estimated IHR of 160. If you are new to taking your heart rate in this manner, it will take some trial and error to get good at it. It is easier to find your pulse after physical exertion than when you are at rest, because the beats are stronger and are thus easier to feel.

You can become more accurate at manually taking your heart rates by borrowing a heart-rate monitor and doing some testing. You'll need a buddy to help you. While wearing the monitor, swim several different distances at various intensities. Immediately upon completing each swim, your buddy reads your monitor (but does not tell you the result just yet) as you take your heart rate manually. Compare your reading with the reading your buddy took. Repeated experimentation like this can help you determine whether 2 is the correct adjustment for you. You may find that an adjustment of 1 or 3 (or more) gets you closer to the electronic readings. It is good to revisit this exercise every few months, because as your conditioning improves, your adjustment may change.

If you do not have access to a heart-rate monitor or if you are unable to consistently match your manual readings to electronic readings, then you should not take your heart rate manually to gauge exercise intensity. Either buy and use your own monitor or else use the RPE method described earlier in this chapter. RPE is also the preferred method to assess intensity among people who take medications that affect heart rate or pulse. Comparing heart rates taken manually during workouts to benchmarks calculated from electronic readings will likely yield unreliable results. If you choose to go the manual route, you should use manual heart rates both during workouts and for the calculations you'll be doing soon.

You will often see the acronym IHR in the following chapters. IHR is your heart rate taken *immediately* after completing a period of exertion. When you use an HRM, simply glance at it as soon as possible after touching the wall. The first number you see is your IHR. If you are taking your heart rate manually, use the method detailed in the How to Take a Manual Heart Rate sidebar.

SLTHR: Swimming Lactate-Threshold Heart Rate

During nearly all exercise, some combination of carbohydrate and fat is used for fuel. Lactate (lactic acid) is a by-product of carbohydrate metabolism in working muscles. If too much lactate accumulates in your muscles or blood, it begins to cause discomfort or pain and to limit performance. During exercise, your aerobic system clears lactic acid from your muscles and blood. At rest and at low and moderate levels of exertion, there is a balance between lactate production and lactate removal. As exercise intensity increases, however, there is a tipping point at which the body produces lactate faster than it can be removed. This causes an accumulation of lactate in the muscles and blood, which soon limits performance. This tipping point is called the anaerobic threshold or lactate threshold. Lactate-threshold work is the highest intensity of exercise that you can continue for an extended time, and it is a very effective work range for improving your aerobic fitness. A good portion of the training detailed in the practices is performed just at and just above your swimming lactate threshold. Other training intensities called for in the practices are also expressed as a percentage of your SLTHR.

In chapter 3, you were exposed to the T-20 swim. If you gave this swim your best effort, without stopping (or with only very short pauses) and without speeding up in the last two minutes, then the IHR you took at the end of this swim is your lactate-threshold heart rate for swimming. In fact, throughout your swimming career, your best-effort T-20 (or T-30) IHR will be your best indicator of your current SLTHR. But for those of you who are in poor condition, are new to sustained exercise, or are new to sustained swimming, your perception of a best effort may be well short of your true physical ability. Your T-swim IHR will thus fall short of your true swimming lactate-threshold heart rate. That's okay, though, because you'll have lots of opportunity to retest yourself and to get more accurate results. As you move through the workouts, the program will call for you to do T-swims on a regular basis. Each time you do a T-swim, the goal is to improve upon previous performances. If you approach each T-swim in that manner and if your conditioning and performances improve over time, your SLTHR will increase.

Training-Intensity Zones

Beneficial training adaptations will result from swimming at your lactate threshold, but beneficial adaptations will result from training at both lower and higher intensities as well. In fact, whenever you exercise at a heart rate greater than 70 percent of your SLTHR for at least 10 minutes, you can be sure that you will benefit from your efforts. Below 70 pecent of your SLTHR, any benefits will be negligible.

Above 70 percent of SLTHR, different training intensities produce different effects. Exercise intensity determines the training adaptation as well as the sensations you can expect during that training. There are five generally accepted training zones that are delineated by the different percentages of SLTHR. The workout levels in this book include work in each training zone.

Easy- or Active-Recovery Zone: IHR 70 to 80 Percent of SLTHR, RPE 9 to 11

This is the lowest intensity of exercise that has some fitness benefit. Beginners and people who have not exercised for a long time should start in this zone. It is a good recovery zone for people who need a break from hard training. It is also the correct intensity for recovery swims between intense exercise bouts and for cool-downs at the end of practice sessions. Easy work allows you to recover from hard work more rapidly than total rest does. Easy aerobic training stimulates circulation and growth-hormone release, which speeds the healing of tissues that have been damaged by hard training. The main source of fuel used by the muscles at this intensity is body fat. Work in this zone is perceived as very light to light and is comfortable for long durations.

Low-Aerobic Zone:
IHR 80 to 90 Percent of SLTHR, RPE 11 to 13

This is a good zone for long, slow distance swimming. Exercise done in this zone improves the ability of your heart to pump blood and of your muscles to utilize oxygen. The body becomes more efficient at metabolizing stored body fat, still the main source of fuel for your muscles. Training in this zone is an effective way to overload endurance muscle fibers, and training above this intensity is less beneficial for this purpose.

This intensity is perceived as easy to moderate, depending on your fitness level—comfortable enough that you may not feel like you are actually training. Because of this, the most difficult part of following a heart-rate training program is keeping the intensity low on easy days and in long workouts. Performing basic aerobic workouts at too high of an intensity reduces the effectiveness of harder workouts on subsequent days. Working too hard on easy days is a primary cause of overtraining.

High-Aerobic Zone:
IHR 90 to 95 Percent of SLTHR, RPE 13 to 14

This zone is effective for improving overall cardiorespiratory fitness. Working here improves your ability to transport oxygenated blood to the muscle cells and carbon dioxide out of the cells. Glycogen (glucose) and fat are both utilized for fuel here, but as you do more training at this level, your body will burn less glucose and more stored fat. Since lactic acid is a by-product of glycogen

© Icon Sports Media

Effective conditioning for swimming requires work at a variety of intensities while maintaining excellent technique.

metabolism in working muscles, you will experience some effects of lactic acid. But because this work is not very intense, your aerobic system is able to clear the lactic acid from the muscles before enough accumulates to cause pain or limit performance. This zone is also somewhat effective for increasing muscle strength. Training in this zone can be perceived as moderate and comfortable to somewhat hard and somewhat uncomfortable, depending on your fitness level.

Lactate-Threshold Zone: IHR 95 to 100 Percent of SLTHR, RPE 14 to 15

Lactate-threshold exercise is the highest intensity of exercise that you can continue for an extended time. Training near your lactate threshold increases your lactate threshold, which means that you'll be able to maintain a faster swimming pace for a longer time. The closer to your actual lactate-threshold heart rate you train, the greater this training effect. Training in this zone is perceived as difficult but tolerable: your muscles will feel tired, your breathing will be heavy, and you will be uncomfortable.

Red-Line Zone: IHR Above SLTHR, RPE 16 and Up

In this zone, you push your body to its limit. Only train in this zone if you are very fit and have your physician's blessing. It is possible to stay in this zone only for a short time since lactic acid accumulates rapidly, limiting performance. Training in this zone improves your body's ability to buffer and clear lactic acid. It also improves the contractility of your fast-twitch muscle fibers, which increases speed. Your body can tolerate a relatively small amount of this type of work, but a little goes a long way. This intensity of training is perceived as extreme: your muscles will burn, your breathing will be very heavy, you will be in pain, and you may feel like you are going to vomit.

Putting RPE, IHR, and Heart-Rate Training Zones Together

For most people, there is a good correlation between RPEs and exercise heart rates. You can easily calculate your heart rates for each of the different RPEs and training zones by filling in the Personal Training-Zone Chart using your SLTHR from your T-20 swim.

Over time, your swimming lactate-threshold heart rate will change in response to your level and volume of training. Each time you do a T-swim, you are, in effect, retesting for your SLTHR (assuming that you do the swim according to the instructions and truly give your best effort—you should finish knowing you gave it everything you had). It is important, though, that you do not speed up or slow down during the last few minutes of your T-swim. This will ensure that your IHR at the end of the swim represents your average level of effort during the swim. If you have an HRM that will give you an average heart rate across a given interval, you can stop swimming for a few seconds at about the halfway point of the T-swim to start that interval. This will allow you to simply go for it through the rest of the swim and not have to worry about the "don't speed up near the end" restriction (just be sure to stop the interval as soon as you finish the swim). In this case, use the HRM average for that interval as your SLTHR.

As you experience higher SLTHRs in your T-swims, you should recalculate your heart-rate training zones. Similarly, if after a period of reduced training you experience lower SLTHRs in your T-swims, you should recalculate your chart entries. But if you simply have an off day or if you give your T-swim something less than your best effort, do not recalculate your chart entries.

Personal Training-Zone Chart

Date of T-swim: _____   Circle one: T-20   T-30

RPE	Feeling	Percent of SLTHR	Training zone
6	No exertion at all		Couch potating
7			
7.5	Extremely light		Canasta/poker
8			Easy recovery
9	Very light	SLTHR × .70 = _____	Easy recovery
			Easy recovery
10		SLTHR × .75 = _____	Easy recovery
			Easy recovery
11	Light	SLTHR × .80 = _____	Low aerobic
			Low aerobic
12		SLTHR × .85 = _____	Low aerobic
			Low aerobic
13	Somewhat hard	SLTHR × .90 = _____	High aerobic
			High aerobic
14		SLTHR × .95 = _____	High aerobic
			Lactate threshold
15	Hard (heavy)	SLTHR × 1.00 = _____	Lactate threshold
			Lactate threshold
16			Red line
			Red line
17	Very hard	SLTHR × 1.05 = _____	Red line
			Red line
18			Red line
			Red line
19	Extremely hard	SLTHR × 1.10 = _____	Red line
			Red line
20	Maximal exertion	SLTHR × 1.??	Red line

Workout Levels

The workouts in the following chapters are arranged into six workout levels according to duration and intensity. Workouts in the first four levels have a suggested range of effort, which is expressed as a percentage range of SLTHR and RPE. This is your target heart rate and RPE range for most of the practice. You will take an IHR or RPE several times during each practice. In general, your goal should be to monitor your exertion level and rest periods so that your heart rate or RPE stays in the recommended target range. Sets in many practices will produce heart rates and RPEs that are somewhat higher than this range. These peaks will last for short periods and will usually be accompanied by rest or easy activity that is built into the practice, allowing your heart rate or RPE to return to within the specified target range. In levels 5 and 6, use of IHRs and RPEs will be a bit different. We'll talk more about that later.

Moving from one exercise level to the next either increases the average intensity of the workout or increases the duration of the workout. Within each level, there are 10 practices that are arranged roughly in order of increasing difficulty. The degree of difficulty varies from practice to practice and is affected by skill and drill complexity; by length, number, and intensity of swims; by amount of rest; and by target-heart-rate range. A summary of each workout level is given in the following table.

Level	Training Zone	RPE	Percentage of SLTHR	Duration
1	Recovery and low aerobic	9-11	70-90%	20-30 min
2	Recovery and low aerobic	9-11	70-90%	30-40 min
3	Low and high aerobic	11-14	80-95%	30-40 min
4	Low aerobic to lactate threshold	11-15	80-100+%	40-50 min
5	Red line and mix of others	9-19+	70-110+%	40-50 min
6	Red line and mix of others	9-19+	70-110+%	50-60 min

Warming Up and Cooling Down

The warm-up is your first in-water activity of each training session. The three important aspects of the warm-up are overcoming the chill of the water, getting your body ready for the workout, and tuning your mind in to the task. The best way to warm up is to get into the water and to start swimming *slowly* for several laps. Immediately, you are presented with a problem—water temperature that is comfortable during a workout is usually uncomfortably cool when you first get in. The urge to start sprinting can be strong, with heart-stopping, lung-gripping semipanic that only gives way to relative comfort after a few laps or more. But this can be a short path to injury. Better to do a dryland warm-up—calisthenics, Pilates, a brisk jog, or something similar to raise your body temperature and get you moderately sweaty—and then to jump into the water before you have a chance to cool down.

After adjusting to the water temperature, focus your mind and neuromuscular system. Going through a progression of swimming-skill drills will force your swimming muscles to move through all the ranges of motion that are required for full-stroke swimming. The drills also allow you to focus on proper execution. This is an excellent time to work on drills that are difficult to execute properly when you are tired. Your brain also takes a while to get fully involved, and skill drills focus it effectively. Adding full-stroke swimming by alternating a length of drilling with a length of swimming (that is, making what you correctly executed in the drill show up in your stroke) is an ideal way to transition into the main part of the workout. Avoid the tendency to just swim garbage yardage as your warm-up. The warm-ups throughout this book call for a mix of skill drills and swimming.

Actively cooling down at the end of a training session is like warming up in reverse—returning the body and all its functions to near-resting levels by doing some easy swimming or drilling. For a while after a strong exercise effort, your muscles continue to clear lactic acid into your bloodstream. Easy activity helps keep oxygenated blood flowing rapidly, thereby transporting lactic acid away from the muscles. Otherwise, lactic acid continues to accumulate even after you stop exercising. Listen to your car after you've turned it off following a long, hard drive; those sounds of ticking metal and passing vapors go on for minutes. In the same way, your body protests when you swim it hard and then come to a sudden stop. An active cool-down avoids extra strain on the heart and lessens postexercise cramping and soreness.

The cool-down is often treated as a waste due to the common misconception that moving at a low intensity offers no training effect. Ignorance is bliss. The most important training you do in swimming is the training of your neuromuscular system (doing it *right* rather than just doing it). The cool-down is an excellent time to do some high-quality drill work. In fact, coaxing your muscles to go through specific skill drills when they are fatigued presents an effective motor-learning opportunity. Choose drills and skills you have mastered for cool-downs rather than ones you have difficulty executing when rested.

CHAPTER 7

Level 1:
Basic Skills Workouts

Level 1 workouts consist primarily of posture, balance, and swimming-skill drills with a small amount of full-stroke swimming. The workouts in this chapter will take approximately 20 to30 minutes to complete. You will use each of the level 1 drills in the other levels. If you have trouble with a specific drill, spend extra time on it to get it right. Often the real problem is that you haven't mastered an earlier drill. Regardless of your ability, even the simplest drills in this book will enhance your neuromuscular knowledge. Until you are familiar with each drill, you might want to photocopy the drill descriptions and put them in watertight sandwich bags so that you can have them for quick reference at poolside while you practice.

You may do the workouts in this chapter with full-size or short-blade training fins. If you make good forward progress when kicking without fins, you can also do these workouts with bare feet. Assuming that you start with full-size fins, you will want to switch to short-blade fins and eventually to bare feet as you become more comfortable with various drills and exercises.

You will want to spend as much of your swimming time as possible emphasizing the fundamentals you have been learning. Use the focus points throughout the swim to keep your mind engaged. A photocopy of the focus-point list (page 220) in a plastic bag can come in handy.

After you have completed all of the practices in this chapter once, repeat the T-20 swim from chapter 3. The goal is to swim farther in the allotted 20-minute period than you did originally. Do the T-20 without fins so that you'll be comparing apples to apples. If you were unable to complete the initial T-20 swim without stopping, then you may improve significantly simply by taking shorter rests. After you complete the T-20, record your results with your original results, and be sure to recalculate your training-zone heart rates if your SLTHR has increased.

You should plan on going through the level 1 practices at least twice before moving to the next level. After your first pass through level 1, reread the descriptions of each drill and focus point that appear in the practices. Chances are you'll absorb new concepts and nuances that you may not have noticed when you first read them. After completing your second pass through level 1, repeat the T-20 and record the results before going on to level 2.

Reading the Workouts

I use some notation shortcuts throughout the practice sections of this book. At first glance they may be confusing, but after you've read through a couple of the examples that follow, you'll catch on.

6 × 25 swim TS on :15R

This means to swim six lengths (each length is 25 yards or meters) of the pool with your training snorkel (*TS*), taking 15 seconds rest at each end of the pool. In general, the rest duration is a suggestion rather than a requirement. The idea is to allow yourself enough time to regroup your thinking and to recover enough physically that you can continue with success. If you need more rest, take it. If your skills and conditioning allow you to take less rest, that's fine too.

1 × 100—alt 25 FB, 25 BB, 25 SGB, 25 SGSS

This means to do four lengths without stopping, moving from one drill to the next with each length.

6 × 25 on :15R—alt 25 FB, 25 BB

This means to swim six lengths of the pool, taking 15 seconds rest after each length. Alternate one length of front-balance drill and one length of back-balance drill.

4 × 50 SGNU on :15R as 25 rt, 25 lft

This means to do the SGNU (side-glide nose-up) drill for 50—two lengths of the pool with no rest at the far end—and then to rest for 15 seconds. Repeat three more times for a total of four 50s. On each 50, alternate doing the first length on your right side with doing the second length on your left side.

6 × :15 VK on :10R—odd: hands on your chest; even: hands out of the water

This notation asks for six 15-second periods of vertical kicking with different hand positions on odd and even repeats. There are 10-second rests between each 15-second VK period.

IHR or RPE

Immediate heart rate or rating of perceived exertion. When you see this, take your heart rate as quickly as possible after completing the activity. If you are using the Borg RPE scale instead, assess your level of exertion as you are completing the activity.

1 × 100 SGB-alt 25 good, 25 weak

Many skills involve doing something on one side, then repeating the action on the other side (e.g., side-glide balance, breathing, and the like). You will usually find that you are better at performing a skill on one side than on the other. On that side, you'll be more relaxed and better able to get into a proper position quickly. You may also be able to hold that position longer and with less effort. This is your good side. The side on which you experience more problems is your weak side.

Continuing Technique Education

In the original drill descriptions I included a number of focus points, each of which bring together two or more skills and feedback tools in a short, easy-to-remember phrase. These are intended to direct your thinking to important areas while swimming or drilling. You'll see them mentioned often in the workouts. As you progress through the levels and as your skills improve, I will introduce more focus points. Following are a few you are likely ready for now.

FOCUS POINT ➤ Downhill Swimming

When you are organized in a tight-line posture, maintain enough buoy pressure to keep your hips and legs at the surface. It should feel as if your entire body is tilted slightly downhill. You really want to be horizontal, but if your habit is to be in a somewhat uphill position—head and shoulders a bit higher than your hips and legs—then when you are in a horizontal position, it will *feel* like you are tilted slightly downhill.

FOCUS POINT ➤ Side Skating

As you take strokes, you should turn all the way onto your side, or nearly so, with each rotation of your body, so that your navel is pointed toward the side wall. Try to "skate" on that side with your bottom arm extended at a slightly downward angle. Continue skating in that position while the recovering arm moves forward past your head to the laser-beam rotation-trigger point.

FOCUS POINT ➤ Hand Swapping

This is one step short of the glove focus point. The idea is to keep your extended arm in front of your body until your recovering, or entering, hand is ready to take its place. Always use one of your hands as the front of your moving vessel; never use your head as the front. This is another way to think of front-quadrant swimming. See chapter 5, page 50 for a more complete description.

FOCUS POINT ➤ Stroke Count

One indicator of technical proficiency and swimming efficiency is the distance you travel with each stroke. Counting the number of strokes it takes to swim each length of the pool gives you excellent feedback about the distance you are traveling with each stroke—the fewer you take, the further you travel with each one. Count one for each hand as it enters the water. The last hand entry at the end of the pool counts as well, even though you touch the wall instead of taking another stroke.

1 Posture and Static Balance

Training zone: Recovery and low aerobic

Target RPE range: 9 to 11

Target heart-rate range: 70 to 85% of SLTHR

This entire practice is done at warm-up and cool-down intensity

2 × 25 FB on :20R *TS*

2 × 25 BB on :20R

4 × 25 on :15R—alt 25 FB, 25 BB

2 × 25 swim on :20R *TS* (focus: tight line)

IHR or RPE

2 × 25 SGND on :20R *TS*—alt 25 rt, 25 lft

4 × 25 on :15R—alt 25 FB, 25 BB—tight-schlumpy-tight on each length. Start each length with tight-line posture, then at about the halfway point, purposely relax into schlumpy posture for a few seconds, then lengthen again into tight-line posture to complete the length. Note the changes that take place in balance and water flow over your body.

2 × 25 swim on :20R *TS* (focus: buoy pressure)

IHR or RPE

2 × 25 SGNU on :15R (focus: tight line)

4 × 25 on :15R—alt 25 FB, 25 SGNU lft, 25 BB, 25 SGNU rt—tight-schlumpy-tight on each length

1 × 25 swim *TS* (focus: tight line)

1 × 25 swim *TS* (focus: buoy pressure)

IHR or RPE

Total distance: 650

Comments: This is mainly a static-balance and posture-skills practice session. Do it all at an easy and comfortable pace. The focus is on executing each drill flawlessly. If you are having success keeping a tight line and balance, it is okay to reduce the amount of rest. If you feel that you need more rest, take it.

Posture, Static Balance, and Vertical Kick 2

Training zone: Recovery and low aerobic

Target RPE range: 9 to 11

Target heart-rate range: 70 to 85% of SLTHR

This entire practice is done at warm-up and cool-down intensity

4 × 25 on :15R *TS*—alt 25 FB, 25 SGND (focus: tight line)

4 × 25 on :15R—alt 25 BB, 25 SGNU rt, 25 BB, 25 SGNU lft (focus: downward angle of extended arm)

2 × 25 on :15R *TS*—alt 25 SGND rt, 25 SGND lft (focus: buoy pressure)

IHR or RPE

2 × 25 swim on :20R *TS* (focus: downhill swimming)

4 × 25 on :15R—alt 25 BB, 25 SGNU lft, 25 BB, 25 SGNU rt

4 × :15 VK on :15R (focus: tight line)

IHR or RPE

4 × 25 on :15R *TS*—alt 25 FB, 25 SGND lft, 25 FB, 25 SGND rt—tight-schlumpy-tight on each length

4 × :20 VK on :10R—tight-schlumpy-tight during each repeat

2 × 25 swim on :20R *TS*—tight-schlumpy-tight on each length

IHR or RPE

Total distance: 750 (includes estimated equivalent for VK)

Comments: This, again, is mainly a posture and static balance-skills practice session. Do it all at an easy and comfortable pace, except that the vertical kicking will likely be a bit more intense. The focus is on executing each drill flawlessly. Feel free to shorten the rest intervals on the drills that you are sure you are executing properly. If at any time you feel that you need more rest to successfully execute a drill, take it.

3 Static and Dynamic Balance and Core Rotation

Training zone: Recovery and low aerobic

Target RPE range: 9 to 11

Target heart-rate range: 70 to 85% of SLTHR

This entire practice is done at warm-up and cool-down intensity

8 × 25 on :15R *TS*—alt 25 FB, 25 SGND rt, 25 FB, 25 SGND lft (focus: tight line)

2 × 25 swim on :15R *TS* (focus: pierce down to extension)

2 × 25 BBR on :15R *TS* (focus: tight line)

IHR or RPE

2 × 25 SGNU good on :15R (focus: downward angle arm extension)—tight-schlumpy-tight on each length

2 × 25 SGB good on :15R (focus: red dot)

4 × 25 BBR on :15R *TS* (focus: red dot)

IHR or RPE

2 × 25 SGB weak on :15R (focus: red dot)

4 × :20 VKR on :15R (note that the kicking is done with rotations this time)

4 × 25 LAR on :15R *TS* (focus: patches and cheeks)

2 × 25 swim on :20R (focus: the glove)

IHR or RPE

Total distance: 800 (includes estimated equivalent for VKR)

Comments: This practice includes both static and dynamic balance skills. As with the previous practices, perform all drills at an easy, comfortable pace. On the VKR, reread the description of the drill to be sure that you are doing it correctly. Reread the description of proper breathing for the long-axis rotation (LAR) drill. If you are breathing incorrectly, you'll simply create a hard-to-break bad habit. Flawless execution of the drill is more important than speed. If you are using fins and if you feel comfortable and confident about some of the drills, you might want to try them with short-blade fins or with bare feet. Remember, the long-term goal is to be able to do all these drills comfortably without using fins.

Stroke Integration

Training zone: Recovery and low aerobic

Target RPE range: 9 to 11

Target heart-rate range: 70 to 85% of SLTHR

Warm-Up
4 × 25 on :10R *TS*—alt 25 BBR, 25 SGND rt, 25 BBR, 25 SGND lft

4 × 25 on :15R *TS*—alt 25 SGND, 25 swim (focus: tight line)

IHR or RPE

Main Set
4 × :20 VKR on :10R—tight-schlumpy-tight during each repeat

4 × 25 on :10R LAR *TS*—tight-schlumpy-tight on each length

2 × 50 on :15R—alt 25 SGB good, 25 SGB weak

2 × 25 SGSS on :15R *TS* (focus: laser-beam rotation trigger)

2 × 25 on :10R—alt 25 SGB weak, 25 SGB good

2 × 25 SGSS on :15R *TS* (focus: neutral shoulder)

IHR or RPE

4 × :20 VK on :10R—odd: hands on your chest; even: hands out of the water

Cool-Down
4 × 25 on :15R—alt 25 SGB, 25 swim (focus: tight line), 25 SGNU, 25 swim (focus: marionette recovery)

IHR or RPE

Total distance: 850 (includes estimated equivalent for VK or VKR)

Comments: This practice introduces the first stroke-integration drill, side-glide single strokes (SGSS), and still includes posture and balance skills. On the VK, with your hands out of the water, increase the intensity of your kick in order to keep your blow-hole dry without tipping your head back. Note that some of the rest intervals have been shortened. As you become more skilled at these drills, you should need less rest. Our goal is still flawless execution, though, so if you feel that you need more rest in order to execute well, then take extra time between repeats at the walls.

5 More Stroke Integration

Training zone: Recovery and low aerobic

Target RPE range: 9 to 11

Target heart-rate range: 70 to 85% of SLTHR

Warm-Up

6 × 25 on :10R—alt 25 SGB rt, 25 SGB lft, 25 SGSS (focus: sliding-board entry)

4 × 25 on :10R *TS*—alt 25 SGSS, 25 swim (focus: side skating)

IHR or RPE

Main Set

2 × 50 on :15R *TS*—alt 25 SGND, 25 SGSS (focus: patches and cheeks)

2 × 50 on :15R *TS*—alt 25 SGSS, 25 3S&G (focus: patches and cheeks)

4 × 25 on :10R *TS*—alt 25 SGSS, 25 3S&G (focus: patches and cheeks)

2 × 25 swim on :10R (focus: patches and cheeks)

IHR or RPE

4 × :20 VKR on :10R—odd: hands on your chest; even: hands out of the water

2 × 25 on :10R LAR *TS*—tight-schlumpy-tight on each length

Cool-Down

6 × 25 on :10R *TS*—alt 25 SGND, 25 SGSS, 25 swim (focus: downhill swimming)

IHR or RPE

Total distance: 900 (includes estimated equivalent for VKR)

Comments: This practice introduces another stroke-integration drill, 3 strokes and glide (3S&G). The main set takes a single focus point, patches and cheeks, and applies it to a progression of increasingly complex activities—from a single-stroke drill up to full-stroke swimming. You can apply this pattern to other focus points as well. Take more rest than indicated if you feel out of breath or if you feel that you need more rest to execute well. Have you tried using short-blade fins or bare feet for some of your drills?

More Stroke Integration and Core Rotation 6

Training zone: Recovery and low aerobic

Target RPE range: 9 to 11

Target heart-rate range: 70 to 85% of SLTHR

Warm-Up

4 × 25 on :10R *TS*—alt 25 FB, 25 SGND rt, 25 SGND lft, 25 swim (focus: neutral shoulder)

4 × 25 on :10R—alt 25 SGNU, 25 SGB rt, 25 SGB lft, 25 SGSS (focus: over the keg)

IHR or RPE

Main Set

4 × :20 VKR on :10R (focus: tight line, but go schlumpy for a few seconds a few times in the set)

2 × 50 on :15R—alt 25 SGSS, 25 3S&G (focus: over the keg)

2 × 25 on :10R—alt 25 LAR, 25 3S&G (focus: snappy hips)

2 × 50 on :15R *TS*—alt 25 3S&G, 25 swim (focus: pierce down to extension)

4 × 25 on :10R *TS*—alt 25 LAR (easy), 25 LAR (faster)

IHR or RPE

2 × 25 swim on :10R *TS* (focus: wide tracking)

4 × :20 VK on :10R—odd: hands on your chest; even: hands on your head (focus: tight line)

IHR or RPE

Cool-Down

6 × 25 on :10R—alt 25 SGSS, 25 SGB, 25 swim (focus: the glove)

IHR or RPE

Total distance: 900 (includes estimated equivalent for VK or VKR)

Comments: This practice continues stroke-integration drills and adds more core-rotation work. Note that the distance and frequency of full-stroke swimming is gradually increasing. Reread the descriptions of each of the focus points indicated. Note the change in hand/arm positions on the VK set. "Hands on your head" means that one hand should be fully on top of the other on top of your head, and both elbows should be out of the water.

7 Drill Review

Training zone: Recovery and low aerobic

Target RPE range: 9 to 11

Target heart-rate range: 70 to 85% of SLTHR

Warm-Up

4 × 25 on :10R—alt 25 SGNU, 25 SGB, 25 SGSS, 25 swim (focus: finish your strokes)

4 × 25 on :10R—alt 25 SGB, 25 SGSS, 25 3S&G (focus: wide tracking), 25 swim (focus: risky breathing)

IHR or RPE

Main Set

2 × 50 on :15R—alt 25 BB, 25 SGB (focus: red dot)

4 × 25 on :10R *TS*—alt 25 FB, 25 SGND, 25 BBR, 25 SGSS (focus: buoy pressure)

2 × 75 on :30R *TS*—alt 25 SGSS, 25 3S&G, 25 swim (focus: hand swapping)

IHR or RPE

2 × :30 VK on :15R—hands out of the water

6 × 25 on :10R—alt 25 LAR (focus: tight line), 25 3S&G (focus: pierce down to extension), 25 swim (focus: downhill swimming)

2 × :30 VKR on :15R—odd: hands on your chest; even: hands on your head

IHR or RPE

Cool-Down

3 × 50 on :10R *TS*—alt 25 SGSS, 25 LAR (focus: tight line)

IHR or RPE

Total distance: 950 (includes estimated equivalent for VK or VKR)

Comments: This practice includes each of the skill drills introduced so far. Note that you are gradually stringing together a longer and longer series of drills and swim lengths without rest. The VK part of this workout is the most demanding yet. You may have noted that the SGND, SGNU, and SGB drills appear without an explicit indication of which side you should be on. Do half of each drill on your right side and half on your left side, either by taking a single stroke at mid-pool to switch sides, or, when you do multiple lengths of the drill, alternating one length on your right, one on your left.

Adding Some Speed 8

Training zone: Recovery and low aerobic

Target RPE range: 9 to 11

Target heart-rate range: 70 to 85% of SLTHR

Warm-Up

4 × 25 on :10R—alt 25 SGNU, 25 SGB weak, 25 SGSS, 25 swim (focus: side skating)

2 × 50 on :10R—alt 25 SGB weak, 25 swim (focus: snappy hips)

IHR or RPE

Main Set

1 × 100 *TS*—alt 25 SGND, 25 LAR, 25 3S&G, 25 swim (focus: tight line)

1 × 75 SGB—alt 25 weak, 25 good, 25 weak

1 × 75—alt 25 SGSS, 25 3S&G, 25 swim (focus: hand swapping)

1 × 50 LAR—Start each length easy, gradually increase speed, and finish the length fast.

IHR or RPE

1 × 50 *TS*—alt 25 swim fast (focus: tight line), 25 SGND weak

1 × 25 swim fast (focus: hand swapping)

1 × 25 SGB weak

1 × 50—alt 25 3S&G, 25 swim fast (focus: tight line)

4 × :15 VK on :15R—hands on your head

IHR or RPE

Cool-Down

3 × 50 on :10R *TS*—alt 25 BBR, 25 LAR (focus: tight line)

IHR or RPE

Total distance: 950 (includes estimated equivalent for VK)

Comments: This is the first practice in which you are asked to swim fast for a couple of lengths. Don't be alarmed if your new technique improvements seem to fall apart the first few times you try to swim fast—this is normal. Take extra rest after these lengths if you need to. Also, note the emphasis on *side-glide* drills on your weak side. Try to pinpoint what you are doing differently on your weak side that prevents it from feeling the same as your good side. The difference usually involves head position, buoy pressure, posture, or some combination thereof.

9 Focused Swimming

Training zone: Recovery and low aerobic

Target RPE range: 9 to 11

Target heart-rate range: 70 to 85% of SLTHR

Warm-Up

2 × 50 on :10R—alt 25 SGB weak, 25 swim (focus: neutral shoulder)

4 × 25 on :10R *TS*—alt 25 SGSS, 25 BBR, 25 SGSS, 25 swim (focus: side skating)

IHR or RPE

Main Set

1 × 100 *TS*—alt 25 BBR, 25 SGND, 25 5S&G, 25 swim (focus: over the keg)

2 × 75 on :15R *TS*—alt 25 LAR, 25 3S&G, 25 swim (focus: red dot)

3 × 50 on :10R *TS*—alt 25 SGSS, 25 swim (focus: patches and cheeks)

IHR or RPE

1 × 50—alt 25 SGB, 25 swim fast (focus: tight line)

1 × 50—alt 25 SGSS, 25 swim fast (focus: hand swapping)

1 × 50—alt 25 LAR, 25 swim fast (focus: downhill swimming)

4 × 25 on :15R—alt 25 swim (focus: tight line), 25 swim (focus: risky breathing)

IHR or RPE

Cool-Down

3 × 50 on :10R—alt 25 LAR, 25 5S&G (focus: red dot)

IHR or RPE

Total distance: 1,000

Comments: Reread the description for each focus point called for in this practice—then apply them. Turning your brain off (or, conversely, trying to focus on 15 things at once) decreases your ability to perform well and decreases neuromuscular learning potential.

Stroke-Count Awareness

10

Training zone: Recovery and low aerobic

Target RPE range: 9 to 11

Target heart-rate range: 70 to 85% of SLTHR

Warm-Up

4 × 50 on :10R *TS*—alt 25 SGSS, 25 3S&G (focus: red dot)

1 × 100—alt 25 SGB good, 25 SGSS, 25 5S&G, 25 swim (focus: stroke count)

IHR or RPE

Main Set

1 × 100—alt 25 SGB good, 25 3S&G, 25 5S&G, 25 swim (focus: stroke count)

2 × 75 on :10R—alt 25 SGSS (focus: buoy pressure), 25 5S&G, 25 swim (focus: pierce down to extension)

2 × 50 on :10R—alt 25 SGSS (focus: tight line), 25 swim (focus: stroke count)

1 × 50—alt 25 SGNU weak, 25 swim fast (focus: tight line and stroke count)

IHR or RPE

1 × 50 *TS*—alt 25 3S&G (focus: tight line), 25 swim fast (focus: hand swapping and stroke count)

4 × 25 swim on :15R *TS*—each one faster than the previous one (focus: stroke count)

IHR or RPE

Cool-Down

3 × 50 on :10R *TS*—alt 25 LAR, 25 5S&G (focus: tight line)

IHR or RPE

Total distance: 1,000

Comments: Try to move from each part of the workout to the next as quickly as possible. Remember that you want to take about half your breaths on one side of your body and half on the other when you are not using a snorkel. Note the emphasis on stroke counting in this practice. Stroke count is our most useful and immediate feedback tool for improving efficiency. As your speed increases, you want to control any increase in stroke count. Having a physical-skill focus while counting strokes will greatly increase the value of stroke counting.

CHAPTER 8

Level 2: Skill Development Workouts

Assuming that you have worked through the complete set of level 1 practices a couple of times and that you have been completing them easily and within your target heart-rate range, it is probably time to move to level 2 practices. By now you should feel confident with all of the skill drills and focus points presented in level 1. If not, you may want to review and practice any areas of concern. You will need to be proficient in all of the skills and drills presented so far in order to take the next step of connecting your core rotations to your strokes.

Level 2 practices, like level 1 practices, are primarily posture, balance, and swimming drills, but they also have a small amount of full-stroke swimming. These practices will be a bit longer (30–40 minutes rather than 20–30 minutes for level 1 practices). They are very similar to level 1 practices, but there are more repetitions of the various drills and some added focus points.

At various places in the workout notation, I indicate multiple focus points (e.g., focus: tight line and marionette recovery). Initially, this means that you should alternate between the focus points indicated. You should focus on one point for several strokes, then shift your focus to another point for several strokes, and so on. Alternatively, if the length of the activity is sufficient, you could complete a length with one focus, then a length with another, and so on. As you acquire and refine more skills, it will be possible for you to focus on multiple points at the same time.

While training fins are still encouraged for any drills that you have not yet become comfortable with, our long-term goal is to move from long-blade fins to short-blade fins and finally to bare feet in as many of the drills as possible. As you work through these practices, look for opportunities to rely less on fins, especially when you are just swimming as opposed to drilling.

Reading the Workouts

This section introduces a few new notation shortcuts.

1 × 50 swim as 25 @ NSPL, 25 @ -1SPL

SPL means "strokes per length." In level 2 you will need to be aware of and control how many strokes per length you are taking. By 25 @ NSPL, I mean to swim the first 25 at normal SPL—that is, the number of strokes per length that feels normal to you *right now* without trying to do anything special to lengthen the strokes themselves. 25 @ -1SPL means to swim the next 25 yards or meters taking one fewer stroke than you normally would take at that length.

4 × 25 swim @ N, -1, -1, -2SPL

Swim one 25 at normal SPL, the next two 25s taking one fewer stroke than normal, and the last 25 taking two fewer strokes than normal. In this example, if you swim the first 25 using 18 strokes, then the second and third lengths should be swum using 17 strokes each, and the fourth using 16.

4 × 25 swim—descend 1–4 (or desc 1–4)

Level 2 introduces a series of swims in which you vary your speed. Descend 1–4 means that in a set of 4 swims, each swim is to be completed in less time than the previous one. The first one is swum at an easy pace, the second one a bit faster, the third one even faster, and the fourth one faster still. Try to make roughly the same increase in speed from one swim to the next. In this example, if you swim the first 25 in 22 seconds, try to swim the next three in 21, 20, and 19 seconds, respectively.

4 × 25 swim (odd: fast; even: easy)

Odds and evens: Odd-numbered repeats are done with one instruction or focus point; even-numbered repeats are done with a different instruction or focus point. In this example, you would swim the odd repeats fast and swim the even repeats easy.

BOYLFS

Breathe on Your Less Favorite Side: When you see BOYLFS, breathe only on this side, with an eye toward making improvements—imagine the red dot on your head, maintain zero head lift, go more toward nose-up, keep your weightless arm out front, etc. It is not sufficient to simply be *able* to breathe on both sides but, rather, to breathe *well* on both sides. The BOYLFS instruction makes you work on the side on which you have less experience breathing, and thus your habits, good or bad, are not as ingrained. Your weak side is the easier side for learning new, more effective skills and for improving your awareness of how your breathing affects the rest of your swimming technique. As your skills and awareness improve on this side, you will likely find that it becomes your favorite breathing side, indicating that it is time to apply what you have learned to your *new* less favorite side!

Earlier I mentioned half-and-half breathing, or the idea of taking roughly half your breaths on one side and half your breaths on the other side during drills, and that this idea applies to full-stroke swimming as well. Breathing on both sides is important for ensuring that you do not develop lopsided technique. Swimmers often choose to breathe on both sides by taking a breath every third stroke—often called bilateral breathing. But for most adult swimmers, bilateral breathing does not supply enough oxygen for swims over 50 yards or so. The instinctive response to this lack of oxygen is to take more strokes in each length so that more breaths can be taken—and I hope I've conditioned you to recoil at the thought of needlessly adding strokes to your swim. Instead, I encourage you to practice half-and-half breathing by breathing to your right for a 25 (or 50 or 100) and then breathing to your left for a 25 (or 50 or 100). This allows you to take 33 percent more breaths than traditional bilateral breathing without having to shorten your strokes.

Continuing Technique Education

By now, through your core-rotation work in the VKR and LAR drills, you have improved at rotating your core with the largest muscles in the body and transmitting that rotation to your shoulders via tight-line posture. The rotation-connection drills and focus points that follow will help you connect your arms and their motions to this large core engine.

Many Rotations, Three Strokes (MR3S)

This drill is a hybrid of the LAR drill and the 3S&G drill. It is best not to attempt it until you have mastered both the LAR and 3S&G. The following are drill steps for building up to the complete MR3S drill. You'll want to progress through the steps using your training snorkel until you've mastered them before trying them with real breathing.

Step 1: *Many Rotations, One Stroke (MR1S)*   This is the familiar LAR drill with an occasional single-arm freestyle-stroke cycle thrown in. As you work your way down the pool practicing a fully streamlined nose-down LAR drill, use one rotation, initiated by a rotation kick, to power each stroke. Stroke with the arm that is closer to the bottom of the pool at the *beginning* of the rotation. Start the stroke at the same time you start the rotation. Try to finish the stroke at the same time you finish the rotation. Do your marionette arm recovery during the two flutter kicks that follow the rotation kick. Time your recovering arm so that your hand is just passing your head (laser-beam rotation-trigger point) as the next rotation kick initiates body rotation. Remember your hand-entry-to-kick coordination that you established in the SGSS and 3S&G drills. That arm should pierce the surface and extend forward as you rotate—and it should extend at a bit of a downward angle in order to rejoin the arm that remained there throughout the cycle. Continue your long-axis rotations for a while as you assess the stroke, recovery, and entry, and then plan ahead for the next cycle. After some more rotations, repeat the step with a single-arm stroke cycle of the other arm. Your goal is to have a consistent LAR rhythm that continues unchanged through each stroke cycle.

Step 2: *Many Rotations, Two Strokes (MR2S)* We now expand MR1S to add in a stroke with the other arm in each cycle of the drill, instead of just leaving that arm out front. Note that the MR1S drill required two rotations for each single-arm stroke cycle. The MR2S drill requires three rotations to complete a cycle of two strokes as follows: Start as you did in MR1S, using one rotation to power a stroke and using two flutter kicks as you recover that arm to the front of your head.

Here is the addition: as you begin the second rotation, start to stroke with the other arm, so as the second rotation drives the recovering arm to pierce the surface, it also powers the second stroke. As this second rotation is finishing, we want the second stroke to finish by your thigh and, at the same time, to have the entering arm reach full extension in front of the body. Take two more flutter kicks as you recover that second arm forward. As that hand passes the laser-beam rotation-trigger point, initiate the third rotation, which drives the hand through the surface and forward to meet the first arm, which is still extended in front of the body. Continue your long-axis rotations as you assess the cycle of two strokes, and plan ahead for the next cycle. After a few more rotations, repeat with another two-stroke cycle. You should alternate which arm takes the first stroke. Again, we're looking for your long-axis rotations to drive the strokes without changing the rotation rhythm.

Step 3: *Many Rotations, Three Strokes (MR3S)* Now we add a fourth rotation and a third stroke to the cycle in the same way that we added a rotation and a stroke to MR1S to arrive at MR2S. As before, breathe during the segments of rotations that separate stroke cycles. With three strokes in each set of strokes, you will begin to sense a stroking rhythm. Don't let your arms take control of the rhythm of the long-axis rotations away from your legs. Instead, focus on your upper body and arms being driven by the four core rotations that underlie the cycle. Keeping your tight-line posture and using the glove and laser-beam rotation-trigger focus points will help. Also include enough rotations between each set of strokes to give you time to assess each set and to plan ahead for the next cycle. You should alternate which arm takes the first stroke of each cycle as you do this drill.

Step 4: *Add Real Breathing* Set the snorkel aside for this. As you did with the 3S&G drill, you can add a breath on the last stroke of each cycle, though you won't have the luxury of stopping while in a side-glide position. Then follow the pattern you used in the 3S&G drill, moving the breath to the first or second stroke.

Stepping-Stone to MR3S

When you start this progression, I suggest you do each step with regular fins until you can perform that step well, then wean yourself first to short fins and then to bare feet.

Feedback Tools

- Matching your rotation tempo to a tempo beeper (or to a familiar tune with a distinctive beat in your head) can help you determine whether you are changing tempo as you switch from just rotations to rotations with strokes and back. The goal is to have an uninterrupted rotation tempo throughout (even when turning your head to breathe).

- Use the patches-and-cheeks focus point to determine whether you are balanced.

Experiment a Bit

So far, these drills have been performed at very relaxed tempos with an emphasis on maintaining even rhythm and timing. After you have mastered these drills at relaxed tempos, experiment with setting a faster long-axis rotation rhythm and with connecting your strokes to that faster core rotation. This means that your arm motions will be faster as well. The challenge, as before, is to avoid letting your arms take over and set the rhythm. That is the job of your leg-driven core rotations. Increase the tempo only when you are able to maintain your posture, balance, and consistent rotation tempo while taking strokes and only when you are able to finish each set of strokes with a balanced tight line that needs no correcting.

FOCUS POINT ➤ The Tube

The tube is a mental image that helps you become aware of the space through which you are swimming or drilling. The goal is to minimize the size of the tube your body slides through in the water. When you are doing the LAR drill with tight-line posture and perfect balance, your shoulders carve out a tube as you rotate down the lane. Your head, hips, and legs should all stay inside this tube. If you use this mental image when you are swimming full strokes, only your arms should stray outside this tube. If your legs move outside of the tube as they kick, although they somewhat increase the propulsive force of the kick, they generally add more drag than propulsion—an inefficient tradeoff. Using a fast kick during certain drills will help you keep your kicks smaller and inside the tube.

FOCUS POINT ➤ Kick From Hips

We are not just interested in the size of your kick—i.e., keeping it inside the tube. We also want to use the correct muscles for kicking. People instinctively kick from their knees as they learn to swim—generally as an attempt to support sinking hips. Instead, each kick should originate predominantly from your hip, allowing the knee to yield slightly to the resistance of the water as the leg kicks forward. There should be no knee bend *at all* on the leg recovery. You've been practicing this in your vertical kicking drills, which encourage proper kicking motions. You've likely discovered that it is nearly impossible to drive rotation in the VKR drills if you kick from your knees. It is important to carry this focus point into your swimming.

1 Static Balance

Training zone: Recovery and low aerobic

Target RPE range: 9 to 11

Target heart-rate range: 70 to 85% of SLTHR

This entire practice is done at warm-up and cool-down intensity

6 × 25 on :10R *TS*—alt 25 FB, 25 SGND, 25 swim (focus: the tube)

IHR or RPE

3 × 50 on :15R—alt 25 FB, 25 BB (focus: tight line)

2 × 75 on :20R—alt 25 SGNU weak, 25 SGNU good, 25 SGNU weak

1 × 100—alt 25 FB, 25 BB, 25 SGNU weak, 25 SGNU good (focus: kick from hips)

1 × 50 *TS*—alt 25 BBR, 25 swim (focus: kick from hips)

IHR or RPE

6 × 25 on :15R *TS*—alt 25 SGND weak, 25 BBR, 25 swim (focus: downhill swim-ming)

2 × 25 cavort on :10R—kickboard surfing. Standing on a submerged kickboard, propel yourself in any way you can. Keep your feet on the board. Do not use lane ropes. Experiment with different ways to propel yourself.

1 × 50 swim (focus: choice)

IHR or RPE

2 × 25 LAR on :15R (focus: the tube)

4 × 25 on :15R—alt 25 FB, 25 SGB lft, 25 BB, 25 SGB rt

IHR or RPE

Total distance: 1,000

Comments: As with the first level 1 practice, this is mainly a balance- and posture-skills practice session. The focus is on executing each drill flawlessly, with tight-line posture and excellent balance. If you are having success maintaining your posture and balance, it is okay to reduce the amount of rest. If you feel you need more rest, take it.

Static Balance and Vertical Kick

Training zone: Recovery and low aerobic

Target RPE range: 9 to 11

Target heart-rate range: 70 to 85% of SLTHR

This entire practice is done at warm-up and cool-down intensity

12 × 25 on :15R—alt 25 FB, 25 SGB weak, 25 BB, 25 SGB good

IHR or RPE

6 × 25 on :15R—alt 25 SGNU weak, 25 SGB weak, 25 swim BOYLFS (focus: red dot)

4 × :15 VKR on :10R—hands on your chest (focus: tight line and the tube)

6 × 25 on :15R—alt 25 BBR, 25 LAR, 25 swim (focus: risky breathing)

IHR or RPE

4 × 25 swim on :15R (focus: odd: downhill swimming; even: side skating)

4 × :15 VK on :10R—hands on top of your head (focus: tight line and kick from hips)

2 × 50 on :15R—alt 25 SGB weak, 25 swim BOYLFS (focus: the glove)

IHR or RPE

Total distance: 1,000 (includes estimated equivalent for VK and VKR)

Comments: Again, this is mainly a posture- and balance-skills practice session. Do it all at an easy pace (although the VK work might be more intense). If you want to make the drill more difficult, reduce the rest intervals for the drills you are comfortable with. Are you making enough progress on these simplest drills to justify using your fins less?

3 Static and Dynamic Balance

Training zone: Recovery and low aerobic

Target RPE range: 9 to 11

Target heart-rate range: 70 to 85% of SLTHR

Warm-Up

8 × 25 on :15R—alt 25 FB, 25 SGB rt, 25 BB, 25 SGB lft

2 × 25 swim on :15R—tight-schlumpy-tight on each length

IHR or RPE

Main Set

4 × 25 swim on :20R *TS*—desc 1-4 (focus: stroke count. Don't let the SPL increase.)

2 × 25 BBR on :15R *TS* (focus: red dot)

4 × 25 on :10R—alt 25 SGNU weak, 25 SGB weak, 25 SGNU good, 25 SGB weak

IHR or RPE

4 × :15 VK on :15R—odd: hands on your chest; even: hands out of the water (focus: tight line and the tube)

IHR or RPE

6 × 25 on :15R—alt 25 SGB weak, 25 SGB good, 25 swim (focus: red dot)

2 × 25 cavort on :15R—freestyle with underwater recovery. Instead of recovering your arm over the surface of the water, you'll slide it under the water, up along the centerline of your body. Can you maintain good posture and balance?

IHR or RPE

4 × :15 VKR on :10R—odd: hands on your chest; even: hands out of the water (focus: kick from hips)

IHR or RPE

Cool-Down

2 × 25 swim on :15R BOYLFS (focus: marionette recovery)

2 × 25 LAR on :10R (focus: tight line and the tube)

IHR or RPE

Total distance: 1,050 (includes estimated equivalent for VK and VKR)

Comments: Note that you are often asked to do a drill in order to isolate a skill and then to follow the drill with a swim in which the skill is the focal point. This accelerates the neuromuscular learning process. Where no focus point is specified, you should choose your own; you have been doing these drills enough to have an idea of what you need to focus on. Have you tried any of the VK drills with short-blade fins or with no fins at all?

Beginning Stroke Integration

Training zone: Recovery and low aerobic

Target RPE range: 9 to 11

Target heart-rate range: 70 to 85% of SLTHR

Warm-Up

8 × 25 on :10R *TS*—alt 25 LAR, 25 SGND rt, 25 LAR, 25 SGND lft

4 × 25 on :15R—alt 25 SGB, 25 swim (focus: side skating and stroke count)

IHR or RPE

Main Set

4 × 75 on :20R—alt 25 SGNU good, 25 SGNU weak, 25 SGSS (focus: laser-beam rotation trigger)

4 × 25 SGSS on :15R—desc 1–4 (focus: downward angle arm extension)

2 × 25 cavort on :15R—body dolphin. Lying on your belly in the pool, arms extended in front of you, alternate pressing your chest, and then your hips, toward the bottom of the pool. Let your legs transmit that pulse to the water. This is a full-body undulation; it is not kicking with your legs. (Hint: A dolphin is one big swimming muscle with no legs.) Keep your head in tight-line position, and lift it as little as possible when you breathe. Take no strokes. Use fins for this cavort.

2 × 25 swim on :15R BOYLFS—second one faster (focus: over the keg and stroke count)

IHR or RPE

6 × :20 VKR on :15R—odd: hands on your chest; even: hands out of the water (focus: kick from hips)

Cool-Down

6 × 25 on :15R *TS*—alt 25 SGSS, 25 swim (focus: over the keg and the tube)

IHR or RPE

Total distance: 1,100 (includes estimated equivalent for VKR)

Comments: As you become more skilled at these drills, you should need less rest. See how little rest you can get away with—not necessarily recovering completely between repeats. The focus is still on flawless execution, though, so if you feel that you need more rest for proper performance, then take the extra time to get it. Always try to apply an aspect of a drill you have mastered to your full-stroke swimming.

5 More Stroke Integration

Training zone: Recovery and low aerobic

Target RPE range: 9 to 11

Target heart-rate range: 70 to 85% of SLTHR

Warm-Up

6 × 25 on :10R—alt 25 SGNU weak, 25 SGB good, 25 swim BOYLFS (focus: wide tracking)

6 × 25 on :10R *TS*—alt 25 SGSS, 25 swim (focus: patches and cheeks. Go tight-schlumpy-tight and see how this affects the position of your hips.)

IHR or RPE

Main Set

6 × 50 on :15R *TS*—alt 50 SGND, 50 SGSS, 50 3S&G

4 × 25 on :10R *TS*—alt 25 SGSS, 25 swim (focus: hand swapping)

2 × 25 LAR fast on :20R *TS* (focus: tight line and the tube)

2 × 50 on :15R—alt 25 LAR, 25 3S&G (focus: sliding-board entry)

2 × 25 swim on :10R as 1 @ NSPL, 1 @ -2SPL (focus: hand swapping and stroke count)

IHR or RPE

4 × :20 VKR on :10R—odd: hands on your chest; even: hands on top of your head

IHR or RPE

Cool-Down

6 × 25 on :10R—alt 25 SGSS, 25 3S&G, 25 swim (focus: sliding-board entry)

IHR or RPE

Total distance: 1,150 (includes estimated equivalent for VKR)

Comments: Take more rest than indicated if you are out of breath or if you feel that you need more in order to execute well. For which drills have you been using short-blade fins or bare feet? On the fast LAR segment, you will need a bit more tension on your tight line than when you perform a slower-tempo LAR.

Stroke Integration and Rotation Connection

6

Training zone: Recovery and low aerobic

Target RPE range: 9 to 11

Target heart-rate range: 70 to 85% of SLTHR

Warm-Up

4 × 25 on :10R—alt 25 SGB rt, 25 SGB lft, 25 3S&G, 25 swim (focus: downhill swimming)

4 × 25 on :10R *TS*—alt 25 SGND weak, 25 SGSS, 25 MR1S, 25 swim (focus: tight line)

4 × 25 on :10R *TS*—alt 25 3S&G, 25 5S&G, 25 MR1S, 25 swim (focus: finish your strokes)

IHR or RPE

Main Set

2 × 25 swim on :10R (focus: marionette recovery and laser-beam rotation trigger)

2 × 50 on :15R—alt 25 3S&G, 25 MR1S (focus: red dot)

2 × 25 on :15R—alt 25 MR1S, 25 MR2S (focus: buoy pressure and kick from hips)

4 × 75 on :15R *TS*—alt 25 MR1S, 25 MR2S, 25 swim (focus: neutral shoulder)

IHR or RPE

2 × 25 swim on :10R BOYLFS (focus: hand swapping and tight line)

2 × 25 cavort on :10R—double-overarm lollygag. A slow-body dolphin, performed on your back, with your arms extended toward the far end of the pool. Take a stroke with both arms at the same time, and then recover them straight up, over your head, and back into the water. Try it with one dolphin pulse per stroke cycle on the first length, then two dolphin pulses per stroke cycle on the second length. Fins help greatly.

4 × :20 VKR on :20R—hands on your chest. Kick fast enough to raise and keep your shoulders out of the water.

IHR or RPE

1 × 50 *TS*—alt 25 LAR, 25 MR3S (focus: tight line and buoy pressure)

Cool-Down

6 × 25 on :10R *TS*—alt 25 MR1S, 25 3S&G, 25 swim (focus: snappy hips and finish your strokes)

IHR or RPE

Total distance: 1,200 (includes estimated equivalent for VKR)

Comments: Put as much focus into smoothly executing cavorts as you put into doing the serious stuff. Have you reread the descriptions of the drills and focus points? Doing so will improve your understanding of them. On the higher-intensity VKR drill, be careful not to try to help the rotation by throwing your shoulders. Your tight line should simply allow them to go along with what the lower body is doing.

7 Drill Review

Training zone: Recovery and low aerobic

Target RPE range: 9 to 11

Target heart-rate range: 70 to 85% of SLTHR

Warm-Up

4 × 25 on :10R—alt 25 FB, 25 BB, 25 SGNU rt, 25 SGNU lft

4 × 50 on :15R—alt 25 SGB weak, 25 SGB good (focus: buoy pressure)

IHR or RPE

Main Set

2 × 75 on :15R *TS*—alt 25 SGND, 25 BBR, 25 SGSS (focus: red dot)

2 × 75 on :30R *TS*—alt 25 3S&G, 25 5S&G, 25 swim (focus: hand swapping)

IHR or RPE

4 × 25 on :10R—alt 25 MR1S, 25 MR2S, 25 MR3S, 25 swim (focus: kick from your hips)

2 × 25 swim on :05R as 25 @ NSPL, 25 @ -2SPL (focus: downhill swimming and the tube)

2 × 25 swim on :05R as 25 @ NSPL, 25 @ -2SPL (focus: risky breathing)

4 × :30 VKR on :10R—odd: hands on your chest; even: hands on top of your head

IHR or RPE

Cool-Down

4 × 75 on :15R—alt 25 LAR, 25 3S&G, 25 swim BOYLFS (focus: stroke count and finish your strokes)

IHR or RPE

Total distance: 1,250 (includes estimated equivalent for VKR)

Comments: This practice includes at least one length of each of your skill drills. Regardless of your conditioning or ability level, every time you revisit a drill that you think you already know how to do well, your neuromuscular system learns new skills or refines old ones. The VKR part of this workout is the most demanding yet.

Adding Some Speed

Training zone: Recovery and low aerobic

Target RPE range: 9 to 11

Target heart-rate range: 70 to 85% of SLTHR

Warm-Up

6 × 25 on :10R—alt 25 LAR, 25 SGSS. Gradually increase speed as you move through the set.

1 × 100 as 50 swim @ NSPL, 25 SGB weak, 25 swim faster at same SPL used for first 50

IHR or RPE

Main Set

4 × 25 swim on :15R *TS*—desc 1-4 (focus: snappy hips and tight line)

2 × 75 on :15R *TS*—alt 25 MR1S, 25 MR2S, 25 MR3S (focus: kick from hips)

2 × 75 on :15R *TS*—alt 25 SGSS, 25 3S&G, 25 swim fast (focus: hand swapping)

3 × 50 SGB on :10R desc 1–3—alt 25 weak, 25 good

IHR or RPE

6 × 25 on :15R—odd: SGB or SGSS; even: swim fast (focus: tight line)

4 × :30 VKR on :15R—1: hands on your chest; 2: hands out of water; 3: hands on your chest; 4: hands on top of head

1 × 50 cavort—1/1 long-axis combo (focus: tight line and red dot). Take one stroke of freestyle, one stroke of backstroke, one of free, and one of back. Repeat the cycle for the length of the pool. If you do this drill correctly, you'll sort of cork-screw down the lane. Switch rotation direction on the second length.

1 × :30 VKR in full streamline position (focus: tight line and the tube)

IHR or RPE

2 × 50 swim sort of fast on :20R BOYLFS as 25 @ NSPL, 25 @ -1SPL (focus: the tube)

IHR or RPE

Cool-Down

3 × 50 on :10R—alt 25 SGB weak, 25 swim (focus: buoy pressure and downward angle arm extension)

IHR or RPE

Total distance: 1,300 (includes estimated equivalent for VKR)

Comments: You should notice that a few skills are starting to show up in your faster swimming. Take extra rest after the fast ones if you need to. Try to pinpoint what you are doing differently on your weak-side drills that prevents you from performing them in the same way that you perform them on your good side. There is usually a problem with posture, head position, buoy pressure, or some combination thereof.

9 More Focused Swimming

Training zone: Recovery and low aerobic

Target RPE range: 9 to 11

Target heart-rate range: 70 to 85% of SLTHR

Warm-Up

4 × 25 on :10R—alt 25 SGSS, 25 SGB, 25 SGSS, 25 swim BOYLFS (focus: tight line)

4 × 50 on :10R—alt 25 SGB weak, 25 swim (focus: snappy hips. Go tight-schlumpy-tight and see how this affects the transmission of rotation from your hips to your arms.)

IHR or RPE

Main Set

3 × 100 on :20R *TS*—alt 25 FB, 25 SGND, 25 5S&G, 25 swim (focus: hand swapping and stroke count)

2 × 75 on :15R *TS*—alt 25 3S&G, 25 LAR, 25 MR3S (focus: red dot)

3 × 50 on :10R—alt 25 SGNU, 25 swim (focus: marionette recovery)

IHR or RPE

4 × 25 on :10R—alt 25 SGSS (focus: sliding-board entry), 25 swim fast (focus: stroke count. Second fast 25 should be at a lower count than the first fast one.)

IHR or RPE

4 × 25 on :15R—alt 25 3S&G easy (focus: over the keg), 25 swim fast (focus: hand swapping)

4 × 25 swim on :15R (focus: stroke count)

IHR or RPE

Cool-Down

3 × 50 on :10R—alt 25 LAR, 25 5S&G (focus: tight line and the tube)

IHR or RPE

Total distance: 1,350

Comments: Do you know what each of the focus points means? If you don't know one well enough to teach it to someone else, study the description again. Remember that when you see either SGND, SGNU, or SGB, with no indication of which side to do it on, you should do half on one side and half on the other, either by taking a single stroke at midpool to get to your other side or by alternating lengths. Are your stroke counts lower than when you started these practices?

Stroke-Count Awareness 10

Training zone: Recovery and low aerobic

Target RPE range: 9 to 11

Target heart-rate range: 70 to 85% of SLTHR

Warm-Up

4 × 50 on :10R—alt 25 SGB weak, 25 5S&G

2 × 50 on :10R—alt 25 LAR, 25 swim BOYLFS (focus: stroke count)

IHR or RPE

Main Set

4 × :15 VKR on :10R—odd: hands on chest; even: full streamline (focus: tight line and kick from hips)

1 × 100—alt 25 SGB good, 25 3S&G, 25 5S&G, 25 swim (focus: stroke count)

2 × 75 on :10R *TS*—alt 25 LAR, 25 LAR fast, 25 swim (focus: stroke count)

2 × 50 on :10R *TS*—alt 25 SGSS, 25 swim (focus: stroke count)

2 × 25 swim fast on :30R *TS* (focus: snappy hips and stroke count)

4 × 25 on :10R—alt 25 SGB weak, 25 SGB good

IHR or RPE

4 × 25 on :15R—swim @ N, -1, -1, -2SPL (focus: tight line)

1 × 50 as MR3S

4 × 50 swim on :30R—desc 1–4 (focus: tight line and stroke count. Can you keep your stroke count from increasing?)

IHR or RPE

Cool-Down

3 × 50 cavort on :10R—Swim freestyle with underwater recoveries. From your hip, try to sneak each arm forward to full extension, keeping it as close to the body as possible. How much of your posture, balance, core rotation, swapping hands, risky breathing, and over-the-keg stroke can you maintain?

IHR or RPE

Total distance: 1,400 (includes estimated equivalent for VKR)

Comments: Try to move from one part of each workout to the next as quickly as possible. Note the emphasis on stroke counting in this practice. Always try first to control, and later to lower, stroke counts. This practice has the longest string of uninterrupted swimming (4 × 50 descending) so far. You'll have to start this series at a slower pace than you might think you should in order to descend the times.

CHAPTER 9

Level 3: Full-Stroke Swimming Workouts

In level 2, you continued to focus on learning and refining skill drills in a workout format. The amount of swimming was restricted to no more than 30 percent of the distance of any practice. If you have cycled through the level 2 practices a couple of times and can stay within your target heart-rate range most of the time (except during a fast swim or during vertical kicking), it is time to move on to level 3.

Practices will involve more full-stroke swimming but will still include any-where from 30 to 50 percent skill drills. The duration of these practices will remain in the 30- to 40-minute range, though more accomplished swimmers will complete them in less time. The intensity will increase, either by reduc-ing rest, increasing speed, or both. Therefore, the total distance you cover will be greater than in level 2. You will note that the target heart-rate range has increased to 80 to 95 percent of SLTHR and that the target-RPE range has moved up to 11 to 14 (light to somewhat hard). In general, you should stay within those target ranges throughout the main set of each of the level 3 workouts—though, as before, there will be instances when the activity will get your heart rate above those ranges for short periods. If you need to lengthen or shorten the amount of rest that is suggested, do so.

Although I encourage you to use training fins for drills that you are not yet comfortable with, you should have at least moved on to using short-blade fins for most of them. The upcoming practice notation will tell you when to use fins. Unless you need them, do not use fins unless the practice notation calls for them.

Reading the Workouts

This section introduces some new notation shortcuts. Equipment, drill, and focus options and choices are offered in order to increase variety in your training. They are not intended to help you avoid the skills, drills, and foci you don't like. If anything, you should do more of the skills and drills that give you trouble, since they usually alert you to something that is lacking in your swimming.

Fins, SBFins

Fins means that you should use fins of any type. *SBFins* means that you should use short-blade fins.

FinsOpt, SBFinsOpt, TSOpt

Opt means that you should feel free to use the specified piece of equipment, or not, as you choose.

SPBDchoice

You choose the static-posture balance drill (FB, BB, SGND, SGNU).

DPBDchoice

You choose the dynamic-posture balance drill (SGB, BBR, LAR).

SIDchoice

You choose the stroke-integration drill (SGSS, 3S&G, 5S&G).

RCDchoice

You choose the rotation-connection drill (MR3S and its lead-up drills, or 3R3S, which you'll read about shortly).

Dchoice, Dmix

Dchoice means drill choice. This means that you may substitute any skill drill I have presented. *Dmix* means that you may choose and mix more than one drill (example: completing one length of FB, one length of SGB, and two lengths of 3S&G).

Focus: choice

This means that you may substitute any of the focus points I have presented.

SLSSS

This means super-low-and-slow stealth swimming. The objectives are to swim at a super-low stroke count, to use super-slow movement through each stroke cycle, to make as little noise as possible, and to disturb the surface as little as possible. SLSSS exposes the gaps in your posture, balance, and motion skills. If you are unable to maintain perfect balance and coordination while taking full strokes at very slow tempos, then you need to work to bridge those gaps. Slower tempos expose precisely *where* the gaps are. If you feel the need to hurry up during any part of the stroke, you are either losing balance or are simply glossing past a portion of the stroke in which posture, balance, and/ or position are iffy. Noise, chop, and wake signal that you are losing precious kinetic energy to the water.

8-minute set of 50s on IHR or RPE (stay in target range)

Swim a 50, then take an IHR or RPE. As soon as you determine the IHR or RPE, swim another 50, and then take another IHR or RPE. Repeat this pattern for 8 minutes. If you have time to start another 50 before time expires, then do the whole 50. On this set, the final instruction is to swim at a pace that keeps your IHR or RPE in the target range indicated for the practice.

2 × 75 swim—alt 25 fists, 25 fingers, 25 hands

Fists means to ball your hands into fists and swim. Fist swimming, by dramatically decreasing the sensory impulses from the bazillions of nerve endings in your hands, helps you figure out how to use your arms, rather than your puny hands, as your paddles. You become much more aware of the pressure and flow that your arms—especially your forearms—experience. As the sensitivity in your forearms increases, you can more accurately move them to where they most effectively hold onto the water.

Fingers simply refers to a partial fist. Open the three fingers on the pinkie side of the hand (you'll be holding your hand roughly in the "OK" position). This is a stepping-stone to swimming with open hands. As you swim, remember that your forearms are the largest, most predominant part of your paddle.

What matters most is what happens once you release your fingers and return to normal swimming with your hands open. You will probably find that after a lot of fist swimming, the first few lengths you swim with open hands will be at significantly lower stroke counts than you normally swim with open hands. The awareness, sensitivity, and technique of fist swimming will remain with you as your unfettered hands act as an extension of your newly discovered and sensitized forearms. Your paddles will feel big and you will swim farther with every stroke, which, of course, is the primary ingredient of faster swimming (not to mention of simply looking more like an accomplished swimmer). But you will soon return to the habit of using only your hands and your old motions—unless, of course, you do enough fist swimming on a regular basis to create new, more effective habits.

4 × 50 swim fast on 2:00

You are used to seeing exercises listed in the form of, for example, "4 × 50 swim on :20R," where a specified amount of rest follows each repeat. Beginning in this level, you will see exercises listed in a format called interval notation. A training interval is a specified time during which you perform an activity and get some rest before repeating the activity.

4 × 50 swim fast on 2:00 means to swim four 50s fast with two minutes between the beginning of one 50 and the beginning of the next. This is referred to as swimming on a 2-minute interval. If it takes you 1:15 to swim a 50, then you would rest for 45 seconds before beginning the next 50. If it takes you only 55 seconds to swim a 50, then you'd rest for 1 minute and 5 seconds. The whole set would take 8 minutes. I should specify that with long rests like this, I mean active rest—easy swimming or drilling, treading water, bobbing, or other low-intensity water exercises. Keep moving and you'll speed recovery.

4 × 50 SGolf on 1:45

Swim four 50s SGolf on a 1:45 interval. For each 50, count the total number of strokes you take, note your elapsed swim time on the clock, and use part of the rest period to compute your swimming golf score for the swim. The goal of any SGolf set is to lower your score. (See chapter 3, p. 23 for a detailed description of swimming golf.)

4 × 50 SGolf on 1:45 (or :45RMin)

Swim four 50s SGolf on a 1:45 interval. In parenthesis is an alternative for slower swimmers. *:45RMin* means that you should rest for *at least* 45 seconds. If a 1:45 interval doesn't allow for at least 45 seconds of rest, then use a longer interval that does. Again, long rest periods should be *active* rest.

Continuing Technique Education

In the previous level, the MR3S drill progression taught you to occasionally mix a few strokes and breaths into a long series of core rotations. Here we will refine that process in order to bring you as close as possible to full-stroke swimming while still drilling. I also will add some more advanced focus points, and I will discuss how you should think about swimming faster.

Three Rotations, Three Strokes (3R3S)

This second rotation-connection drill progression is an extension of the MR3S drill. You will make just three rotations between sets of strokes. Even though you have practiced the MR3S drill in the level 2 practices, it would be useful to reread the learning progression for the MR3S drill before continuing here. The following are the learning steps for 3R3S:

1. Start by doing the MR3S drill, taking a breath on the second stroke of each three-stroke cycle and making many rotations between sets of strokes. Remember to be risky as to how deep you keep your head when you turn for a breath. The goals are to have zero head lift (remember the red-dot focus point), to avoid introducing a hitch into the rhythm

of rotations, and to maintain your posture and balance. If you find that you need more air, you may add an additional breath during the rotations that occur between each set of strokes.

2. Once you are comfortable with step 1, you can switch to taking two breaths in each cycle by breathing on the first and third strokes. Depending on how much air you need, you will want to be able to switch easily from breathing on the second stroke only to breathing on the first and third strokes and then back to breathing on the second stroke only.

3. As you become comfortable with breathing during each set of three strokes, make fewer rotations between each set. In the finished form of the drill, we want to make only three long-axis rotations between each set of strokes, and we want to breathe only during the sets of strokes.

So the 3R3S drill goes as follows: Push off the wall in a streamline position with tight-line posture. Do three long-axis rotations without strokes, take three strokes with rotations, do three more rotations without strokes, take three more strokes with rotations, and so on, with all your breaths coming during the strokes. Since each cycle of three strokes requires four rotations and since there are three more rotations before the next set of strokes, the entire pattern repeats every seven rotations. This means that each set of strokes begins with the opposite arm from the previous set. As before, the goal is to seamlessly add strokes (and breaths) to your long-axis rotations. If I were to watch just your legs, hips, and torso as you do this drill, I should not be able to tell when you are just rotating and when you are rotating with strokes.

In the workout descriptions, when 3R3S appears with *TS*, the drill is simpler since you don't have to turn your head to breathe. When you move through this progression to 3R3S, I suggest that you do each step with regular fins until you can do the step well. Then wean yourself first to short fins and then to bare feet.

Feedback Tools

- Matching your rotation tempo to a tempo beeper (or to a familiar tune with a distinctive beat in your head) can help you determine whether you are changing tempo as you switch back and forth between rotations only and rotations with strokes. The goal is to have an uninterrupted rotation tempo throughout (even while letting your head turn with your body to breathe).

- Use the patches-and-cheeks focus point to determine whether you are balanced.

Experiment a Bit

After you have mastered 3R3S at an easy tempo, experiment with setting a faster long-axis rotation rhythm. Then connect your strokes to that faster core rotation. Your arm motions will be faster as a result of the faster core-rotation tempo. But if you find your arms setting the rhythm instead of your leg-driven core rotations, then slow down to a tempo that you can control with your rotations. Also, as you improve at the 3R3S drill, you can take more strokes in each set of strokes, effectively turning this into a 3R5S or 3R7S drill in which you can take more breaths during each set of strokes. Increase the number of strokes only if you are able to maintain your posture, balance, and rotation tempo as you take strokes and breaths and only if you can finish each set of strokes in a fully balanced tight line that needs no correction.

○ FOCUS POINT ➤ Hand and Hip Connection

You might recall from chapter 5 (Your Swimming Machine, pages 48 to 50) that the engine that drives truly effective swimming is in the legs and the core, not the arms. Highly effective swimmers use their arms primarily to transmit energy, which is generated by core rotation, to the water. An effective mental image is that of an internal connection between your hand and your hip. In reality, your right hand is firmly connected to your right hip via the tension of your tight-line posture and paddle linkage. Your left hip and hand are similarly connected. We want to exploit those connections in order to power the stroke on one side of your body and, at the same time, to drive the entry and extension on the other side.

Stroke and Hip Connection If you are practicing front-quadrant swimming, you have one arm extended underwater at a slightly downward angle as your recovering arm moves forward to enter the water. Just after the recovering hand passes your head and then passes through the laser-beam rotation trigger, the legs initiate body rotation. As your hips and core begin to rotate, you should feel your tight-line tension tugging your extended arm back just as you reach over the keg to make your catch. Only once your lead arm is fully over the barrel, with your elbow close to the surface of the water and your forearm nearly vertical, should that arm and shoulder add some backward stroking force of their own. The arm and shoulder should put only enough pressure on your paddle to complete the stroke at the same instant that the hip-and-body rotation finishes.

You should feel the internal connection of the rotating hip pulling the stroking hand throughout the stroke. Start stroking too early and you will feel no connection—and your shoulders will end up doing most of the work (an analogous scenario would be of a baseball pitcher making his arm motion first and then turning his hips). If you swim schlumpy instead of using a tight internal-core line, you will have no effective connection. If you put too much pressure on the paddle with your arm and shoulder muscles, the stroke will get ahead of and finish before the core rotation, and you will not have a working connection. Maintaining a feeling of internal connection, however, allows most of the force that you apply to the paddle to come from your core-rotation engine.

Entering Arm and Hip Connection   You also want to maintain a connection between the entering arm and its hip. From the moment the recovering arm passes the head and begins to move toward the spot where it will pierce the surface, you should feel as though the arm is extending as a result of the core's rotation, rather than just stabbing the hand forward from the shoulder. The forward extension of the arm begins as the core's rotation begins, and it ends as the rotation ends.

FOCUS POINT ➤ Weightless Arm

When breathing to one side, you want the arm on your other side to remain extended in front of you at a slightly downward angle. The tendency, unless you have ingrained good habits, is either to push down on the water with the extended arm or to start the next stroke too early. Instead, throughout your inhalation, the extended arm should remain *weightlessly* extended. This way, it will be in the right place to start the next stroke as you begin the next rotation (which comes *after* you've taken a full breath of air).

FOCUS POINT ➤ Stealth

How quiet can you be and how little can you disturb the water as you swim? A highly skilled swimmer swimming at an easy pace should be able to make a wake so small that it does not move past the wave-eating lane lines into adjacent lanes. Noise, chop, and wake give up precious kinetic energy to the water.

FOCUS POINT ➤ Two-Beat Kick

Until now, all of our discussion on kicking while swimming has been about six-beat kicking—three kicks per stroke, in which one kick rotates your body as you take a stroke and two flutter-kick beats follow; another kick rotates you back as you take the next stroke; and two more flutter-kick beats complete a cycle of two strokes. There are two possible purposes for those flutter kicks between the rotation kicks. For poorly balanced swimmers, flutter kicks prevent the hips and legs from sinking. For well-balanced swimmers, they provide direct motorboat, push-you-forward-style propulsion.

By now, as a well-postured, well-balanced swimmer, the former point should be moot for you. The second point, however, warrants further inspection. Kicking in order to produce this type of direct propulsion, even when done by the most accomplished swimmers, requires *a lot* of energy for a small (or zero) return in extra speed.

Kicks that primarily rotate you do not propel you forward in the same way that flutter kicks do. Used correctly, low-intensity rotation kicks properly timed with your arm strokes will *indirectly* net you far more propulsion than *any* amount of motorboat flutter kicking will—and with a much smaller energy expenditure. For this reason, most distance swimmers opt for a two-beat kick—one kick beat for each rotation and arm stroke. The only purpose of these kicks is to drive the rhythmic core-body rotation. A good two-beat kick may not feel like normal kicking. Many swimmers say they feel like they are using the legs to alternately shift the hips around the core as opposed to making deliberate kicking motions.

Switching from six-beat to two-beat timing is, for some, as simple as just saying no to the extra flutter kicks between each rotation kick. For others, switching is best accomplished by swimming at first with no kick whatsoever, then adding only the single-kick beats needed to drive the rotations. In either case, focusing on the hand-entry-to-kick coordination that you developed in earlier drills will be a key to learning and getting the most from a two-beat kick. Once you become comfortable with using two-beat, rotation-only kicking without losing your balance, you may find that you *never* need to go back to six-beat kicking.

Moving at Faster Speeds

Easy-paced swimming and drilling allow you to practice skills at a fairly slow speed. Practicing these skills at faster paces, though, is more challenging. Think of learning to play a complicated, fast-paced piece of music on the piano. First, you learn which notes to play. Then you have a lot more learning and practicing to do in order to play the notes at the right speed and with the right emphasis and nuance. Now that you've made some attempts to swim at faster speeds, I want to address a couple of concerns.

Rotate all the way onto your side?   During drills and when you are swimming at slow speeds, there is plenty of time to rotate entirely onto your side—and it is easy to do. But as you start swimming faster, you will find that rotating onto your sides is more difficult to do. At higher stroke tempos, there simply isn't enough time to complete one rotation before the next stroke (and hence the next rotation) begins. This is okay. A little less rotation will produce a little more resistance, but that resistance won't decrease the amount of power available from your core engine.

How tight is your line?   Whether your power is fully transmitted from your core engine to your arms depends on your tight-line posture. As you increase your rotation tempo (and thus your stroke tempo), your core rotates faster. This requires more core tension (a tighter line) to instantly and completely transmit that rotation energy—the higher the tempo, the greater the core tension necessary to keep a tight line. The challenge, then, is to experiment in order to determine the amount of tension required for each swimming speed—enough to keep your head, torso, and hips all firmly connected, but not so much that you waste energy.

What about stroke count?   All swimmers take more strokes at faster speeds than at slower speeds. But the most effective swimmers tend to take fewer strokes at their fastest speeds than less effective swimmers take at their fastest speeds. Your job, at each of your swimming speeds, is to figure out how to take fewer strokes. When you learn to take fewer strokes without slowing down, you become a more effective swimmer.

Where do you set the tempo?   The instinct when swimmers try to increase their speed is to move the arms faster. Instead, you should try to set a faster long-axis rotation tempo, and then connect your strokes to that faster core rotation. When you do this, your arms *will* move faster. The challenge is to prevent them from setting the tempo instead of your leg-driven core rotations setting it. More about this later.

Back to Fundamentals

1

Training zone: High aerobic

Target RPE range: 11 to 14

Target heart-rate range: 80 to 95% of SLTHR

Warm-Up

4 × 50 on :10R *TS FinsOpt*—alt 25 MR3S, 25 3R3S (focus: over the keg)

1 × 100 Dmix *TS*

IHR or RPE

Main Set

4 × 25 swim on :10R fists—desc 1-4 (focus: tight line)

6 × 50 on :15R—alt 25 Dchoice, 25 swim (odd: fists; even: hands) (focus: over the keg)

3 × 100 on :20R *TS*—alt 25 SGND, 25 swim SLSSS, 25 SGSS good, 25 swim fast (focus: stealth)

4 × 25 cavort on :15R desc 1-4 *FinsOpt*—360-degree somersault at midpool. On each length, execute a forward somersault approximately at midpool. Try to use your momentum to turn yourself through the somersault rather than using your arms to help turn you. Swim out of the somersault as smoothly as possible.

IHR or RPE

Cool-Down

2 × 75 swim on :15R—alt 25 fists, 25 fingers, 25 hands (focus: weightless arm)

4 × 25 on :15R *TS FinsOpt*—alt 25 FB, 25 SGND, 25 BBR, 25 swim (focus: stealth)

2 × 25 swim on :15R *TS* (focus: hand and hip connection)

IHR or RPE

Total distance: 1,400

Comments: This practice requires more full-stroke swimming than any of the level 1 or level 2 practices. The emphasis should be on swimming well rather than on swimming fast. As some of the swim and drill combinations get longer, it is important to turn quickly at the walls and to make good, long, streamlined push-offs. The SLSSS is full-stroke swimming, but it is done at a tempo that one doesn't normally equate with swimming—as if you were watching yourself swim in slow motion on a video camcorder. Highly skilled swimmers are able to take SLSSS tempos into the 4- to 5-seconds-per-stroke range without additional kicking and without losing their balance.

2 Rotation Kick Emphasis

Training zone: High aerobic

Target RPE range: 11 to 14

Target heart-rate range: 80 to 95% of SLTHR

Warm-Up

4 × 25 on :10R *FinsOpt*—alt 25 FB, 25 LAR (focus: tight line)

4 × 25 on :10R *SBFins*—alt 25 LAR, 25 swim (focus: the tube)

4 × 25 on :10R swim BOYLFS (focus: hand and hip connection)

IHR or RPE

Main Set:

4 × 25 on :10R—alt 25 FB, 25 SGSS, 25 LAR, 25 swim (focus: stroke count and stealth)

4 × :20 VKR on :10R—hands on your chest

IHR or RPE

4 × 75 on :10R *FinsOpt*—alt 25 LAR, 25 MR3S, 25 swim (focus: two-beat kick)

4 × :20 VKR on :10R *SBFins*—hands out of the water

IHR or RPE

2 × 50 swim SLSSS on :10R (focus: 25 two-beat kick, 25 laser-beam rotation trigger)

4 × :20 VKR on :10R *Fins*—hands on top of your head

1 × 100 cavort—Cross back and forth under the lane rope as you swim. After taking a few strokes on one side of the lane rope, cross under the rope and take three to five strokes on the other side, then cross back and finish each length in your lane. Try to switch from lane to lane smoothly, without touching the lane rope, and with as little break in your rhythm as possible. Be careful of traffic.

IHR or RPE

Cool-Down

2 × 100 on :15R—alt 25 SGB weak, 25 swim (focus: weightless arm and stroke count)

Total distance: 1,400 (includes estimated equivalent for VKR)

Comments: Experiment with the size and speed of your kick as a way to prevent your heart rate from rising during the VKR sets. As you progress through the level 3 practices, try to switch from one set or activity to the next as quickly as possible. Ideally, you should take short enough breaks that your heart rate does not drop below the bottom of the target heart-rate range during the entire main set. Taking too much rest decreases the aerobic benefit of the workout.

Consistent Stroke Counting

Training zone: High aerobic

Target RPE range: 11 to 14

Target heart-rate range: 80 to 95% of SLTHR

Warm-Up

2 × 100 on :15R *TS FinsOpt*—alt 25 FB, 25 SGND rt, 25 BBR, 25 SGND lft

4 × 50 swim on :10R *TS*—desc 1–4 (focus: 25 patches and cheeks, 25 two-beat kick)

IHR or RPE

Main Set

10 × 25 swim on :10R (focus: stroke count. Don't let SPL increase as set progresses.)

IHR or RPE

6 × 50 on :15R—alt 25 3R3S, 25 swim (focus: stroke count. Don't let SPL increase as set progresses.)

IHR or RPE

8 × :15 VKR on :10R *SBFins*—odd: hands on your chest; even: hands on top of your head (focus: tight line)

IHR or RPE

1 × 100 swim (focus: stroke count. Don't let it increase from length to length.)

IHR or RPE

Cool-Down

3 × 50 swim SLSSS on :10R (focus: tight line and weightless arm)

4 × 25 Dchoice on :10R *SBFins*

IHR or RPE

Total distance: 1,500 (includes estimated equivalent for VKR)

Comments: Longest sets yet appear in this practice. The VKR activity will likely be fatiguing—can you keep your tight line despite your fatigue? WIth SLSSS, you want to have the lowest stroke count possible without resorting to drilling or extra kicking. A six-foot-tall, highly skilled swimmer should expect, over time, to venture into the single-digit SPL range with SLSSS in 25-yard or -meter pools and into the low-20s SPL range in 50-meter pools.

4 IHR or RPE Set

Training zone: High aerobic

Target RPE range: 11 to 14

Target heart-rate range: 80 to 95% of SLTHR

Warm-Up

1 × 100 swim SLSSS (focus: 50 weightless arm, 50 two-beat kick)

1 × 100 swim—alt 25 fists, 25 fingers, 25 hands, 25 hands (but lower SPL)

1 × 100 Dmix

IHR or RPE

Main Set

1 × 100—alt 25 SPBDchoice, 25 swim (focus: two-beat kick and stroke count)

8-minute set of 50s swim on IHR or RPE (focus: odd: hand and hip connection; even: stealth)

4 × 25 cavort on IHR or RPE—submarine. Do this as LAR with fins. Start each length on the surface, slide under the surface partway down the lane and head toward the bottom of the pool at an angle, come within an inch or two of the bottom, and then return to the surface at an angle and finish the length normally. The goal is to perform this sequence gracefully, without breaking your tight line or interrupting the rhythm of rotations.

IHR or RPE

2 × 50 swim fast on IHR or RPE (focus: tight line and hand swapping). Wait until HR or RPE returns to the low end of your target range before doing the second 50.

6 × 50 LAR on IHR or RPE *SBFinsOpt*

IHR or RPE

Cool-Down

4 × 75 on :15R *SBFins*—alt 25 swim SLSSS, 25 SIDchoice, 25 swim SLSSS (focus: weightless arm)

IHR or RPE

Total distance: approximately 1,500

Comments: Note that there are fewer 25s and some longer drills and swims. As you become more skilled, you should need less rest. Always try to apply a part of a drill you have mastered to your full-stroke swimming. Remember that on sets done on IHR or RPE, the goal is to stay in the target range assigned for the workout.

50s or Longer

Training zone: High aerobic

Target RPE range: 11 to 14

Target heart-rate range: 80 to 95% of SLTHR

Warm-Up

4 × 75 on :15R *SBFins*—alt 25 SGSS, 25 3R3S, 25 swim BOYLFS (focus: stealth)

IHR or RPE

Main Set

6 × 50 on :15R *TS*—alt 50 SGSS, 50 3S&G, 50 3R3S (focus: hand and hip connection)

IHR or RPE

6 × 50 on :15R *Fins*—alt 25 3S&G (focus: over the keg), 25 swim fast (focus: weightless arm)

IHR or RPE

8 × :20 VKR on :10R—odd: hands out of the water; even: hands on top of your head

IHR or RPE

Cool-Down

6-minute set of 50s swim on IHR or RPE (focus: odd: hand swapping; even: two-beat kick). Keep HR or RPE below target range.

IHR or RPE

Total distance: approximately 1,600 (includes estimated equivalent for VKR)

Comments: Note this is the first practice in which the shortest distance with no rest is 50 yards/meters rather than 25. Take more rest than indicated or slow down a bit if you are out of breath, out of your target heart-rate range, or if you think you need it. Fast swimming with fins is a great way to become aware of how you may be swimming with more resistance than necessary. Faster speeds make turbulence and resistance more noticeable.

6 Swimming Golf

Training zone: High aerobic

Target RPE range: 11 to 14

Target heart-rate range: 80 to 95% of SLTHR

Warm-Up

1 × 100—alt 25 DPBDchoice, 25 swim (focus: tight line)

1 × 100—alt 25 SIDchoice, 25 swim (focus: weightless arm)

1 × 100—alt 25 RCDchoice, 25 swim (focus: hand and hip connection)

IHR or RPE

Main Set

3 × 50 SGolf on 2:00 (or 1:00RMin)

IHR or RPE

3 × 100 on :20R *FinsOpt*—alt 25 Dmix, 25 swim (focus: two-beat kick)

IHR or RPE

4 × 25 cavort—dogpaddle. This is the opposite of over the keg. Instead you swim with your elbows totally dropped and with an underwater recovery. Do some fast; do some slow; do some schlumpy with your head out of the water and some with full tight-line posture and balance. Does proper posture and balance make even the dog-paddle more efficient? Only truly self-secure people can handle doing this in public.

3 × 50 SGolf on 1:45 (or :45RMin) (focus: over the keg)

IHR or RPE

1 × 150 swim SLSSS (focus: 50 tight line, 50 the tube, and 50 two-beat kick)

IHR or RPE

3 × 50 SGolf on 1:30 (or :30RMin)

1 × 100 swim SLSSS (focus: neutral shoulder and sliding-board entry by 25s)

IHR or RPE

Cool-Down

4 × 50 on :10R *TS*—alt 25 SGSS, 25 3R3S (focus: hand and hip connection and stealth)

IHR or RPE

Total distance: 1,600

Comments: Expect higher IHRs after SGolf sets. After today's practice, be sure to write down your best (lowest) SGolf scores and how you got them—number of strokes, number of seconds, and what you were focusing on to get those scores. In fact, writing down all of your SGolf scores as you do them will come in handy in the next level, when you will repeat these swims for comparison. Remember that easy movement or easy swimming during those longer rests will help you recover faster. There are several places where you can choose your focus or drill; you should make a different choice each time.

Longest Swim Yet

7

Training zone: High aerobic

Target RPE range: 11 to 14

Target heart-rate range: 80 to 95% of SLTHR

Warm-Up

4 × 50 on :10R—alt 50 DPBDchoice, 50 swim (focus: two-beat kick)

4 × 50 on :10R—alt 25 SGSS, 25 swim BOYLFS (focus: red dot)

IHR or RPE

Main Set

3 × 150 on :30R desc 1–3 *FinsOpt*—alt 25 SIDchoice, 50 swim (focus: choice), 25 DPBDchoice, 50 swim (focus: choice)

IHR or RPE

1 × 200 swim *SBFinsOpt* (focus: 25 two-beat kick, 25 hand swapping)

IHR or RPE

2 × 50 SGolf on :10R (focus: neutral shoulder)

IHR or RPE

1 × 100 *TS*—alt 25 LAR, 25 3R3S, 50 swim (25 @ NSPL, 25 @ -1SPL) (focus: stealth)

1 × 50 *TS* swim fast (focus: tight line)

1 × 50 *TS* Dchoice

1 × 50 *TS* swim fast (focus: hand and hip connection)

IHR or RPE

Cool-Down

4 × 75 on :15R—alt swim 25 @ NSPL, 25 @ -1SPL, 25 @ -2SPL (focus: odd: weightless arm; even: over the keg)

IHR and RPE

Total distance: 1,700

Comments: Longest uninterrupted full-stroke swim yet—200. After your turn, you'll want to have at least enough air in your lungs to blow your snorkel clear (if you are wearing one) once you surface from your underwater push-off.

8 Focus Switching

Training zone: High aerobic

Target RPE range: 11 to 14

Target heart-rate range: 80 to 95% of SLTHR

Warm-Up

3 × 100 swim on :15R *FinsOpt* (focus: 25 the tube, 25 the glove, 25 hand swapping, 25 red dot)

IHR or RPE

Main Set

2 × 100 swim *SBFins* (focus: two-beat kick and hand and hip connection)

1 × 100 swim (focus: tight line and patches and cheeks)

IHR or RPE

4-minute continuous VKR *Fins*—alt :15 hands on chest, :15 hands out of the water (focus: tight line)

10-minute set of 50s swim on IHR or RPE (focus: mix. Cycle at least three different focus points × 50s.)

4 × 25 cavort on IHR or RPE—reverse-video freestyle. This is swimming in reverse, feet first, as if you were watching a videotape of yourself swimming normally and then played it in reverse. You'll want to point your toes without kicking much or at all. Keep a tight line. The suntanned side of the hand and forearm is used as a propelling surface instead of the usual side. You must keep the elbow high throughout the "pull" in order to make backward progress.

Cool-Down

2 × 100 on IHR or RPE *TS Fins*—alt 25 SPBDchoice, 25 DPBDchoice, 25 LAR, 25 swim (focus: kick from hips)

IHR or RPE

Total distance: approximately 1,700 (includes estimated equivalent for VKR)

Comments: It's likely that your first attempt at reverse-video freestyle will be a humbling experience. Using a pull-buoy can make it less so. Notice the emphasis on switching your focus from one mental image to another. Remember, on VKR, it is important not to tilt your head back but rather to kick fast enough that your blowhole stays above the water.

Drill Review

9

Training zone: High aerobic

Target RPE range: 11 to 14

Target heart-rate range: 80 to 95% of SLTHR

Warm-Up

10 × 50 on :05R—one each of FB, BB, SGND, SGNU, SGB, BBR, LAR, SGSS, 3S&G, swim (focus: choice)

IHR or RPE

Main Set

3 × 100 on :20R—alt 25 Dchoice, 25 swim (focus: hand swapping and two-beat kick)

3 × 100 on :15R—alt 25 5S&G, 25 MR3S, 25 3R3S, 25 swim (focus: stroke count. Each should be at a lower SPL than the previous one.)

IHR or RPE

4 × 50 on :10R *TS*—alt 25 SGSS, 25 swim (focus: marionette recovery)

1 × 100 *TS*—alt 25 SGSS, 25 swim fast (focus: tight line), 25 SGND weak, 25 swim fast (focus: tight line. Go tight, schlumpy, tight.)

2 × 50 SGolf on 2:00 (or 1:00RMin) *TS*

1 × 100—alt 25 SGB good, 25 swim fast @ NSPL, 25 SGNU weak, 25 swim fast @ -1SPL

IHR or RPE

Cool-Down

4 × 50 on :10R—alt 25 SGNU weak, 25 5S&G (focus: weightless arm and neutral shoulder)

IHR or RPE

Total distance: 1,800—Just over one mile!

Comments: It is good to revisit the fundamental drills from time to time. How was your experience with the drills today compared to the first time you tried them? Did you miss your fins today?

10 Stroke Counting Expanded

Training zone: High aerobic

Target RPE range: 11 to 14

Target heart-rate range: 80 to 95% of SLTHR

Warm-Up

3 × 100 swim on :10R *SBFinsOpt*—alt 25s @ N, -1, -2, -3SPL

IHR or RPE

Main Set

4 × 25 swim fists on :10R @ N, -1, -2, -3SPL (focus: weightless arm and laser-beam rotation trigger)

IHR or RPE

1 × 100 Dchoice *FinsOpt*

4 × 50 swim fingers on :15R @ N, -1, -2, -3SPL (focus: hand and hip connection)

IHR/RPE

1 × 100 Dchoice

4 × 75 swim on :20R @ N, -1, -2, -3SPL (focus: stealth and the glove)

4 × :30 VKR on :15R

IHR or RPE

1 × 100 Dchoice *TS*

2 × 50 SGolf on 1:00RMin *TS* (focus: two-beat kick)

IHR or RPE

Cool-Down

2 × 100 on :10R *TSOpt FinsOpt*—alt 50 LAR, 25 SGSS, 25 swim (focus: stealth and wide tracking)

IHR or RPE

Total distance: 1,800 (includes estimated equivalent for VKR)

Comments: Greatly emphasize stroke counting in this practice. You should try to lower your stroke counts at all speeds. Until you gain better control of your stroke length, some of those low-stroke-count swims may feel more like drills. Plan for which drills you will choose. Choose drills that might help you do the next swim correctly. Are you noticing fewer differences between the weak and good sides? If not, review the drill descriptions. Ask someone to read the description, watch you execute the drill, and then give you feedback. Note that since all fin use was optional, you could have done this entire practice with bare feet.

CHAPTER 10

Level 4: Lactate Threshold Workouts

If you have gone through the workouts in level 3 a couple of times and can stay within the RPE and target heart-rate ranges most of the time (except during a fast swim or vertical kicking), it is time to move on to level 4. Workouts in this chapter include from 25 to 50 percent skill drills at moderate intensity. These workouts extend into the 40- to 50-minute range, though, so the total distance you cover in these practices will be greater than in level 3. Unless you absolutely need to use short-blade fins for a drill, do not use fins unless the practice notation calls for them.

Intervals and the Pace Clock

In chapter 9, you were briefly introduced to swimming on intervals. Practices will now rely more heavily on interval training and will include a wider variety of intervals. The faster you swim an interval, the more rest you get before starting the next swim. Different types of work require different amounts of rest. This is called the work-to-rest ratio. The following table shows the various types of interval work you'll be doing and their components—work-to-rest ratio, exercise intensity, RPE, and aerobic versus anaerobic contribution.

Type of work	Work-to-rest ratio	Intensity	RPE	% Aerobic vs. anaerobic
Recovery	5 or more to 1	Very low	9-11	95/5
Low aerobic	5 or more to 1	Low	11-13	90/10
High aerobic	5 or more to 1	Moderate	13-14	85/15
Lactate threshold	4 or more to 1	High	14-15	80/20
Lactate endurance	1 to 1	Very high	16-18	65/35
Lactate tolerance	1 to 2 or more	Extremely high	18+	<60/>40

You will need to become better acquainted with the pace clock in order to negotiate some of the complex intervals that will follow. Because most lap pools have analog pace clocks, my descriptions of how to use a clock as you train will assume that you are using an analog pace clock. The concepts are easily applied to a digital clock, however, whether the clock is on the wall or on your wrist. At first, using a pace clock to do intervals may cause confusion, but once you've done it a few times, you will become comfortable with the process. Consider the following set:

4 × 50 swim on 1:15 desc 1–4 *Fins*

Swim four 50s with fins on a 1:15 interval, with each 50 swum in less time than the previous one. Start the first 50 when the second hand hits the 60-second mark (figure 10.1a)—this is referred to as "going on the 60". As you finish the swim, note where the second hand is. It tells you how long it took you to swim the 50. Let's say you finish on the 55-second mark. Because the interval is 1:15, swim 2 (figure 10.1b) will start on the 15-second mark (1:15 after the 60-second mark at which you started the first swim), giving you 20 seconds rest. Try to swim the second 50 a bit faster than the first. If swim 2 is done at the same speed as swim 1, you would finish on the 10-second mark (55 seconds after the 15-second mark at which swim 2 started). Instead, you swim a 53 (2 seconds faster) and arrive at the wall at the 8-second mark. Swim 3 (figure 10.1c) will start on the 30-second mark (1:15 after the 15 mark), so you have 22 seconds rest. Let's say your third swim is another 2 seconds faster (51 seconds), which puts you at the wall as the second hand passes the 21-second mark. Finally, your fourth swim (figure 10.1d) starts on the 45-second mark. You swim the 50 in 50 seconds, your fastest repeat of the set, and you finish as the second hand hits the 35 mark.

Note that the send-off (another name for when the next swim begins) for each swim jumps forward on the clock by 15 seconds—60, 15, 30, 45. If the set had called for five 50s instead of four, the next repeat would start on the 60 again. If the set had been a 4 × 50 swim on 1:10, the send-off would move forward by 10 seconds on each repeat—60, 10, 20, 30. Had the interval been 50 seconds, the send-off would move backward on the clock face by 10 seconds for each repeat—60, 50, 40, 30.

Reading the Workouts

Swimming allows you to incorporate an array of physical and mental challenges into your workouts. As the sets become more complex, the workout notation can start to look more like math homework than a description of exercises. But once you understand the notation, the workouts are easy to follow.

This chapter introduces two closely related types of interval-training sets: cruise pace sets and cruise interval sets. To perform either of these sets, you'll need to know your cruise pace. This number is derived directly from your T-swim performances. Each time you complete a T-20, use the T-20 Cruise Pace Per 100 Chart in the appendix to determine the average pace per 100

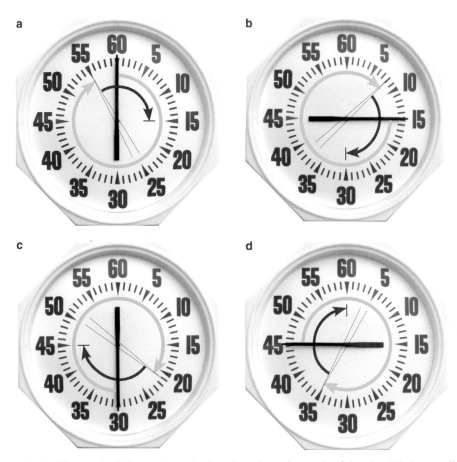

Figure 10.1   These clock faces show the hand positons for each of the 4 × 50 descending swims on 1:15 interval described in the text. Solid hand shows where the repeat begins; green arrow shows duration of swim; hollow hand shows where the swim finishes; and red arrow shows the rest period before the next swim.

that you maintained during the T-20. Similarly, when you complete a T-30, you should use the T-30 Cruise Pace Per 100 Chart. Once you know your cruise pace, you can use two other charts in the appendix—the Cruise Times Chart and the Cruise Interval Chart—to determine your aerobic- and lactate-threshold-training paces for various distances. Many workouts in this chapter require you to swim at your cruise pace or on a cruise interval.

Cruise Times

Workouts designed around cruise pace can provide excellent, basic aerobic-endurance training. The workouts are not overly stressful because adequate rest is incorporated into them. The Cruise Times Chart in the appendix shows the time it takes to swim various distances, from 25 up to 500 at any cruise pace. Simply locate your cruise pace in the cruise pace per 100 column, then look left or right on that row to find your cruise time for various distances.

11-minute set. Swim 200s @ CPace on :10–:15R

This example asks you to swim an 11-minute set of 200s at your cruise pace (let's say your pace is 1:37 per 100) and to take between 10 and 15 seconds rest after each 200. Locate 1:37 in the cruise pace per 100 column on the Cruise Times Chart and look across to the 200 column. The entry there is 3:14. In other words, if you swim at your cruise pace, you'll swim the 200 in 3:14. Starting the next 200 at 3:25 would give you between 10 and 15 seconds rest. The fourth 200 would begin at 10:15. Because the 11:00 period is not yet complete, either complete the lap that the 11:00 mark falls in or complete the entire 200 at cruise pace.

1 × 7-minute swim @ CPace

For a set written in this form, choose the shortest distance for which your cruise time equals or exceeds 7:00, then swim that distance at your cruise pace. If you swim exactly at your cruise pace, you will finish at the cruise time you read from the chart. If your line on the Cruise Times Chart doesn't have an entry for 7:00, simply add two cruise times from your line together (for example, if your cruise pace is 1:12 per 100, the most amount of time on your line is 6:00 for 500; therefore, you would simply add the time for one more 100 to arrive at 7:12 for a swim of 600).

Cruise Intervals

Your cruise pace is also used to determine challenging anaerobic-threshold-training intervals called cruise intervals. Cruise intervals include both an interval to swim each repeat at and a target time to match or beat on each repeat. The target time for a cruise interval will usually be from 1 to 4 percent faster than your cruise pace, and the interval will be at least 5 percent longer than your cruise pace for that distance.

A section of the Cruise Interval Chart (appendix D) is shown here.

Cruise intervals					
Cruise pace per 100	50	75	100	150	200
1:49	1:00-54	1:30-19	2:00-45	2:55-40	3:55-32
1:48	1:00-53	1:30-18	2:00-44	2:55-37	3:50-32
1:47	1:00-52	1:30-16	1:55-45	2:55-34	3:50-29

A cruise interval set will look something like this:

12-minute set. Swim 200s on CInt.

Let's say that the cruise pace per 100 you looked up after your most recent T-swim is 1:48 and that you want to know your cruise interval for 200s. To find it, do the following:

1. Find 1:48 in the cruise pace per 100 column of the Cruise Interval Chart.

2. Look across the 1:48 line to the cruise interval 200 column.

3. The entry in the 200 column is 3:50-32. This means that your interval is 3:50 and that your target time to match or beat on every swim is 3:32. This will give you about 18 seconds of rest before you start your next 200. (Note that the cruise interval entry in the 100 column on this same line—2:00-44—means an interval of 2:00 for 100s with a target time of 1:44, not 2:44.)

4. Since your interval is 3:50, you'll have time to complete four full repeats and a portion of repeat number five in the 12-minute set. Always swim for the entire time indicated, finishing either the entire repeat or at least the lap during which 12 minutes ticks by at the same pace as the rest of the swim (or faster).

In a cruise interval set, it is okay to swim some or all of the repeats faster than the target time as long as you don't swim any of them slower than the target time. Note that as your T-swim performances improve, your cruise pace will be faster. Your cruise intervals will change (meaning that either the interval gets shorter or the target time requires you to swim faster, or both) in order to keep in step with your improvement. You may find that reaching your new target time for the interval is difficult to do for more than a few repeats. That's okay. The idea behind cruise intervals is to push you just beyond your comfort zone. If you are able to consistently swim the cruise interval sets faster than the target times, then you should be able to improve your next T-swim.

Last One Fast One (LOFO)

On cruise pace and cruise interval sets, you will often see LOFO in the set description. This means that you should swim the last repeat at a significantly faster pace than the preceding repeats. When you see LOFO, prior to the last repeat, you may take up to twice the amount of rest that was prescribed for the other repeats in that set.

Negative Split (NS)

A negative-split swim is one in which each portion of a continuous swim is swum faster than the previous one. Negative-split segments can be written like this:

$$1 \times 300 \text{ NS}$$

This means that the second 150 is swum faster than the first 150—say, 2:05 for the first 150 and 2:01 for the last 150 (a 4-second negative split) for a total of 4:06 for the 300.

$$1 \times 300 \text{ NSx100s}$$

Each 100 in the 300 is swum faster than the previous one—say, 1:25, 1:22, and 1:19. You finish with the same 4:06 time as in the previous example, but you swim the 300 a little differently.

The average swimmer often starts a swim too fast, then soon experiences fatigue, pain, and a loss of speed control as lactate accumulates in the muscles. Coaches often call this positive-split or sucker-split swimming. The athlete who swims negative splits enjoys greater control, increased confidence, and increased speed as the swim progresses. For any distance that requires more than 60 seconds to swim, slightly negative splits give the best tradeoff between speed and energy consumption.

Until you have *a lot* of experience with negative splitting, you cannot judge your pace by feel—so use the pace clock. To simplify the math of negative splitting, try this: As you turn at the halfway point of a repeat, glance at the clock in order to get your first-half split (if you usually use flip turns, there is no shame in using an open turn so that you can see the pace clock). As you swim that next length, figure out what your finish time will be if you swim the second half in exactly the same time as the first half. (For example, if you swim the first 100 of a 200 in 1:22, simply add 1:22 + 1:22 to get 2:44.) Remember that time! At the end of the swim, look at the clock as you touch the wall.

- If you hit the wall *after* that 2:44 mark, then you've done a positive- or sucker-split swim (for example, a 2:47 means the second half was 3 seconds slower than the first half, or 1:25).

- If you finish *exactly at* 2:44, the second half was swum in the same time as the first half, or 1:22. We call this an even split. Better.

- But if you finish *before* the 2:44 mark—say, 2:42—then you swam the second half 2 seconds faster than the first half. That's a 2-second NS. Now, *that's* what I'm talkin' 'bout!

The following are the two most common mistakes that people make when they first try to swim negative splits:

1. Misjudging the correct pace for the start of the swim. You'll likely need to start out at a pace that feels *much* slower than you think you'll need. The slower pace will allow you to swim faster later.

2. Increasing the stroke tempo in the second half with no attention to maintaining your distance per stroke. The usual result is *harder* swimming in the second half, not *faster* swimming.

Once you have learned the basics of swimming a negative split, the next step is to swim the first half faster but to still swim the second half faster than the first. As you gain more skill and confidence, try to negative-split every swim longer than 60 seconds. Eventually, you will negative-split longer swims automatically, finishing them faster than before and with more control and less fatigue.

Continuing Technique Education

You already know that full-stroke swimming requires the coordination of various skills and movements. The previous chapter introduced the final technique drill in the step-by-step progression to full-stroke swimming. By now, you should be comfortable with all of the drills and be a master of most. Each of the following focus points describes a different way to think about and assess your execution of skills.

FOCUS POINT ➤ Shift and Skate

With every stroke of a drill or swim, there is a period when you surge forward in the water and a period when you glide on one side of your body as you prepare to take the next stroke. I liken this to a speed skater's experience—each time she pushes off with one skate and shifts her weight onto the other skate, there is a noticeable surge of speed (this correlates to a swimmer's body rotation and to the stroke she takes during that rotation). After the weight shift, there is a period of gliding with no propulsion as the skater prepares to make the next weight shift (this correlates to a swimmer's streamlined side-lying position, as the recovering arm moves toward the laser-beam rotation-trigger point). In swimming, the surge is greatest when you maintain the hand and hip connection, and the skating action is most effective when you swim in a balanced, streamlined position, which best conserves speed.

FOCUS POINT ➤ Forward Lunge

This is an extension of the hand and hip connection focus point. You already know that each core rotation is connected to a stroke on one side of the body and, simultaneously, that an entry and extension is connected to the rotation on the other side. Try this: As you rotate, think of your stroking arm as a fulcrum point from which your rotation drives the other side of your body aggressively forward. This lunging action drives the hand and arm forward through the surface of the water, straight to your extension point. As with the stroke, the lunge happens during, and because of, a snappy rotation of the body's core. This shift in focus allows you to concentrate on what's moving forward.

FOCUS POINT ➤ Kayak Paddling

When you paddle a kayak, you place one blade of the paddle in the water and then use torso rotation to apply backward force through the lower hand and forward force through the upper hand. The forces that you apply to the upper hand are transmitted through the rigid link of the paddle handle, across the fulcrum created by the lower hand, and finally to the blade in the water. You use a similar chain of actions in swimming.

You will recall that the muscular tension of your tight-line posture firmly connects your head, torso, and hips into a kayaklike vessel. You will also recall that we use a line of muscular tension to firmly connect your whole-arm paddle to your tight line—your paddle linkage. Finally, you will recall from the sliding-board-entry focus point that the kinetic energy of the falling or extending arm adds to the energy of the core's rotation and thus is transmitted to the stroking arm through your tight line. Expanding upon these ideas, if you time your over-the-keg catch correctly, you should feel the muscular tension of your paddle linkage extend all the way across your back and through the tight line of your core to your other shoulder and the entering arm.

This uninterrupted line of muscular tension from one hand to the other provides a firm, internal linkage that is functionally similar to the external link provided by the rigid kayak paddle. Thus, the force of the entering arm is transmitted directly to the stroking arm, much like the force applied to the upper hand on a kayak paddle is transmitted to the blade in the water.

Now that you are primed with new training and technique concepts, move on to the level 4 practices. Before you do, though, turn to the appendices and copy down two sets of numbers for quick reference. From the Cruise Times Chart, copy down the row of times and associated distances for your most recent cruise pace per 100. On the Cruise Interval Chart, find your cruise pace per 100 and copy the row of cruise intervals and target times for each distance across the chart. Put these in a zipper sandwich bag that you can keep on the pool deck during your practice sessions.

Now get yourself to the pool.

Introducing Cruise Pace

1

Training zone: High aerobic and lactate threshold

Target RPE range: 13 to 15

Target heart-rate range: 90 to 100+% of SLTHR

Warm-Up

4 × 25 on :10R *SBFinsOpt*—alt 25 Dchoice, 25 swim

4 × 50 on :10R—alt 25 3S&G, 25 3R3S

IHR or RPE

Main Set

1 × 200 swim NS *SBFinsOpt* (focus: tight line and red dot)

4 × 50 on :15R—alt 25 3R3S, 25 swim (focus: stroke count. Each one should be lower than the last.)

8-minute set. Swim CPace 50s on :10–:15R (focus: downhill swimming and tight line)

2 × 25 swim fast on :20R (focus: shift and skate)

IHR or RPE

3 × 100 on :20R—alt 25 SPBDchoice, 25 swim (focus: kayak paddling), 25 swim easy (focus: stealth), 25 swim (focus: kayak paddling)

1 × 4-minute swim @ CPace

IHR or RPE

Cool-Down

1 × 50 swim *TS FinsOpt* 25 @ NSPL, 25 @ -2SPL (focus: shift and skate)

4 × 25 on :10R *TS FinsOpt*—alt 25 FB, 25 BBR, 25 SGSS, 25 3S&G

1 × 50 swim *TS FinsOpt* @ -2SPL (focus: downhill swimming)

IHR or RPE

Total distance: Approximately 1,800

Comments: If you would like to swim some cruise pace and cruise interval sets with fins, you will need to do a T-swim with fins so that you'll have an appropriate set of times to work with. Same goes for using a training snorkel. Throughout the remainder of the practices in this level, the total distance shown is for a person with a cruise pace of 1:50 per 100. Faster swimmers will rack up more distance—slower swimmers, less.

2 Introducing Cruise Intervals

Training zone: High aerobic and lactate threshold

Target RPE range: 13 to 15

Target heart-rate range: 90 to 100+% of SLTHR

Warm-Up

1 X 300 *TSOpt SBFinsOpt*—alt 25 Dchoice, 25 swim (focus: choice). Use many different choices, one for each cycle, for both the drill and the focus.

IHR or RPE

Main Set

8 X 25 on :15R—alt 25 FB, 25 SGB good, 25 BB, 25 swim (focus: kayak paddling)

IHR or RPE

4 X 50 LAR on :10R *SBFinsOpt*—desc 1–6

4 X 50 on :10R *SBFinsOpt* as 25 SGB weak, 25 swim (focus: shift and skate)

2 X 25 cavort on :10R—kickboard surfing, backward. Same as the kickboard surfing you did in level 2, only backward. Again, experiment with different ways to propel yourself.

6-minute set. Swim 50s at CPace on :05–:10R LOFO

IHR or RPE

6 X :20 VKR on :10R *Fins*—shoulders up and down. (Within each 20-second repeat, gradually increase your kicking speed so that your shoulders come up out of the water, then gradually decrease your kicking speed and return to your starting position.)

IHR or RPE

6-minute set. Swim 50s on CInt

IHR or RPE

Cool-Down

4 X 50 on :15R—alt 25 LAR, 25 swim (focus: forward lunge)

Total distance: Approximately 1,900 (including estimated equivalent for VKR)

Comments: You can see the difference between a CPace set and a CInt set. These types of sets have been rather short so far. As the workouts progress, the duration of the sets will increase in order to make them more of an aerobic workout. Be sure to move from one part of the practice to the next as quickly as possible so that your heart rate, or RPE, doesn't drop below the target range.

Counting Strokes While Cruising 3

Training zone: High aerobic and lactate threshold

Target RPE range: 13 to 15

Target heart-rate range: 90 to 100+% of SLTHR

Warm-Up

1 × 100 *FinsOpt*—alt 25 FB, 25 SGB rt, 25 BBR, 25 SGB lft

1 × 100 *FinsOpt TSOpt* LAR build (*build* means to get steadily faster)

1 × 100 *FinsOpt TSOpt* swim (focus: 50 tight line, 50 kayak paddling)

IHR or RPE

Main Set

10 × 25 swim on :10R (focus: stroke count. Don't let the SPL increase as the set progresses.)

IHR or RPE

6-minute set. Swim 100s @ CPace on :10-:15R (focus: stroke count. Don't let it increase.)

IHR or RPE

6-minute set. Swim 50s on CInt LOFO (focus: stroke count. Don't let it increase, except maybe a little on the LOFO.)

IHR or RPE

4 × 50 on :10R *SBFinsOpt*—alt 25 5S&G, 25 3R3S (focus: tight line. Go tight-schlumpy-tight several times during the set.)

1 × 50 swim SLSSS

2 × 200 swim NS with as much rest as you want between each repeat. On each repeat, swim the first 100 slower than your CPace, then see how fast you can swim the second 100.

IHR or RPE

Cool-Down

8 × 25 swim on :10R 2 @ NSPL, 4 @ -1SPL, 2 @ -2SPL (focus: downhill swimming)

IHR or RPE

Total distance: Approximately 2,000

Comments: Going right from the CPace set to the CInt set may be quite challenging. Try to keep the same stroke count per length throughout both sets.

4 Cruising and Drilling

Training zone: High aerobic and lactate threshold

Target RPE range: 13 to 15

Target heart-rate range: 90 to 100+% of SLTHR

Warm-Up

4 × 50 on :10R *SBFins*—alt 25 BBR, 25 SGB

1 × 100—alt 25 SGB, 25 swim (focus: shift and skate)

IHR or RPE

Main Set

8-minute set. Swim 50s on IHR or RPE (Keep HR in target range.) (focus: choice/mix)

1 × 100 as 50 SGB, 50 MR3S

IHR or RPE

8-minute set. Swim 50s on CInt LOFO (focus: odd: forward lunge; even: kayak paddling)

1 × 100 *TS SBFins*—alt 50 5S&G, 50 3R3S

IHR or RPE

8 × 25 LAR on :20R—alt 25 build, 25 fast underwater (Can you complete the length without coming to the surface to breathe?)

1 × 100 cavort—side swimming. Start from side-glide position. Staying entirely on that side (no rotation), swim by using your extended arm to take short strokes with underwater recoveries, while your top arm takes longer strokes and over-the-water recoveries. Alternate sides on each length. Experiment with the timing of your strokes to find out what works best. Keep your balance and tight line.

IHR or RPE

1 × 4:00 swim @ CPace

Cool-Down

4 × 50 on :10R *SBFins*—alt 25 SGB, 25 3S&G (focus: red dot)

IHR or RPE

Total distance: Approximately 2,000

Comments: Always try to use an aspect of a drill you have mastered in your full-stroke swimming. Are you becoming more comfortable with CPace and CInt swims? On CInt sets, it is okay to swim faster than the target time indicated on the chart during some of the repeats, but only if you swim *none* of them slower than the target time.

Negative Splitting and Stroke Counting at Cruise Pace

Training zone: High aerobic and lactate threshold

Target RPE range: 13 to 15

Target heart-rate range: 90 to 100+% of SLTHR

Warm-Up

6 × 50 on :15R desc 1–6 *TSOpt SBFinsOpt*—alt 25 LAR, 25 swim (focus: stroke count; don't let it increase as the set progresses)

IHR or RPE

Main Set

4-minute (or longer) swim (distance evenly divisible by 100) NS (Swim this at a speed you can negative split comfortably. Record your splits and finish time.)

IHR or RPE

4 × 50 on :15R *Fins*—alt 25 3S&G, 25 swim fast (focus: tight line. Go tight-schlumpy-tight on one of the fast ones.)

IHR or RPE

4-minute swim (same distance as above) NS (This swim should be faster than the previous one. Try to start with the same first-half split, but swim a faster second split for a faster elapsed time. Record your splits and finish time.)

8 × 25 fast on :20R *Fins*—alt 25 LAR, 25 swim (Go tight-schlumpy-tight on several of the LARs and swims.)

IHR or RPE

4-minute swim (same distance as above) NS (This one should be faster still. Can you start this one a bit faster than you did the others and still NS with a faster elapsed time?)

1 × 100—alt 25 Dchoice, 25 swim SLSSS (Active recovery. You'll recover faster doing easy work than by just standing still.)

10-minute set. Swim 100s @ CPace on :10–:15R LOFO (focus: stroke count. Try to keep it consistent throughout the set.)

IHR or RPE

Cool-Down

4 × 50 3R3S on IHR or RPE (focus: choice/mix). Keep IHR/RPE below target ranges.

Total distance: Approximately 2,100

Comments: Fast swimming or drilling with fins is a great way to become aware of whether you are swimming with more resistance than necessary. Were you able to do the LOFO at the end of the CPace set without adding strokes?

6 Swimming Golf Revisited

Training zone: High aerobic and lactate threshold

Target RPE range: 13 to 15

Target heart-rate range: 90 to 100+% of SLTHR

Warm-Up

100—alt 25 DPBDchoice, 25 swim (focus: tight line)

100—alt 25 SIDchoice, 25 swim (focus: choice)

100—alt 25 RCDchoice, 25 swim (focus: choice)

IHR or RPE

Main Set

3 × 50 SGolf on 2:00 (or 1:00RMin)

IHR or RPE

3 × 100 on :20R *FinsOpt*—alt 25 Dmix, 25 swim (focus: choice)

IHR or RPE

4 × 25 cavort—dogpaddle. Does keeping a tight line and good balance make this drill any easier than the last time you did it? Have you made improvements that you should let your best friends know about?

3 × 50 SGolf on 1:45 (or :45RMin)

IHR or RPE

1 × 150 swim SLSSS (focus: tight line and the tube by 50s)

IHR or RPE

3 × 50 SGolf on 1:30 (or :30RMin)

IHR or RPE

12-minute set. Swim (your choice of 75s, 100s, or 150s) on CInt LOFO (focus: choice/mix)

Cool-Down

4 × 50 on :10R—alt 25 SGB, 25 5S&G (focus: kayak paddling)

IHR or RPE

Total distance: Approximately 2,100

Comments: Compare your SGolf scores to the ones you wrote down after level 3, practice 6. Because this practice is exactly the same as that practice (until you come to the 12-minute CInt set after the SGolf swims), you will be comparing apples to apples. What focus choices make it easier to swim your target times in the CInt set?

Longer Cruise Pace Work

Training zone: High aerobic and lactate threshold

Target RPE range: 13 to 15

Target heart-rate range: 90 to 100+% of SLTHR

Warm-Up

1 × 300 swim NSx100s

IHR or RPE

Main Set

3 × 100 on :40R desc 1–3 *SBFins*—alt 25 SGB weak, 25 swim (focus: choice), 25 SGB good, 25 swim (focus: choice)

IHR or RPE

1 × 150 swim *SBFinsOpt* (focus: forward lunge)

16-minute set. Swim 200s @ CPace on :15–:20R (focus: 50 tight line, 50 hand swapping, 50 hand and hip connection, 50 kayak paddling)

IHR or RPE

1 × 50 swim fast (focus: tight line and red dot)

1 × 100 SGB *Fins*—alt 25 rt, 25 lft

1 × 50 swim fast *Fins* (focus: snappy hips)

IHR or RPE

6-minute set. Swim your choice of 25s @ CPace on :5–:10R, or 50s @ CPace on :10–:15R

IHR or RPE

Cool-Down

4 × 50 on :15R as 25 SGB, 25 SGSS

IHR or RPE

Total distance: Approximately 2,200

Comments: Longest CPace set yet. Changing your focus points regularly will help you maintain your technique and will help you pass the time quickly.

8 Lots of 50s

Training zone: High aerobic and lactate threshold

Target RPE range: 13 to 15

Target heart-rate range: 90 to 100+% of SLTHR

Warm-Up

3 × 100 swim on :15R *FinsOpt* (focus: 1: shift and skate, 2: forward lunge, 3: kayak paddling)

IHR or RPE

Main Set

1 × 400 speed-switching swim—alt 75 @ CPace, 25 fast (How fast can you swim the fast 25s and still swim the 75s at CPace?)

20 × 50 on :10R—odd: Dmix; even: swim @ CPace (focus: choice/mix)

IHR or RPE

4 × 25 cavort on :20R desc 1–4—seated kickboard surfing. Sitting on a kickboard, propel yourself in any manner that does not involve touching lane ropes. Along each length, make three 360-degree turns, at roughly one quarter, half, and three quarters of the length. Your 360s may be either somersault 360s or turn-around 360s. Don't always turn in the same direction.

IHR or RPE

8 × :20 VKR on :10R *Fins,* shoulders up and down (as in practice 2 in this level). How high can you get your shoulders?

Cool-Down

100 strokes for distance *TSOpt.* (How far can you swim with 100 freestyle strokes—each arm counts as a stroke—without extra kicking without it looking like a drill? Effective swimmers can swim 200 or more in a short-course pool.)

IHR or RPE

Total distance: Approximately 2,200 (includes estimated equivalent for VKR)

Comments: As you do that set of 20 × 50, alternating between drill and CPace swimming, try to do the drill fast enough that your heart rate doesn't drop much. By the way, did you have to look up your CPace time for 50s or did you remember it? Eventually, you will be very familiar with most of your shorter CPace times.

Drill Review

9

Training zone: High aerobic and lactate threshold

Target RPE range: 13 to 15

Target heart-rate range: 90 to 100+% of SLTHR

Warm-Up

1 × 100 *TS*—alt 25 FB, 25 SGND, 25 BBR, 25 LAR

1 × 100—alt 25 BB, 25 SGNU, 25 SGB, 25 SGSS (focus: forward lunge)

1 × 100—alt 25 3S&G, 25 3R3S, 25 swim fists, 25 swim

IHR or RPE

Main Set

2 × 100 on :20R—alt 25 Dchoice, 25 swim (focus: wide tracking and stroke count)

2 × 50 on :10R—alt 25 3R3S, 25 swim (focus: pierce down, not push down)

2 × 25 on :5R—take the fewest strokes possible, but still look like you are swimming, not drilling.

20-minute set. Swim choice of 100s, 150s, or 200s on CInt LOFO (focus: choice and different choice. Alternate them either between swims or between 50s.)

IHR or RPE

1 × 100 swim SLSSS *TSOpt*

1 × 150 swim BOYLFS *TSOpt*—alt 50 fists, 50 fingers, 50 hands

8 × 25 swim fast on :30R *TSOpt Fins* (focus: stroke count, odds @ NSPL, evens @ -2SPL)

IHR or RPE

Cool-Down

4 × 50 on :10R—alt 25 SGB weak, 25 5S&G

IHR or RPE

Total distance: Approximately 2,300

Comments: Again, the warm-up revisits the fundamental drills—also an excellent way to spend some time in a hotel pool that is not conducive to normal practices. During that set of fast 25s with fins on, a longer-than-normal rest may drop your heart rate a bit out of target range.

10 Stroke-Count Awareness

Training zone: High aerobic and lactate threshold

Target RPE range: 13 to 15

Target heart-rate range: 90 to 100+% of SLTHR

Warm-Up

4 × 75 on :10R—alt 25 SGB weak, 25 3R3S (focus: shift and skate), 25 swim BOYLFS (focus: stroke count)

IHR or RPE

Main Set

6-minute set. Swim 50s CInt LOFO—alt 1 @ NSPL, 1 @ -1SPL

IHR or RPE

1 × 100 Dchoice *FinsOpt*

3 × :30 VKR on :10R *SBFinsOpt*—hands on your chest

8-minute set. Swim 75s CInt LOFO—alt 1 @ NSPL, 1 @ -1SPL

IHR or RPE

1 × 100 Dchoice *FinsOpt*

1 × 100 swim SLSSS *FinsOpt* (focus: kayak paddling)

10-minute set. Swim 100s CInt LOFO—alt 1 @ NSPL, 1 @ -1SPL

IHR or RPE

4 × 25 cavort *Fins*—underwater kick. Start each length kicking underwater with schlumpy posture and in an iron-cross position (arms straight out to the sides), looking straight ahead. Slowly draw yourself into a tight-line position so that you finish the last third of the length streamlined. During that last third, rotate 360 degrees using just your legs to drive a series of ¼-turn rotations, each going in the same direction. Try to perform every rotation completely underwater. Take as much rest as needed between each 25 and descend them.

3 × 50 3R3S fast on :30R (focus: 25 forward lunge, 25 shift and skate)

IHR or RPE

Cool-Down

2 × 100 on :10R 3R3S—alt 50 fists, 25 fingers, 25 hands

IHR or RPE

Total distance: Approximately 2,300 (Includes estimated equivalent for VKR)

Comments: Big emphasis on stroke counting while keeping your speed on target. Always try to lower your stroke counts. When you have drill choices, don't always pick the easiest ones—get out of your comfort zone. The fast-3R3S set shows that drills can be used as high-intensity training too—but strict attention to proper execution and bodily feedback is still vital! That underwater-kick cavort provides lots of learning opportunities.

CHAPTER 11

Level 5:
Speed Workouts

As much as 50 percent of the moderate-intensity practices in level 4 were skill drills. As you move into this chapter, there will be less drilling and more swimming. Yet the focus will still be on technique, rather than on just slogging out laps. This chapter is composed of 40- to 50-minute workouts. Each practice in this chapter involves either one highly anaerobic set (very fast swimming with a moderate to long rest) or a large amount of cruise pace or cruise interval work. Attempt the practices in this level only after you've done the practices in levels 3 and 4 long enough to be comfortable with them. By now you should have mastered all the drills.

Level 4 introduced the concept of cruise intervals as a method of improving endurance at the highest aerobic speeds. Level 5 introduces three new types of sets that are specifically designed to help develop faster, more anaerobic speeds. Short sprint sets help develop maximum, very short-term explosive speed. Lactate-endurance and lactate-tolerance sets improve pain tolerance and your body's ability to deal with lactic-acid accumulation while swimming fast. These last two types of sets require maximum efforts and maximum or near-maximum speeds. I offer them as test sets to help motivate you to do them at the appropriate intensity.

Each of the practices in this chapter has an approximation of total distance based on three cruise paces. You can interpolate or extrapolate based on your personal CPace.

Reading the Workouts

The sets introduced here will be used to train the two anaerobic systems—the alactic system, in which lactic acid does not accumulate, and the anaerobic lactic system, in which high levels of lactic acid accumulate. These sets may require close inspection and attention the first few times you see them.

Short-Sprint Sets

You have already seen a few places where very short repeats are to be done at a fast pace. Let's expand on that idea:

6 × 25 short sprint OACI

This type of set calls for very fast swimming (or kicking) with lots of rest. *Short sprint* will always mean that you should swim as fast as possible. *On Any Comfortable Interval (OACI)* means that you should use an interval that allows enough rest (or easy swim and drill) between repeats so that you can do each repeat fast, without fatigue or pain. The amount of rest needed will vary from person to person. If in doubt, err on the side of too much, rather than too little, recovery. If it takes you more than 15 seconds to swim a full length of the pool, then you should sprint only a portion of the length, perhaps three-fourths or one-half of the length, and slow down for the rest of the length. There are a variety of activities that will qualify as short sprints, and each will be explained in the workout. This type of set—very short, fast repeats with lots of recovery—trains the alactic-anaerobic system.

Test Sets

From the beginning, you have been doing T-swims and recording your results. This is referred to as a *test set*—a set that you repeat from time to time, recording your results each time (see chapter 15 for charts). The goal is to see improvements over time in your technique, speed, and endurance. In the set notation, the word *test* precedes all test sets. In addition to describing the work being done, each set will ask for specific information to be recorded, which will be indicated in brackets.

Level 5 introduces two new types of test sets: lactate-endurance sets and lactate-tolerance sets. These types of sets, if done correctly, are very stressful. Only well-conditioned swimmers can tolerate doing them two or three times per week. Unlike the workouts from previous levels, do not try to do a series of workouts from this level or the next level in consecutive training sessions. By the time you graduate to doing these workouts, you should be following one of the training programs in chapter 13, paying particular attention to the section on rest and overtraining beginning on page 183. Before starting either of these types of sets, check with your physician to be sure that you are healthy enough to engage in maximum-intensity exercise.

Lactate-Endurance Sets

Lactate-endurance (LEnd) sets call for swimming high-intensity repeats with moderate amounts of rest. This allows you to recover partially but not completely between repeats, which will result in rising lactic-acid levels and high heart rates throughout the set. This type of work increases your ability to perform consistently for an extended time at high speeds even when you are fatigued. It improves your body's ability to buffer and metabolize lactic acid. The rest should be active rest—do drills, easy swimming, bobbing, and so on—in the 9 to 11 RPE range in order to speed recovery. The set notation will sometimes suggest a specific recovery activity.

> TEST (LEnd), 16-minute set. Swim 50s 1:1 W/RInt :02Range
> [interval, fast2, slow, avgSPL, HHR]

This notation calls for a 16-minute set of very fast 50s. *1:1 W/RInt* means to choose a one-to-one work-to-rest ratio interval (the rest period between swims should be roughly the same length as the work period). For instance, if each swim takes about 34 seconds, a 1:10 interval allows 36 seconds rest—roughly a 1:1 ratio. If your average swim time is 32 seconds, then 1:05 would be an appropriate interval. When in doubt, choose an interval that allows for slightly less rest.

The *:02Range* means to allow no more than two seconds difference between the slowest and fastest swims in the set. Take an IHR after each fast swim. Count strokes for 8 to 10 lengths, spaced evenly across the set duration but excluding the first length of any repeat. If your interval would have the next repeat begin before the 16 minutes is up, then swim the whole repeat, even though it ends after the 16-minute mark. The bracketed part, *[interval, fast2, slow, avgSPL, HHR]*, means that at the end of this set, you should record your interval, the times of the two fastest swims, the time of the slowest swim, your average number of strokes per length, and the highest heart rate achieved during the set. Test sets for 75s, 100s, and 200s have similar notation:

> TEST (LEnd), 18-minute set. Swim 75s 1:1 W/RInt :03Range
> [interval, fast2, slow, avgSPL, HHR]

> TEST (LEnd), 20-minute set. Swim 100s 1:1 W/RInt :04Range
> [interval, fast2, slow, avgSPL, HHR]

> TEST (LEnd), 24-minute set. Swim 200s 1:1 W/RInt :06Range
> [interval, fast2, slow, avgSPL, HHR]

Lactate-Tolerance Sets

Lactate-tolerance (LTol) sets improve your body's ability to tolerate and buffer high levels of lactic acid. Repeated swims at maximum speeds with longer rests allow more recovery from one swim to the next than LEnd sets. The swimming speeds are faster, the lactic acid levels are higher, and, as a consequence, LTol sets are more painful than LEnd sets.

> TEST (LTol), swim 4 × 100 (or 75—2:00Cut) on 6:00
> [fast2, slow, avgSPL, HHR]

This set notation asks for four all-out 100s on a 6-minute interval with as much active rest as you have time for between each. The *or 75—2:00Cut* means that if you can't finish 100 under 2:00, then you should opt for 75s instead. Count strokes for 6 to 8 lengths, spaced evenly across the set duration but excluding the first length of any repeat. Take an IHR immediately after each fast repeat. Record the times of the two fastest swims, the time of the slowest swim, your average number of strokes per length, and the highest heart rate achieved during the set.

The intervals for LTol sets allow for a lot of recovery time, *most* of which should be active rest. Check your heart rate often to see how quickly and how far it comes down. As your fitness improves, your heart rate will come down faster and farther between LTol set repeats. Because this work is of high intensity and because you are allowed anywhere from two to five times as much rest as work, this set is highly anaerobic in nature. LTol sets for 50s and 200s use similar notation:

TEST (LTol), swim 8 × 50 on 3:00 (or 6 on 4:00—1:00Cut)
[fast2, slow, avgSPL, HHR]

TEST (LTol), swim 3 × 200 (or 150—4:00Cut) on 12:00
[fast2, slow, avgSPL, HHR]

On the set of eight 50s, if you can't make the 1:00 cut, swim 6 × 50 on 4:00 rather than swimming a shorter distance. On the shorter-distance sets (50s and 100s), it's a good idea to have someone else time you with a stopwatch in order to get precise times. You may miss speed improvements that come in fractions of seconds if you time yourself with a pace clock.

Continuing Technique Education

Even though the workouts in this level may appear to be focused on conditioning, it is important to understand that they are meant to condition the muscles and ranges of motion that are necessary for highly effective swimming.

◯ FOCUS POINT ➤ Core-Rotation Tempo

The technique we have been learning uses core rotation around the long axis of the body as the primary engine of propulsion. It relies on the shoulders, arms, and hands to serve as the transmission that links that power source to the water. You have been doing long-axis rotation (LAR) drills at various tempos since level 1. Through your rotation-connection drills (MR3S and 3R3S), you have learned to connect your strokes to your core so that they transmit rotational forces to your whole-arm paddles.

Now, if you want to increase your swimming speed, you have to increase your stroke tempo. To do this, instinct tells you to simply move your arms faster. But *how* you move your arms faster is crucial. An increase in stroke tempo must begin as an increase in core-rotation tempo. The goal then is to move your arms in sync with this faster long-axis rotation while maintaining your hand to hip connections. If you instead follow your instinct and simply move your arms faster, you will lose the hand-to-hip connection as well as the surge of speed that your core long-axis rotation should add to every stroke. Set your swimming tempo with your core rotation, not with your shoulders or arms.

Now that you are primed with new training and technique concepts, let's move to the workouts. Feel free to use a training snorkel at any point in these sections, though according to the restrictions listed here (and not on those drills and swims that obviously designate breathing motions as an essential component—SGNU, SGB, BOYLFS). Also, do not use fins unless the practice notation calls for them, or unless the following conditions are met:

- Cruise pace and cruise interval sets: If you have done a T-swim with fins and/or training snorkel, then it is okay to do CPace and CInt sets, in moderation, with the same equipment.

- Lactate-endurance and lactate-tolerance sets: Once you have performed each test set with no equipment, you may repeat any of the test sets with any combination of equipment you desire in order to add variety and training stress to your program.

It is important to record equipment-aided test-set results separately from your no-equipment test-set results so that on subsequent performances you'll be comparing apples to apples.

1 Drill Review and Cruise

Training zone: Alactic sprints, high aerobic and lactate threshold

Target RPE range: 13 to 15+

Target heart-rate range: 90 to 100+% of SLTHR

Warm-Up

10 minutes. Move continuously through all the drills (except VK and VKR), doing at least 25 of each and 50 or more of those for which you have room for improvement. Then swim 25s descending on :10R (focus: choice/mix) to finish the 10 minutes.

IHR or RPE

Main Set

4-minute set. 25s on :10R *FinsOpt*—alt 25 swim (focus: core-rotation tempo), 25 LAR (focus: tight line). Alt two fast lengths and one very easy length.

IHR or RPE

16-minute set. Swim 200s or 150s on CInt (focus: stroke count. Try to take one fewer stroke on the last length of each repeat.)

IHR or RPE

8 × 12 short sprints on OACI—kick/turn/swim. Each of these short sprints is a hard push to a tight-line sprint kick to just past the near backstroke flags (about six yards/meters). Turn any way you can without touching the bottom or the lane ropes and sprint swim back to the wall (attack the wall).

IHR or RPE

10-minute set. Swim 75s or 50s on CInt LOFO (focus: mix)

IHR or RPE

Cool-Down

4-minute set *Fins*. A continuous swim starting at a fairly fast pace. Gradually *decrease* your core-rotation tempo (and keep your strokes in sync with those rotations) throughout the swim.

IHR or RPE

Total distance:	@ Cruise pace per 100:	1:20	1:40	2:00
	Approximate distance:	2,900	2,350	2,000

Comments: In revisiting the fundamental drills, were you able to remember them all or did you need to see the drill list? Were you able to work through the whole list without stopping? Remember to move quickly from one segment of the practice to the next; you should need no more rest between segments than what is necessary for taking heart rates and making equipment changes.

Long Cruise

Training zone: Alactic sprints, high aerobic and lactate threshold

Target RPE range: 13 to 15+

Target heart-rate range: 90 to 100+% of SLTHR

Warm-Up

100 SPBDchoice *SBFins*. Choose your least favorite ones.

100 DPBDchoice *SBFins*. Choose your least favorite ones.

6-minute set. 75s swim on :10R—alt 25 fists, 25 fingers, 25 hands (focus: over the keg)

IHR or RPE

Main Set

IHR or RPE

20-minute set. Swim 300s (or any longer distance) on CInt LOFO

IHR or RPE

8 × short sprints OACI—odd: 25 sprint swim; even: 12½ sprint kick underwater and swim easy for the rest of the length

IHR or RPE

6-minute set. Swim 50s at 3–4 seconds faster than CPace and see how little rest you can take for each repeat.

Cool-Down

6-minute set. 50s on :10R *TSOpt FinsOpt*—alt 25 Dchoice, 25 swim (focus: shift and skate and hand swapping)

Total distance:	@ Cruise pace per 100:	1:20	1:40	2:00
	Approximate distance:	3,200	2,600	2,200

Comments: For the 20-minute cruise interval set, it's okay to choose a different distance for the last repeat of the set so that your finish time is closer to 20 minutes. If you decided to swim 400s and your CInt is 7:45, your third repeat would start at 15:30 and end at 23:15. You might instead choose to swim a 250—CInt 4:50—on the last repeat, which would allow you to finish the set at 20:20—much closer to the intended set duration.

3 Even Longer Cruise

Training zone: High aerobic and lactate threshold

Target RPE range: 13 to 15+

Target heart-rate range: 90 to 100+% of SLTHR

Warm-Up

4-minute set. 50s on :10R—alt 25 SGNU, 25 SGB

4-minute set. 50s on :10R *TS*—alt 25 SGND, 25 3R3S (focus: core-rotation tempo)

4-minute set. Swim 50s on :10R desc *TS*. Can you prevent your SPL from increasing much?

IHR or RPE

Main Set

6-minute set. Swim @ CPace (Choose the shortest chart distance with a cruise time of 6:00 or longer and try to swim your cruise time exactly.)

IHR or RPE

14-minute set. Swim 200s (or longer) on CInt. Try for a lower SPL on the last length of each repeat.

IHR or RPE

10-minute set. Swim 100s (or shorter) on CInt LOFO

IHR or RPE

Cool-Down

6-minute set. 100s on :10R BOYLFS *FinsOpt*—alt 25 LAR, 25 RCDchoice, 50 swim (focus: red dot)

IHR or RPE

Total distance:	@ Cruise pace per 100:	1:20	1:40	2:00
	Approximate distance:	3,000	2,400	2,000

Comments: During the main set, there is no extra rest between segments. By now you should have done enough breathing on your less-favorite side that when you see BOYLFS, you should have to think about which side to choose—if not, you would profit from choosing your less-favorite side more often.

16-Minute Lactate Endurance   4

Training zone: Alactic sprints, lactate threshold, and red line

Target RPE range: 9 to 18+

Target heart-rate range: 70 to 105+% of SLTHR

Warm-Up

5 minutes. Continuous drill/swim—alt 25 SIDchoice, 25 LAR, 50 swim (focus: 25 tight line, 25 kayak paddling)

5 minutes. Repeat above with *TS*

IHR or RPE

Main Set

5-minute set. Short sprints on OACI *Fins*—odd: 25 swim; even: 25 LAR (focus: core-rotation tempo)

IHR or RPE

TEST (LEnd), 16-minute set. Swim 50s on 1:1 W/RInt :02Range [interval, fast2, slow, avgSPL, HHR] (Easy swimming, bobbing, or exhaling underwater against some resistance is more effective for recovery than just standing still.)

4 × 25 cavort OACI—sculling over the keg. Lay prone in the water with both arms in front of you. Reach into the over-the-keg position with both arms. Use only sculling motions (side-to-side sweeps of your forearms in a single vertical plane, alternating the pitch of your hands so that they deflect water toward your feet with each sweep, in or out) to propel yourself. No kicking! If you have something less than perfect posture and balance, a pull-buoy between your legs can be a useful crutch.

IHR or RPE

5-minute set. Swim 50s @ CPace on :10–:15R LOFO (focus: stroke count. Don't let it increase.)

IHR or RPE

Cool-Down

5-minute set. 50s on :10R *SBFinsOpt*—mix Dchoice and swim as desired (focus: core-rotation tempo)

IHR or RPE

Total distance:	@ Cruise pace per 100:	1:20	1:40	2:00
	Approximate distance:	2,300	1,900	1,600

Comments: If you do the test set correctly, you will hit near-maximal heart rates and an RPE of 18 or more. You should be able to keep a lower stroke count during the CPace set than during the test set. If you haven't acquired a waterproof notebook yet, you'll need to cut up a Tyvek envelope that you can use for recording your test-set results at the pool's edge.

5 18-Minute Lactate Endurance

Training zone: Lactate threshold and red line

Target RPE range: 9 to 18+

Target heart-rate range: 70 to 105+% of SLTHR

Warm-Up

10-minute set. Swim 50s on IHR or RPE *TSOpt* (focus: stroke count. Can you prevent it from increasing much?). Start slow and gradually increase intensity so that HR increases slowly.

Main Set

TEST (LEnd), 18-minute set. Swim 75s on 1:1 W/RInt :03Range [interval, fast2, slow, avgSPL, HHR]. Perhaps swim an EZ 50 BOYLFS during the recovery period between each fast 75.

IHR or RPE

1 × 100 EZ swim SLSSS (or double-overarm lollygag if you prefer)

IHR or RPE

8-minute set. Swim 100s on CInt LOFO (focus: stroke count and shift and skate)

IHR or RPE

Cool-Down

6-minute set. 50s SIDchoice on IHR or RPE *FinsOpt*. Try for a lower IHR or RPE on each repeat.

Total distance:	@ Cruise pace per 100:	1:20	1:40	2:00
	Approximate distance:	2,550	2,050	1,750

Comments: Start the warm-up at a slower pace than you think you'll need. Move from one section of the main set to the next with no extra rest—just check your HR and go. How much faster are you able to swim when you see LOFO?

20-Minute Lactate Endurance   6

Training zone: Alactate sprints and red line

Target RPE range: 9 to 18+

Target heart-rate range: 70 to 105+% of SLTHR

Warm-Up

8-minute set. 50s on :10R *FinsOpt*—alt DPBDchoice, SIDchoice, RCDchoice, swim (focus: choice) BOYLFS

IHR or RPE

Main Set

3 × 50 SGolf on :45R (focus: core-rotation tempo)

IHR or RPE

4-minute set. Short sprints on OACI—kick/turn/kick. These are just like the short sprints in practice 1 in this level—just past the backstroke flags and back— except that now you sprint kick in both directions. Drum your hands as fast as you can on the deck, then take off on your sprint. Try to use the same kick tempo as the tempo you made when you were drumming.

IHR or RPE

TEST (LEnd), 20-minute set. Swim 100s on 1:1 W/RInt :04Range [interval, fast2, slow, avgSPL, HHR]. Swimming an easy backstroke is great for recovery between high-intensity freestyle repeats because it allows you to breathe freely.

4 × 25 cavort on :10R—swim flat. Swim entirely on your stomach with no body roll whatsoever. On even lengths, spread your legs wide at the surface like a drag chute. Breathe by lifting your head, not by turning it. See how balanced you can remain and how smoothly you can swim.

IHR or RPE

3 × 50 SGolf on :30R (focus: two-beat kick)

IHR or RPE

Cool-Down

6-minute set. Swim 50s on CInt+5sec (Just make the interval instead of hitting target times.) (focus: two-beat kick)

IHR or RPE

Total distance:	@ Cruise pace per 100:	1:20	1:40	2:00
	Approximate distance:	2,450	2,000	1,700

Comments: Try to keep your scores in the second set of SGolf at or below your scores in the first SGolf set. Use the cool-down as an opportunity to perform your swimming skills correctly despite your fatigue.

7 24-Minute Lactate Endurance

Training zone: Alactic sprints and red line

Target RPE range: 9 to 18+

Target heart-rate range: 70 to 105+% of SLTHR

Warm-Up

6-minute set. Continuous *FinsOpt TSOpt*—alt 25 LAR, 25 swim (focus: two-beat kick), 25 RCDchoice, 25 swim (focus: two-beat kick). As the set progresses, each 25 swim should be a tad faster than the previous one.

IHR or RPE

Main Set

4 × 12.5 short sprints on :30RMin. Sprint swim or kick a half length, swim easy for the rest of the length, and then rest for at least 30 seconds or swim an easy 25 before doing the next 12.5.

IHR or RPE

100 strokes for distance *TSOpt*. See how far you can swim with 100 freestyle strokes, just as you did in level 4, practice 8.

TEST (LEnd), 24-minute set. Swim 200s on 1:1 W/RInt :06Range [interval, fast2, slow, avgSPL, HHR] (perhaps alternating 25 swim—low stroke count—and 25 lollygag between fast 200s)

IHR or RPE

100 strokes for distance *TSOpt*. Can you swim further on this one than on the one you did a half hour ago?

IHR or RPE

1 × 200 swim fast. Can you swim faster on this one than on the fastest one in the test set?

IHR or RPE

Cool-Down

100 strokes for distance *TSOpt* (Last chance to swim even farther.)

IHR or RPE

Total distance:	@ Cruise pace per 100:	1:20	1:40	2:00
	Approximate distance:	2,600	2,150	1,800

Comments: In the test set, if your interval allows you to start the last 200 anytime before the 24-minute mark, go ahead and swim the whole distance even though it takes you past 24 minutes. The last fast 200, if you really go for it, should take you to a higher lactate peak than the test set did and maybe to a new highest heart rate.

Lactate Tolerance—50s

Training zone: Alactic sprints and red line

Target RPE range: 9 to 19+

Target heart-rate range: 70 to 110+% of SLTHR

Warm-Up

8-minute set. Swim 50s desc on IHR or RPE. Try to finish the 8 minutes with fairly fast swimming (focus: alt finish your strokes, downhill swimming, kayak paddling, and core-rotation tempo)

IHR or RPE

Main Set

8 × 12.5 short sprints *Fins*. Start these from a prone position at midpool. Lying horizontally on your front, start with a compact, fast kick and try to accelerate as quickly as possible. After 6 to 10 kick beats, add strokes and sprint swim to an aggressive finish. Swim EZ 62.5 or more, returning to midpool for the next repeat.

IHR or RPE

TEST (LTol), swim 8 × 50 on 3:00 (or 6 on 4:00—1:00Cut) [fast2, slow, avgSPL, HHR] (perhaps 25s EZ drill and swim mix on short rest between repeats)

IHR or RPE

4 × 25 cavort—sculling variety. On each length, try sculling in a different body position and hand position—on your back, side, or front; head first or feet first; hands sculling in the same plane or on two different planes—you choose. Again, a pull buoy may help if you have posture or balance issues.

Cool-down

4-minute set. EZ 50s on :10R *TSOpt*—alt 25 SGSS, 25 swim (focus: tight line and two-beat kick). Try to reduce your SPL on each swim.

IHR or RPE

Total distance:	@ Cruise pace per 100:	1:20	1:40	2:00
	Approximate distance:	3,000	2,500	2,100

Comments: Although the main set doesn't look like it asks for much distance, if you do the repeats properly with all-out-effort 50s, this set will be very stressful. Be sure to do the entire cavort and to cool down after the main set. Do more EZ swimming if you have not substantially recovered by the end of the cool-down.

9 Lactate Tolerance—100s

Training zone: Alactic sprints and red line

Target RPE range: 9 to 19+

Target heart-rate range: 70 to 110+% of SLTHR

Warm-Up

6 minutes of continuous 25s *TSOpt*—alt 25 swim @ NSPL, 25 swim @ -1SPL, 25 swim @ -2SPL, 25Dchoice

IHR or RPE

Main Set

4 × 25 swim fast OACI

IHR or RPE

1 × 100 swim SLSSS (focus: shift and skate)

IHR or RPE

TEST (LTol), swim 4 × 100 (or 75—2:00Cut) on 6:00 [fast2, slow, avgSPL, HHR]. Some of the cavorts you've done would make good recovery work between high-intensity repeats.

IHR or RPE

1 × 100 swim SLSSS (focus: two-beat kick)

4 × 25 swim *Fins* fast OACI (focus: stroke count descending)

IHR or RPE

Cool-down

6 minutes continuous 25s *TSOpt*—alt 25 swim @ NSPL, 25 swim @ -1SPL, 25 swim @ -2SPL, 25 Dchoice

IHR or RPE

Total distance:	@ Cruise pace per 100:	1:20	1:40	2:00
	Approximate distance:	2,450	2,000	1,700

Comments: Use fast fin swimming in order to become more aware of when you are working against more resistance than necessary. Have you recalculated your SLTHR target heart-rate ranges lately? As you get in better aerobic shape, your SLTHR will change.

Lactate Tolerance—200s   10

Training zone: Lactate threshold and red line

Target RPE range: 9 to 19+

Target heart-rate range: 70 to 110+% of SLTHR

Warm-Up

1 × 300 swim *TSOpt*—alt 100 fists, 100 fingers, 100 hands (focus: two-beat kick)

4 × 25 swim on :10R *TSOpt* (focus: minimum stroke count)

IHR or RPE

Main Set

6-minute set. Short sprints *FinsOpt*—These are called breakaways. This is a continuous swim, most of which is done at a very easy pace, but occasionally you'll sprint furiously from midpool to the wall (as if you just realized that you were being chased by a shark). Be sure to do enough easy swimming to be ready for the next all-out sprint.

TEST (LTol), swim 3 × 200 (or 150—4:00Cut) on 12:00 [fast2, slow, avgSPL, HHR]. Easy swimming or drilling with fins is good for recovery between high-intensity repeats.

IHR or RPE

4 × 25 cavort on :15R—underwater freestyle. This is similar to the freestyle with underwater recoveries that you did in practice 3 of level 2, but now you should minimize the number of times you surface for air on each length. Can you do any or all of the repeats entirely underwater?

Cool-Down

4-minute set. Swim 50s IHR or RPE *TSOpt* (focus: two-beat kick). Start @ CPace and swim each one 2 to 3 seconds *slower* than the preceding one. Try to decrease your stroke count throughout the set.

Total distance:	@ Cruise pace per 100:	1:20	1:40	2:00
	Approximate distance:	3,200	2,600	2,200

Comments: During the long rest periods between the test-set swims, you should evenly divide your time with EZ swimming and your choice of drills—fins are okay here. Active-rest activities (HRs near 70 percent of SLTHR) between high-intensity repeats are an excellent opportunity for focusing on your technique.

CHAPTER 12

Level 6: High-Intensity Workouts

This chapter is composed of 50- to 60-minute workouts. The high-intensity practices in level 5 introduced a variety of challenging anaerobic test sets. The longer (up to 60 minutes) level 6 practices use these same test sets, but they add more aerobic swimming at various intensities. These are the most challenging and stressful practices and should only be undertaken when you are feeling fresh and rested. To do the workouts in this level, you should be following one of the training programs from chapter 13, paying particular attention to the section on rest and overtraining. Before starting the workouts, check with your physician to be sure that you are healthy enough to engage in maximum-intensity exercise.

As in level 5, you are asked to record information and results from various swimming sets. In the level 6 practices, use your fins and training snorkel according to the same permissions and restrictions in level 5.

FOCUS POINT ➤ Easy Speed

In a way, this idea combines all the other focus points. Quite simply, this is the nirvana of swimming—going fast but making it look easy. The goal is to hide the effort. Start with your face. When you are trying to swim fast, are you grimacing or is there a look of tranquility on your face? Then work down your body. Release tension, not part of your posture or linkage. How little tension can you use to maintain your tight line while keeping your critical masses connected and working together? See how little effort you can put into each motion and still have it happen rapidly. Make every movement flow smoothly into the next, swimming *casually* rather than frantically. At first, the idea of easy speed may seem at odds with the idea of swimming fast, but the more you practice it, the more sense it will make. Most people first experience easy speed while swimming fast with fins, later with short-blade fins, and eventually with bare feet.

SGolf and Cruise   1

Training zone: Alactic sprints and lactate threshold

Target RPE range: 13 to 15+

Target heart-rate range: 90 to 100+% of SLTHR

Warm-Up

6-minute set. Continuous *SBFinsOpt*—alt 25 SPBDchoice, 25 LAR, 25 swim (focus: easy speed). Each 25 swim should be faster than the previous one.

IHR or RPE

Main Set

6-minute set. Short sprints *FinsOpt*—These are called speedturns. This is a continuous swim, most of which is done very EZ, but occasionally you'll sprint from just before the backstroke flags to the wall, turn, and sprint three or four strokes (without breathing). Be sure to do enough EZ swimming to recover completely before the next all-out speedturn. Feel for easy speed on those fast strokes out of the speedturn.

IHR or RPE

6-minute set. Swim 75s (or 50s) on CInt LOFO (focus: easy speed)

12-minute set. Swim 200s (or 150s) on CInt LOFO (focus: easy speed)

6-minute set. Swim 75s (or 50s) on CInt LOFO (focus: easy speed)

IHR or RPE

9 × 50 SGolf (see the comments section). How little rest can you take and still swim the drill correctly?

Cool-Down

6-minute set. Continuous—alt 25 SIDchoice, 25 LAR, 25 swim

Total distance:	@ Cruise pace per 100:	1:20	1:40	2:00
	Approximate distance:	3,550	2,850	2,400

Comments: Do not take more rest between the CInt sets beyond the few seconds necessary to do IHR or RPE checks. Easy speed is more difficult to accomplish as fatigue increases. Before you start this practice, look up the results of your previous SGolf sets and calculate an average score per 50 repeat. Use this as your par score on the 9 × 50 SGolf set and try to swim through this 9-hole course, finishing at or under par for the course.

2 Review and Cruise

Training zone: Alactic sprints and lactate threshold

Target RPE range: 13 to 15+

Target heart-rate range: 90 to 100+% of SLTHR

Warm-Up

10 minutes *Fins*. Move continuously through the drills (except VK and VKR), doing 25 of each. Then swim 50s or 25s descending on :10R (focus: easy speed) to finish the 10 minutes.

IHR or RPE

Main Set

3 × :10 VKR *Fins* with easy 50 swim between each. These count as short sprints, which means that you are trying to lift yourself as high as possible out of the water and to stay up there for the full 10 seconds. Can you smile while you do these?

20-minute set. Swim choice of distance 200 or more on CInt

IHR or RPE

3 × :10 VKR *Fins* short vertical sprints with an easy 50 swim between each

IHR or RPE

10-minute set. Swim 100s (or 50s) on CInt (focus: stroke count. Occasionally swim the last length of a repeat at a lower count.)

IHR or RPE

4 × 25 LAR fast on :10R *Fins* in full streamline position

IHR or RPE

5-minute set. 50s swim (focus: stroke count). Do the first one fairly fast. Keep track of your stroke count and elapsed time. Then see how little rest you can repeat that performance with, hitting or improving *both* stroke count and time.

IHR or RPE

Cool-Down

6-minute cavort. Your choice of any of the cavorts already described—or be creative and make up your own. Cavorts can be very low-intensity. The goal is to get out of your comfort zone and do something different in the water.

IHR or RPE

Total distance:	@ Cruise pace per 100:	1:20	1:40	2:00
	Approximate distance:	3,900	3,200	2,700

Comments: By now you know that when I do not suggest a specific focus point, you should choose one of the many we've talked about—cycling through all of them repeatedly over time—right? No extra rest in the main set; go immediately from one item into the next—same for the warm-up. If you would like to do some CInt and CPace sets with fins or a snorkel, you'll need to do T-swims with them in order to establish chart-listing benchmarks.

Golf and Cruise

3

Training zone: Lactate threshold

Target RPE range: 13 to 15+

Target heart-rate range: 90 to 100+% of SLTHR

Warm-Up

8-minute set. *TS*—alt 50 Dchoice, 50 swim. The swims should be descending, but do not allow the total stroke count for the 50 to increase faster than the time (in seconds) decreases.

IHR or RPE

Main Set

6-minute set. Swim @ CPace. Choose a distance for which your cruise time is 6 minutes or more.

2 × 50 SGolf on :20R. Try for a lower score on the second one.

IHR or RPE

14-minute set. Swim 150s (or 100s) on CInt (last length of each at lower SPL)

2 × 50 SGolf on :30R *TS*. Try for a lower score on the second one.

IHR or RPE

10-minute set. Swim 75s (or 50s) on CInt

2 × 50 SGolf on :40R. Try for a lower score on the second one.

IHR or RPE

6-minute set. Swim 50s CInt—alt 1 @ NSPL, 1 @ -1SPL

2 × 50 SGolf on :50R *TS*. Try for a lower score on the second one.

IHR or RPE

Cool-down

5-minute continuous EZ swim *TSOpt*. Start out taking way too many SPL. Gradually trim strokes off each length and try to end with too few SPL at the end of 5 minutes.

IHR or RPE

Total distance:	@ Cruise pace per 100:	1:20	1:40	2:00
	Approximate distance:	3,900	3,200	2,700

Comments: No extra rest during the main set; this will make the swimming golf 50s quite challenging.

4 16-Minute Lactate Endurance

Training zone: Alactic sprints, lactate threshold, and red line

Target RPE range: 9 to 18+

Target heart-rate range: 70 to 105+% of SLTHR

Warm-Up

6 minutes of continuous drill/swim mix. How much of a variety of drills and focus points can you include in the 6 minutes?

IHR or RPE

Main Set

6-minute set. Swim 75s (or shorter) on CInt

IHR or RPE

6 minute cavort *Fins*—dolphin launches. Swim easily to the deep water, then kick down to the bottom, push off the bottom in full tight-line, streamline position, sprint-kicking straight up so that you launch through the surface as high as possible, like a dolphin. Continue kicking hard in order to slow your descent back into the water. The complete launch and slow descent should require 6 to 8 seconds of sprint kicking. Swim easy until you recover and then repeat. If swimming in deep water is not an option, choose any previous short-sprint activity.

IHR or RPE

TEST (LEnd), 16-minute set. Swim 50s on 1:1 W/RInt :03Range [interval, fast2, slow, avgSPL, HHR]. Perhaps do an EZ 25 of a drill or another stroke between each fast 50 instead of just standing still.

IHR or RPE

1 × 100 swim SLSSS

IHR or RPE

12+-minute set. Choose a distance with a CInt just over 6 minutes and do two repeats.

IHR or RPE

Cool-Down

6-minute cavort. Your choice of past cavorts, or make up your own.

IHR or RPE

Total distance:	@ Cruise pace per 100:	1:20	1:40	2:00
	Approximate distance:	3,250	2,650	2,250

Comments: Two cavorts in one practice, though the first one is just a different way to get some alactic sprint kicking in. On the SLSSS, which are you better at: the super-low count, the slow speed, or the stealth? Which do you most need to improve?

18-Minute Lactate Endurance   5

Training zone: Alactic sprints, lactate threshold, and red line

Target RPE range: 9 to 18+

Target heart-rate range: 70 to 105+% of SLTHR

Warm-Up

6-minute set. Swim 25s on IHR or RPE (focus: stroke count). Start slow and gradually increase intensity so that your HR moves up steadily. Can you prevent your stroke count from increasing much?

Main Set

8-minute set. Short sprints *Fins*. First sprint is a full 25, and each subsequent sprint is a bit shorter than the previous repeat. Be sure to do enough recovery swimming between each repeat to allow for full sprinting speed on each.

IHR or RPE

TEST (LEnd), 18-minute set. Swim 75s on 1:1 W/RInt :03Range [interval, fast2, slow, avgSPL, HHR]. Perhaps do an EZ 50 drill/swim/lollygag mix during the rest between each fast 75.

IHR or RPE

16-minute set. Swim choice of distance on CInt LOFO

Cool-down

8-minute set. 75s *FinsOpt TS* 3R3S on IHR or RPE. Keep HR near 70% of SLTHR.

Total distance:	@ Cruise pace per 100:	1:20	1:40	2:00
	Approximate distance:	3,450	2,850	2,400

Comments: Try to start the test set at a lower stroke count than your average from the last time you did this test set. Try to not let the stroke count increase.

6 20-Minute Lactate Endurance

Training zone: Alactic sprints, lactate threshold, and red line

Target RPE range: 9 to 18+

Target heart-rate range: 70 to 105+% of SLTHR

Warm-Up

8-minute set. 50s *FinsOpt*—alt 25 Dchoice, 25 swim (focus: mix). Each 25 swim should be faster than the preceding one. As these 25s get faster, the focus should be on easy speed. All the drill lengths should be done at an easy pace.

IHR or RPE

Main Set

4 × 25 short sprints on OACI. On the first one, sprint only for the first three strokes and then swim easily for the rest of the length. On each repeat, sprint for one more stroke than the preceding repeat so that you finish with six strokes on 4.

4 × 25 short sprints on OACI *Fins*—same as the preceding set.

IHR or RPE

5 × 50 SGolf on OACI. Do the first 50 fast at whatever feels like a normal stroke count. Compute your score, then try to decrease SGolf score with each repeat.

IHR or RPE

4-minute set. Swim continuous EZ—alt 50 @ NSPL, 50 @ -2SPL

IHR or RPE

TEST (LEnd), 20-minute set. Swim 100s on 1:1 W/RInt :04Range [interval, fast2, slow, avgSPL, HHR]. Insert active rest with a technique focus between each high-intensity repeat.

IHR or RPE

5 × 50 SGolf on OACI. Do the first one as SLSSS. Compute your score, then decrease SGolf score with each repeat.

Cool-Down

6-minute set of cavort—maximum strokes. Swim a 25, taking the maximum number of freestyle strokes possible while maintaining your continuous forward motion. Then on each subsequent length, reduce your stroke count until you finish with a low count (for you). The maximum number of strokes that I've seen someone take in a 25-yard pool is 135 (with a full push and glide from the wall). How close can you come to that? What can this cavort teach you?

IHR or RPE

Total distance:	@ Cruise pace per 100:	1:20	1:40	2:00
	Approximate distance:	3,200	2,600	2,200

Comments: In the second set of SGolf, the fatigue of the LEnd set will make it more difficult to swim low scores. If you can swim the same low scores that you did on the first SGolf set, consider that an accomplishment.

24-Minute Lactate Endurance

Training zone: Alactic sprints and red line

Target RPE range: 9 to 18+

Target heart-rate range: 70 to 105+% of SLTHR

Warm-Up

8-minute set as follows:

4 × 50 swim on IHR or RPE desc 1–4 *Fins* (focus: tight line)

6 × 25 swim on :05R desc 1–6 *Fins* (focus: easy speed)

Fairly fast LAR *Fins* to finish 8 minutes

IHR or RPE

Main Set

6-minute set. Short sprints *FinsOpt*. Each short sprint starts from a push into a sprint LAR for at least three rotations. Add four strokes while keeping this fast-rotation tempo, and then swim easy until you recover before the next repeat. Before starting each sprint, drum your hands fast on the deck, tuning your kick to this tempo.

IHR or RPE

TEST (LEnd), 24-minute set. Swim 200s on 1:1 W/RInt :06Range [interval, fast2, slow, avgSPL, HHR]. What will you do instead of just standing there and breathing hard? Easy swim? Drill? Cavort?

IHR or RPE

1 × 100 EZ swim. Count your total strokes for this swim.

IHR or RPE

5 × 50 SGolf OACI (See following comments.)

IHR or RPE

1 × 100 swim. How fast can you swim using no more strokes than in the previous EZ 100?

IHR or RPE

Cool-Down

200 SLSSS or your choice of cavort

IHR or RPE

Total distance:	@ Cruise pace per 100:	1:20	1:40	2:00
	Approximate distance:	3,100	2,550	2,150

Comments: Before you start this practice, look up the results of your previous SGolf sets and calculate an average score per 50 repeat. Use this as your par score on the 5 × 50 SGolf set and see if you can swim through this 5-hole course, finishing under par.

8 Lactate Tolerance—50s

Training zone: Lactate threshold and red line

Target RPE range: 9 to 19+

Target heart-rate range: 70 to 110+% of SLTHR

Warm-Up

8-minute set. Drill or swim continuous *TSOpt*—alt 25 Dchoice, 25 swim

IHR or RPE

Main Set

8-minute set of 50s SGolf. First 50 should be swum at a moderate pace. Then see how many different combinations of stroke counts and time you can use to get the same score. Take only the amount of rest you need.

1 × 100 swim SLSSS BOYLFS

TEST (LTol), swim 8 × 50 on 3:00 (or 6 on 4:00, 1:00Cut) [fast2, slow, avgSPL, HHR]. Swim maybe an easy 50 plus add a bit of bobbing to ease your suffering between repeats.

IHR or RPE

1 × 100 swim SLSSS BOYLFS

IHR or RPE

12-minute set. Swim 150s @ CPace on :15R (or 100s @ CPace, :10R) LOFO. Try to reduce your stroke count throughout this set.

IHR or RPE

2-minute cavort—water-aided standing broad jump. In roughly chest-deep water, perform a standing broad jump for distance. You may use only a single sweep or scoop of your arms to assist you. A judicious use of your leap momentum plus the interplay of gravity and buoyancy can carry you quite a distance. Repeat several times and improve on your original leap.

Cool-Down

4-minute set. EZ 50s continuous *FinsOpt*—alt 25 SGB weak, 25 swim BOYLFS (focus: red dot)

IHR or RPE

Total distance:	@ Cruise pace per 100:	1:20	1:40	2:00
	Approximate distance:	3,300	2,700	2,300

Comments: The CPace set, which follows soon after the test set, offers an excellent opportunity to focus on efficient swimming while you are fatigued. Remember that when a focus point is not explicitly indicated, you should select a focus for your stroke. Focus on correcting and refining problem areas rather than on what you already do well.

Lactate Tolerance—100s 9

Training zone: Alactic sprints, lactate threshold, and red line

Target RPE range: 9 to 19+

Target heart-rate range: 70 to 110+% of SLTHR

Warm-Up

6-minute set. Swim 150s (or 100s) desc and NS on :15R *SBFinsOpt*

IHR or RPE

Main Set

12-minute set. Swim 2 × 500 NS (or shorter distance) @ CPace on 1:00R. Choose a distance in which CPace time is 5:30 or less.

IHR or RPE

6 minutes of short sprints. On the first one, push off and swim three long, easy strokes, and then turn and sprint back to the wall, counting your strokes. On each subsequent repeat, add one more full-length easy stroke before the turn. How few returning sprint strokes can you add for each easy stroke you add? Swim an easy 25 or 50 between each repeat.

IHR or RPE

4-minute set. 25s swim on :10R *TSOpt*—alt 25 @ NSPL, 25 @ -1SPL, 25 @ -2SPL, 25 @ -3SPL. Try to look like you are swimming rather than drilling.

IHR or RPE

TEST (LTol), swim 4 × 100 (or 75—2:00Cut) on 6:00 [fast2, slow, avgSPL, HHR]. Active rest early in the set will delay lactate accumulation; so does breathing out against some resistance. What will you do here between repeats? During the last repeat of the set, remember the following: Pain is weakness leaving the body.

Cool-Down

6-minute set. Reswim one repeat of the distance you swam in the CPace set. Swim it at a very easy pace, but negative-split it.

IHR or RPE

Total distance:	@ Cruise pace per 100:	1:20	1:40	2:00
	Approximate distance:	3,200	2,600	2,200

Comments: On the CPace set, negative splitting each swim is challenging, but it will help you swim your best time for the number of heartbeats spent. Be sure to take an IHR or RPE at the beginning of the 1-minute rest as well as at the end in order to see how well you recover.

10 Lactate Tolerance—200s

Training zone: Red line
Target RPE range: 9 to 19+
Target heart-rate range: 70 to 110+% of SLTHR

Warm-Up

8-minute set. Continuous swim *TS*—alt 75 fists, 50 fingers, 25 hands. First cycle is swum at a very easy pace; each cycle is swum faster than the one before.

IHR or RPE

Main Set

4-minute set. Swim 25s @ CPace on :05–10R. Maintain the same stroke count throughout.

IHR or RPE

1 × 200 swim fists SLSSS

TEST (LTol), swim 3 × 200 (or 150—4:00Cut) on 12:00 [fast2, slow, avgSPL, HHR]. For recovery work between these high-intensity repeats, I encourage you to mix easy swimming and your favorite cavorts.

IHR or RPE

1 × 200 swim fists SLSSS

4-minute set. Swim 25s @ CPace on :10–15R LOFO. Use one fewer SPL than in the previous CPace set.

IHR or RPE

Cool-Down

4-minute set. Swim 50s on IHR or RPE. Start @ CPace and swim each one 1–2 seconds slower than the preceding one. Try to decrease stroke count throughout the set.

Total distance:	@ Cruise pace per 100:	1:20	1:40	2:00
	Approximate distance:	3,450	2,850	2,400

Comments: Once you have swum each of the LEnd and LTol test sets with no fins or snorkel, you may swim some of them with equipment for more variety. Be sure to record these results separately from your no-equipment test sets.

PART IV

Training Over the Long Haul

Part III introduced you to a variety of technique and conditioning activities that became progressively longer or more intense. Once you have familiarized yourself with the skill drills, technique concepts, and practice notation, you are ready to embark on a rest-of-your-life aquatic adventure. Part IV will help you do that. In the following chapters, you'll learn how to organize the practices into a training program and how to chart your progress.

Chapter 13 will help you put together a seasonal training program that incorporates different training phases and appropriate amounts of rest. In addition, I give specific examples of how many swimmers, competitive or otherwise, organize their training.

Chapter 14 offers a variety of sample three-week programs that you can use as building blocks for an entire season. The sample programs in chapter 14 are based on three levels of interest and ability—fitness swimming, precompetitive swimming, and competitive swimming. If you choose to use the programs in chapter 14, you will find that they are progressive and that they continually test your skill, endurance, and speed.

Chapter 15 explains how to keep your motivation high by finding training partners, keeping a training diary, varying your swimming environment, and accurately tracking your swimming progress day to day, week to week, and season to season. Several handy progress charts are supplied for you to photocopy and take to the pool.

CHAPTER 13

Swimming Throughout the Year

Fitness swimmers tend to make a habit of doing long swims at the same moderate pace, with little or no technique focus to their workout—a surefire plan for becoming better conditioned to swim slowly with the same ugly stroke they've always used. While competitive swimmers are more likely to plan their practices and to work harder, they often plan for only one practice at a time rather than for a season of practices. If you want to become a better and faster swimmer—a highly effective swimmer—you need a different strategy.

Whether you are a competitive swimmer or a fitness swimmer, your training will be more productive and enjoyable if you do some seasonal planning. This chapter describes the different phases of a training season, shows you how to plan a season of training, explains how your body responds to training, and explains how to avoid the consequences of overtraining. You'll be able use the sample programs in chapter 14 in your seasonal plan. They will tell you precisely which workouts you should do each day throughout your season.

Phases of a Swim-Training Program

There are five phases of a seasonal training strategy: technique acquisition and general endurance, technique refinement and specific endurance, technique maintenance and competition, tapering for a big meet, and the break between seasons. Depending on your ultimate interests, you may use some or all of the phases in your seasonal planning. How you combine these workouts in each phase determines the outcome of your efforts.

Technique Acquisition and General Endurance   Basic endurance for swimming involves swimming effectively at submaximal paces for extended periods of time. Any training season must start at this level if the athlete is to negotiate more demanding training later in the season. Even elite swimmers spend the first several months of each training season learning new skills and increasing their sensitivity to skill nuances. The practices in levels 1 through 3 allow you to learn new skills while developing an aerobic conditioning base using skill drills and focused, low-intensity swimming. The practices should constitute a sizable portion of your early-season training.

Technique Refinement and Specific Endurance Once general endurance is established, we increase the intensity of the aerobic training by introducing and progressively increasing lactate-threshold training with cruise pace and cruise interval work found in level 4. Because we want to continue refining the skills we learned in the general-endurance phase, we continue to mix skill drills and technique-focused swimming sets. "Practice makes permanent" is the technique theme for this training phase. This may be as far as swimmers with no competitive or risk-taking aspirations ever want to venture into swim conditioning.

Technique Maintenance and Competition Those who wish to compete or to simply test the body's limits will add workouts from levels 5 and 6.

© AP Images

Each of the phases of a well-planned training season incorporates a mix of technique and conditioning work aimed at steadily improving performance.

These workouts introduce lactate endurance, lactate tolerance, and anaerobic alactic work. Anaerobic speed is the conditioning focus, but with enough endurance work to maintain your aerobic conditioning. If you compete, schedule most of your competitions during this training period. They will serve as a portion of your high-intensity training. Maintain the skills you have already acquired and refined by continuing your skill-drill work and by including more full-stroke swimming using real-time feedback. Monitoring your execution of effective swimming skills is the technique theme for this phase of training.

Tapering If you are a competitor, you probably have a specific season-ending competition that you are training toward. A training season is planned to allow you to perform your best during this competition. A training taper is a period of reduced training, during which the body is allowed much more rest than usual and is thereby given the chance to fully adapt to training. For example, during a taper, a swimmer may cut his total training volume (yardage and duration) to as little as one-third of his pretaper volume. The key is to work at the same relative intensity as in pretaper practices but to do less of it. It is common for competitive swimmers to report dramatic improvements in their performance after tapering.

Take a Break   Regardless of your reasons for swimming, an occasional break from your training program—from a week to a month—is necessary in order to maintain freshness and enthusiasm. When you return to the pool, you will have a renewed outlook on your workouts.

Planning a Competitive Training Season

Planning a season begins with the end in mind. Here is an example of how we might build a periodized training schedule for a typical Masters training season, which is focused on a peak performance at Short-Course (25-yard pool) Nationals in mid-May. We'll plan backward from that mid-May date. Since Long-Course (50-meter pool) Nationals usually take place in mid-August, and since swimmers often take a month off after the big meet, the earliest we might start a short-course training season would be in mid-September, which would give us 35 weeks to train.

Taper Period   Depending on the intensity and duration of the training season, your taper should last anywhere from two to four weeks. We'll use the three weeks from late April to mid-May. Personal experience over a few seasons will give you a better idea of how long your taper should be.

Technique Maintenance and Competition Period   Depending on the duration of your training season, this training period could last from 6 to 12 weeks. This is the optimum range for concentrated, high-intensity training. After deducting the taper period, we have roughly 32 weeks left in our season. We want each endurance training phase to last longer than our competition phase, so we'll block out the 9 weeks from mid-February to late April, less than one-third of the remaining season, for our competition training.

Technique Refinement and Specific Endurance Period   With 23 weeks left for endurance training, we want to spend about half of that time in each endurance phase. So for our specific endurance period, we'll block out 12 weeks—December through mid-February—knowing that we'll probably lose a week of training around the holidays.

Technique Acquisition and General Endurance Period   This leaves the 11 weeks from mid-September through the end of November for our general endurance training.

The schedule would look like this:

Technique acquisition and general endurance, 11 weeks (mid-September through the end of November)

Technique refinement and specific endurance, 12 weeks (December to mid-February)

Technique maintenance and competition, 9 weeks (mid-February to late April)

Taper, 3 weeks (late April to mid-May)

Short-Course Nationals

Break, 2 weeks (until early June)

If, after completing this competition, you then wanted to go to Long-Course Nationals in mid-August, you would have a very short season of 11 weeks to work with. You might arrange it as follows:

Cut break short, 1 week. This gives you 12 weeks to work with.

Technique acquisition and general endurance, 3 weeks (late May to mid-June)

Technique refinement and specific endurance, 4 weeks (mid-June to early July)

Technique maintenance and competition, 3 weeks (early July to very late July)

Taper, 2 weeks (very late July to mid-August)

Long-Course Nationals

Break, 4 weeks (until mid-September, when the next short-course season begins)

This long-course scenario is not ideal, but it illustrates how the fundamental principles for building a season are applied at the extreme short end of the spectrum. Some swimmers and coaches prefer to plan three seasons in a year rather than two. A three-season yearly cycle might look like this:

Season 1: 15 weeks from early September, culminating in a selected meet in late December

Technique acquisition and general endurance, 4 weeks (early September to early October)

Technique refinement and specific endurance, 5 weeks (early October to early November)

Technique maintenance and competition, 4 weeks (early November to early December)

Taper, 2 weeks (early December to late December)

Selected meet

Break, 1 to 2 weeks

Season 2: 20 weeks from January 1, culminating in Short-Course Nationals in mid-May

Technique acquisition and general endurance, 6 weeks (January through mid-February)

Technique refinement and specific endurance, 6 weeks (mid-February to late March)

Technique maintenance and competition, 5 weeks (late March to late April)

Taper, 3 weeks (late April to mid-May)

Short-Course Nationals

Break, 1 to 2 weeks

Season 3: 11 or 12 week long-course training season as described earlier with 3 to 4 weeks break before the next short-course season

Planning a Fitness Training Schedule

A fitness swimmer can use the same building blocks for planning without the constraint of a specific competition schedule. Some choose to progress through the phases just as a competitive swimmer would, including tapering and taking a break. Others prefer to eschew one or both of the competition or tapering phases, depending on whether a period of high-intensity work is desired. The following are samples of possible fitness-training schedules:

6-week schedule without a high-intensity phase

Technique acquisition and general endurance, 3 weeks

Technique refinement and specific endurance, 3 weeks

Since the physiological stress of such a season is low, it can be repeated several times without taking a break between each cycle. The duration of each phase is not critical, except that they should be roughly equal. For the swimmer who wishes to include a period of high-intensity training, the following plan would work:

9-week schedule including a high-intensity phase

Technique acquisition and general endurance, 3 weeks

Technique refinement and specific endurance, 3 weeks

Technique maintenance and competition, 2 weeks

Taper or break, 1 week

Again, the actual durations of the phases are not as important as following the relative durations as described earlier. Though you won't actually compete, that third phase is when the high-intensity training takes place. Following it with either a short taper period or with a short break, perhaps for cross-training, serves both as a reward and as a method for avoiding overtraining.

Planning for a break when regular training is difficult to maintain—Christmas holiday, for instance—is a great way to avoid the guilt that often arises when one must miss training.

Adaptation

A common misconception is that the work you do in practice makes you a better-conditioned swimmer. In fact, it is what you do *between* work sessions—during your recovery periods—that actually improves your conditioning. Under normal conditions, the body makes adaptations in response to physical demands. Your body seeks a state of fitness for which the physical activities that you regularly engage in are not a great hardship. A furniture mover's body adds muscle mass to help him lift heavy objects. A runner's body increases the aerobic capacity of her leg muscles and improves the cardiovascular system. Exercise sends signals to the brain and body that trigger a variety of physiological adaptations, such as increased strength, more explosiveness, more endurance, and so on.

The operative phrase in the previous paragraph is *under normal conditions*. Normal conditions include proper nutrition, proper hydration, adequate amounts of high-quality sleep, minimal or zero use of cultural pollutants (e.g., alcohol, nicotine, crack, Twinkies), freedom from disease, and relatively low psychological-stress levels.

But when one or more conditions are abnormal, there is a dramatic decrease in the body's ability to adapt normally to exercise. If you go to practice this evening, then eat poorly, party hearty, and don't get enough sleep, you should expect very little adaptation to result from your workout. And you can't get it back. Even if you finally get your act together three days from now by getting plenty of sleep and eating well, you will not reap the benefits of today's workout.

Lack of sleep is probably the most common and most destructive deviation from ideal-adaptation conditions. If you are not getting enough sleep, you'd probably be better off taking the two to three hours you now devote to the workout process (i.e., traveling, training, and traveling again) and investing it in a good nap. Better yet, get to bed earlier. Coupling lack of sleep with one or more of the other negative conditions just compounds the problem. Although an occasional deviation won't devastate your training, consistently infringing on ideal adaptation conditions will give your competition a huge advantage.

Rest and Overtraining

Doing too much high-stress exercise while at the same time not getting enough rest, active and passive, will result in what is called failing adaptation, which, as a protective mechanism, actually decreases your ability to do further exercise. This is often referred to as overtraining, and it potentially has far worse consequences than not training enough. Taking a proactive approach to avoiding overtraining—through planning, awareness, monitoring, and flexibility—is essential.

Planning Because too many days of hard exercise in a row or in a week is the primary cause of overtraining—regardless of your ability level, conditioning level, or interest level—you should plan to take at least one day off from swimming each week. This will help keep both your body and your mind fresher when you are in the pool. Pursuing other physical activities on your day off is fine, as long as you keep the intensity level low. Consider this another form of active rest.

Awareness When you are involved in an exercise regimen, it is prudent to watch for signs of overtraining. Consider one or more of the following subjective indicators a caution flag:

- Feeling tired, drained, or like you have no energy
- General aches or pain in many muscles and joints
- Not recovering from one workout to the next
- Decrease in performance, training capacity, or intensity
- Insomnia
- Headaches
- Moodiness, irritability, decreased enthusiasm, depression
- Diminished appetite

There are more objective measures for overtraining. If you are following the programs in this book, then you are regularly recording your T-swim heart rates—your SLTHR. If you find that your training pace begins to slow down when you are at that heart rate, you may be heading toward overtraining. A training diary in which you include notes about how you feel each day can also help you spot downward trends and decreased enthusiasm.

Monitoring Another indicator of overtraining is an unexpected variation of your resting heart rate (RHR). To make this determination accurately, you must make a habit of checking your RHR regularly, even daily, so that you know its normal range. Wearing a heart-rate monitor and setting it to average your heart rate overnight is ideal for this. The next best option is to take a reading first thing in the morning when you wake up. If you check your RHR manually, count the number of pulses over a full 60-second period and breathe normally throughout. If you notice that your RHR is more than a few BPM out of your normal range, high or low, for more than a day or so, this could indicate either the beginning of overtraining or the first stages of illness.

Flexibility   If you continue to train despite having the warning signs of over-training, you will feel stale at best and sick or injured at worst. Depending on the severity of your symptoms, total recovery can take from a few days to several weeks. Recovery should include proper nutrition, stress reduction, and quality sleep. It would be better to avoid overtraining in the first place. If you suspect that you may be on the edge of overtraining, try altering your training for a few days to a week. Decrease the amount of high-intensity training you do and include more rest and active rest. You may be able to avoid more severe consequences and end up with merely a training blip as opposed to a train(ing) wreck.

The sample programs in chapter 14 lay out training days. They typically alternate between less intense and more intense days and include at least one day of rest per week. Follow these programs or use them as a model for designing your own to ensure that you plan an adequate amount of rest into your training program.

Sample Swimming Programs

Most adults who swim regularly will say that they swim first and foremost for fitness. What varies from person to person is the motivation for continuing to come back to the water when they could be doing something else. Whether you simply want to be aerobically fit, increase the effectiveness of your swimming, or train for the national championships, read on and you will find a set of programs that can help you reach your goals. The programs in this chapter are divided into three interest, or participation, types:

Beginning- and Easy-Swimming Programs (Lap or Fitness Swimming)   As a beginning swimmer, you probably swim on a regular basis for relaxation and enjoyment or as part of an aerobic-fitness plan. The beginning and easy programs provide a variety of learning activities that will improve your aerobic fitness. These programs consist mainly of level 1 and level 2 practices that focus on skill drills. They teach and reinforce the fundamentals of efficient freestyle swimming while providing you with aerobic activities for three or four practices per week. While most of these practices are intended to keep your heart rate at the lower end of the aerobic-training heart-rate range, there are also a few level 3 and level 4 practices that are somewhat more intense.

Frequent-Swimming Programs (Precompetitive)   Swimmers who make a habit of working out regularly often want to increase the frequency and intensity of their workouts—often with an eye toward competing in the future. People who swim frequently go beyond the minimum aerobic-exercise requirements. They train more often, for longer periods, and at higher intensities. Frequent swimmers might also swim in an occasional competition, such as an open-water swim or a distance event at a local Masters meet. If you swim four or five times per week, you are most likely in this category. Precompetitive workouts increase training volume, frequency, and intensity while laying the groundwork for the more intense training that is necessary for competition.

Intense-Swimming Programs (Competitive)   If you already compete, if you want to compete in the near future, or if you just want to know what your body is capable of, a more intense program is for you. These programs assume that swimming is your primary physical activity and that you are willing to commit to more training time each week. Whether you actually compete in meets is irrelevant. A competitive swimmer is one who finds joy and motivation in testing her speed and endurance, whether against the pace clock or against other swimmers. The workouts in these programs are designed for swimmers who want to swim fast now and faster next week. They are intense and they provide a progressive challenge.

The following is a sample of three-week programs for each of the three above categories. Each program focuses on a specific aspect of swimming—i.e., improving technique, building endurance, or building speed. Also included are explanations of the workouts and how you can use the programs most effectively. By reading the explanations and following the examples, you will be able to adapt the programs to fit your schedule or to put together programs of your own.

Beginning- and Easy-Swimming Programs (Lap or Fitness Swimming)

IMPROVING TECHNIQUE

These two programs present the complete set of level 1 and level 2 practices in a logical progression, slowly introducing new skill drills and gradually increasing distance and complexity. If you are new to this system, if you are a beginning swimmer, or if any of the skill drills or training concepts are unclear, I strongly encourage you to start with these programs. The last day of each program calls for you to repeat an easier practice and to follow it immediately with another T-20 swim (recording your results). With all of the programs in this chapter, you can shift the column headings in order to do the first workout of the program on the day of the week you choose. Note that L1•4, for example, means to do practice 4 in level 1 (chapter 7).

If your fitness level is above average but you still need to learn the skill drills in a logical order, consider accelerating the progression by taking fewer days off or by doing two practices on some days. In either case, I recommend that you do the practices in the order indicated. If your schedule allows only enough time for three practices a week, then lengthen these programs to four weeks, but follow the order indicated.

	Sun	Mon	Tue	Wed	Thurs	Fri	Sat
W1	L1•1	—	L1•2	—	L1•3	—	L1•4
W2	L1•5	—	L1•6	—	L1•7	—	L1•8
W3	L1•9	—	L1•10	—	L2•1	—	L1•1 and T-20

	Sun	Mon	Tue	Wed	Thurs	Fri	Sat
W1	L2•1	—	L2•2	—	L2•3	—	L2•4
W2	L2•5	—	L2•6	—	L2•7	—	L2•8
W3	L2•9	—	L2•10	—	L3•1	—	L2•1 and T-20

▪ BASIC SKILLS   ◢ SKILL DEVELOPMENT   ⬭ FULL-STROKE

BUILDING ENDURANCE

After you have worked through all of the level 1 and 2 practices at least once and are familiar with the drills and focus points, it's time to start building your endurance. These two programs give you more flexibility while gradually introducing more challenging practices. Note that L1•1-5, for example, means to select any one of the practices, 1 through 5, from level 1.

	Sun	Mon	Tue	Wed	Thurs	Fri	Sat
W1	L1•1-4	—	L3•1	—	L1•5-7	—	L3•2
W2	L1•8-10	—	L3•3	—	L2•1-4	—	L3•4
W3	L2•5-7	—	L3•5	—	L2•8-10	—	L2•1 and T-20

	Sun	Mon	Tue	Wed	Thurs	Fri	Sat
W1	L2•1-5	—	L3•6	—	L3•7	—	L2•6-10
W2	L3•8	—	L3•9	—	L1•6-10	—	L3•10
W3	L1•6-10	—	L4•1	—	L2•1-5	—	L2•1 and T-20

LACTATE THRESHOLD   SPEED   HIGH-INTENSITY

Frequent-Swimming Programs (Precompetitive)

IMPROVING TECHNIQUE

In these programs, there are five practices per week, including more level 3 and level 4 practices, which require more distance and intensity. These are interspersed with lower intensity, fundamental-skill practices from levels 1 and 2. The first two Saturdays of each program are longer training days, using an easy level 1 practice as a warm-up for a more intense level 3 or 4 practice. As before, the final Saturday of each program calls for a T-20 swim.

	Sun	Mon	Tue	Wed	Thurs	Fri	Sat
W1	L2•1-5	—	L3•1-5	L1•1-4	L2•6-10	—	L1•3 and L3•6-10
W2	L1•5-7	—	L4•2	L1•8-10	L2•1-4	—	L1•6 and L4•3
W3	L2•5-7	—	L4•4	L2•8-10	L3•1-5	—	L3•6-10 and T-20

	Sun	Mon	Tue	Wed	Thurs	Fri	Sat
W1	L3•1-5	L1•1-4	—	L4•5	L3•1-5	—	L1•4-6 and L4•6
W2	L1•7-10	L4•7	—	L2•1-5	L2•6-10	—	L1•1-5 and L4•8
W3	L1•6-10	L4•9	—	L2•1-5	L4•10	—	L3•1-5 and T-20

▢ BASIC SKILLS   ◿ SKILL DEVELOPMENT   ⬭ FULL-STROKE

BUILDING ENDURANCE

These programs call for five practices per week, and they add one or two level 5 practices a week to the mix of levels 1 to 4 practices. Saturdays continue to be longer training days. There will be longer lactate-threshold sets and some lactate-endurance sets. Many level 5 practices include test sets beyond the T-swims, requiring more record keeping to track your progress. Note the final Saturday of the second program calls for a T-30 swim instead of a T-20 swim.

	Sun	Mon	Tue	Wed	Thurs	Fri	Sat
W1	L3•1-5	—	L4•1-4	L1•1-4	L3•6-10	—	L2•1 and L5•1
W2	L2•1-4	—	L4•5-7	L2•1-4	L3•1-5	—	L2•2 and L5•2
W3	L2•5-7	—	L4•8-10	L2•8-10	L5•3	—	L4•1-5 and T-20

	Sun	Mon	Tue	Wed	Thurs	Fri	Sat
W1	L4•6-10	L1•1-4	—	L5•1-3	L3•5-7	—	L2•1-5 and L4•6-10
W2	L2•7-10	L5•1-3	—	L5•4	L3•8-10	—	L6•1-3
W3	L1•6-10	L4•5-7	—	L5•5	L4•8-10	—	L1•1-10 and T-30

LACTATE THRESHOLD   SPEED   HIGH-INTENSITY

BUILDING SPEED

These programs will build your speed with more lactate-endurance work, and they will maximize and test your speed with lactate-tolerance work. Note that each of the high-stress practice days (level 5, practices 4 to 10, and level 6, practices 4 to 10) is followed by either a rest day or by a low- or moderate-intensity level 1, 2, or 3 day.

	Sun	Mon	Tue	Wed	Thurs	Fri	Sat
W1	L3•1-2	—	L5•6	L1•1-4	L4•1-5	—	L2•1-2 and L5•7
W2	L2•8-10	—	L5•8	L2•5-7	L5•1-3	—	L2•3-4 and L5•9
W3	L3•3-4	—	L4•6-10	L1•5-7	L5•10	—	L1•1-10 and T-20

	Sun	Mon	Tue	Wed	Thurs	Fri	Sat
W1	L4•6-10	L6•4	—	L5•1-3	L3•5-6	—	L2•5-6 and L5•4-7
W2	L3•7-8	L6•5	—	L3•9-10	L5•8-10	—	L2•7-8 and L5•1-3
W3	L2•1-5	L6•6	—	L4•6-10	L6•7	—	L2•9-10 and T-30

BASIC SKILLS   SKILL DEVELOPMENT   FULL-STROKE

Intense-Swimming Programs (Competitive)

IMPROVING TECHNIQUE

In these programs, there are six practices per week, including more practices from levels 5 and 6, which require more distance and intensity. These are interspersed with lower-intensity, fundamental skill drills and conditioning workouts from levels 1 through 4. If your schedule does not permit six practices a week, then stretch these programs across four weeks of five practices, but keep the same order. All of the T-swims in these programs are T-30s.

	Sun	Mon	Tue	Wed	Thurs	Fri	Sat
W1	L5•1-3	—	L4•1-3	L3•1-3	L4•4-6	L3•4-6	L2•5-10 and L4•1-5
W2	L5•1-3	—	L3•7-10	L4•7-10	L5•4-5	L2•5-10	L3•1-3 and L5•6-7
W3	L5•1-3	—	L1•5-10	L2•5-10	L3•5-10	L4•5-10	L2•1-5 and T-30

	Sun	Mon	Tue	Wed	Thurs	Fri	Sat
W1	L4•1-3	L4•4-6	L5•4-5	—	L3•5-6	L4•7-10	L2•5-6 and L5•1-3
W2	L3•7-8	L4•6-7	L4•8-10	—	L5•6-7	L3•1-3	L2•7-8 and L6•1-3
W3	L2•1-5	L5•1-3	L4•1-3	—	L4•5-10	L3•4-6	L2•6-10 and T-30

LACTATE THRESHOLD   SPEED   HIGH-INTENSITY

BUILDING ENDURANCE

As before, we add more lactate-threshold activities and some lactate-endurance work. With only one day off each week, it becomes important to watch for signs of overtraining. If you find that you are not recovering between one high-intensity workout and the next, you might want to stretch these programs over four weeks, adding another day of rest each week.

	Sun	Mon	Tue	Wed	Thurs	Fri	Sat
W1	L4•4	—	L6•1-3	L1•1-4	L3•6-10	L4•5-7	L2•1-5 and L5•1-3
W2	L5•4-5	—	L5•6-7	L2•1-4	L3•1-5	L4•8-10	L2•6-10 and L6•1-3
W3	L4•6-10	—	L6•4-7	L2•8-10	L5•1-3	L2•1-10	L2•1-10 and T-30

	Sun	Mon	Tue	Wed	Thurs	Fri	Sat
W1	L4•6-10	L5•4-7	L4•1-4	L3•5-7	—	L5•1-3	L2•1-5 and L6•1-3
W2	L2•7-10	L5•1-3	L3•1-4	L6•4-7	—	L3•8-10	L2•6-10 and L6•1-3
W3	L1•6-10	L4•8-10	L3•5-7	L6•1-3	—	L4•5-7	L1•1-10 and T-30

BASIC SKILLS   SKILL DEVELOPMENT   FULL-STROKE

BUILDING SPEED

More lactate-endurance and lactate-tolerance workouts make these programs challenging and stressful. Do not use these programs for more than 9 to 12 weeks at a time without returning to a stretch of less stressful programs for a few weeks.

	Sun	Mon	Tue	Wed	Thurs	Fri	Sat
W1	L4•6-10	L6•4-7	—	L5•1-3	L6•6	L3•1-5	L2•5-6 and L5•4-7
W2	L3•7-8	L6•7	—	L4•6-7	L6•8	L3•6-10	L2•7-8 and L5•4-7
W3	L3•1-5	L6•9	—	L2•1-10	L6•10	L1•1-10	L2•5-10 and T-30

	Sun	Mon	Tue	Wed	Thurs	Fri	Sat
W1	L4•6-10	L6•4-7	L2•1-10	—	L6•8-10	L3•5-6	L2•5-6 and L5•1-3
W2	L3•1-5	L6•4-7	L4•6-10	—	L6•8-10	L3•1-10	L2•7-8 and L6•4-7
W3	L2•1-5	L4•7-10	L6•7-10	—	L5•1-3	L1•1-10	L2•9-10 and T-30

LACTATE THRESHOLD   SPEED   HIGH-INTENSITY

CHAPTER 15

Staying On Track

Most people who begin exercise programs stop exercising within six months. If that was *your* plan, you wouldn't have purchased this book. Yet we all know that good intentions are not enough. The primary reasons that people drop out of exercise programs are boredom and lack of motivation. When you begin a new program, there is a period of two or three months in which the stimulation of new surroundings, new people, and new experiences keeps you excited about the activity. But as the workout routine gets to be the same old, same old, it becomes more difficult to avoid boredom and to stay motivated. This chapter shows you how to chart and interpret your training progress, encourages you to hook up with a training partner and find different places to swim, and explains how and why to keep a training diary. Any one or all of these may be the key to your continued participation in an exercise program.

Charting Your Progress

If you have a constant supply of accurate feedback about your efforts, you will find that staying motivated is easy. The more positive feedback you can get, the more excited you will be about going back to the pool for your next swim.

Throughout the programs and practices, you often will test various aspects of your swimming. Rather than trusting the results to memory, I strongly encourage you from day one to record your results and to keep these records in an organized and logical fashion. Your efforts will pay off, both in the short term and over the long haul. On a daily or weekly basis, you will see improvements in your results. When you don't see improvements in particular areas, you will become aware of skills or conditioning that need extra attention. As months and seasons pass, you will see a progressive pattern of increased training intensity, because you will do much of your swimming at speeds that are derived directly from the results of your previous test swims. This type of specific, personalized feedback will greatly improve the odds that you stick with the workout program and that you get the results you are looking for.

At the end of this section, there are several charts for recording the results of test sets and swims. Make copies of these charts *before filling them out the first time* so that you will have clean charts for recording results over an extended time. You may want to make several copies of each chart so that you can keep track of different set variations, distances, and equipment. A looseleaf binder (preferably with a built-in calculator) will help you organize and track your swimming progress.

T-Swim-Test Performance Chart

This is the first chart you'll become acquainted with when you initially record your T-20 swim results from the swimming-fitness test in chapter 3. After that, you'll record the results of subsequent T-20 swims. Once you move up to T-30 swims, start a new chart. You should keep separate charts for T-swims that you do with equipment. You'll need to look up your cruise pace per 100 on the appropriate T-swim chart. Progress is indicated by any of the following:

1. Faster cruise pace per 100
2. Same cruise pace but lower IHR
3. Same cruise pace but lower average stroke count
4. Same cruise pace but lower RPE

Charting and tracking your progress provides a powerful feedback mechanism that can keep you motivated and in the pool.

David Madison/Photographer's Choice/Getty Images

As you switch from T-20s to T-30s, do not be alarmed if your cruise pace slows a bit. The longer your T-swims are, the more accurate the estimates of true cruise pace will be, assuming that you give the T-swims your best effort.

Swimming Golf (SGolf) Performance Chart

In chapter 3, you were introduced to swimming golf. Throughout the practices, there are numerous opportunities to do SGolf swims. In addition, any time you feel like testing your technical ability, try a few SGolf repeats. Although SGolf swims in the practices are limited to 50s, you can apply the same method to any distance. Improvements are indicated by any of the following:

1. Lower SGolf score
2. Same SGolf score with lower IHR
3. Same SGolf score with lower RPE

Compute your swimming golf score by adding the total number of strokes to the total number of seconds that are required to complete a distance. You'll note that there is a column for your ASGolf (advanced SGolf) score. This is simply your regular SGolf score plus your IHR. Comparing advanced SGolf scores will give you a more accurate reading of the changes in your swimming efficiency. If you use an HRM, you can substitute ASGolf for SGolf anywhere it appears in the practice descriptions. You should keep separate charts for SGolf swims that you do with equipment.

Lactate-Endurance (LEnd) Test-Set Performance Chart

When you begin doing level 5 and 6 workouts, you'll start using this chart. You'll need to keep four of these charts—one for each of the four LEnd sets that appear in the level 5 and 6 practices. These charts are more complex, but they give you a wealth of progress feedback. You will need to calculate and record the weighted average swim time (add the fastest, next fastest, and slowest swim times and then divide by three) as well as the calculated range of times (subtract the fastest swim time from the slowest swim time). Improvements are indicated by any of the following:

1. Swimming a faster weighted average time
2. Maintaining the same weighted average time but with a smaller range
3. Having a lower average stroke count without sacrificing speed
4. Swimming a faster interval
5. Achieving a new highest heart rate (HHR), which means that you have pushed yourself harder than ever before

As your swimming improves, you can move to faster intervals for LEnd sets. The goal for LEnd sets is to maintain a 1:1 work-to-rest ratio for whatever distance you swim. Let's say you have been swimming 100s on a 2:30 interval. Over time, you have lowered your weighted average time from 1:15s to 1:13s. Until now, you have been swimming on the correct interval. Let's say that on your next couple of performances, you average 1:12s or 1:11s. Assuming that you are swimming all of your sets within the specified range, it is probably time to drop your interval to 2:25, since this would now be closer to a 1:1 work-to-rest ratio. You should keep separate charts for LEnd sets that you do with equipment.

Lactate-Tolerance (LTol) Test-Set Performance Chart

The most intense test sets appear in level 5 and 6 workouts. There are three LTol test sets that you'll keep charts for. As with the LEnd charts, you will need to keep track of average swim times and ranges. You should keep separate charts for LTol sets that you do with equipment. There are four progress-feedback points:

1. Faster weighted average swim time
2. Same weighted average swim time but a smaller range
3. Lower average stroke count without sacrificing speed
4. Achieving a new highest heart rate (HHR), which means that you have pushed yourself harder than ever before

Finding a Training Partner (or Several)

Whether you are learning to swim, swimming for fitness, or training for competition, your experience can be greatly improved by training with others. I encourage you to find at least one training partner with whom you can swim, compare notes, trade feedback, and cross-motivate. Training with a partner has several benefits:

Learning   If you buy your partner a copy of this book, you'll each have the same reference manual to base your workouts on. Observing and analyzing the movements of others allows you to think about your own efforts in a different light. One of the best ways to shorten learning curves is to try to teach something you have a fair grasp on. This will reinforce the ideas you understand and will reveal any remaining gaps in your understanding.

Motivation   The get-to-the-workout nudges that partners give each other can help on the days when you otherwise might skip the trip to the pool. The high-intensity sets in the upper levels of this program will be more productive if you and a partner push each other.

Camaraderie   Swimming with like-minded people helps a workout go more quickly. Even if you and your partner can swim together only occasionally, the partnership can still enhance the overall effort for each of you. Gathering several training partners into an informal training group can be even more effective, particularly if you all follow the same program.

Keeping a Training Diary

I encourage you to start and keep a dedicated swim-training diary or journal. I don't mean a pocket-sized affair where you write down your workout distances and the occasional personal record. I mean a proper notebook where, after every practice session, you write in complete sentences about aquatic skills you worked on, what you learned, questions that arose, answers to those questions, etc. Plan to sit with a notebook and pen for at least 10 minutes, writing continuously in complete sentences about the practice experience. Then, before each practice, reread the entries from at least the last two practices. Whether you are a triathlete, a competitive swimmer, or a fitness swimmer, this will shorten the learning or refining cycle. It will make the time you spend in the water more productive, and it will increase your motivation level. Keeping a training diary helps you do the following:

Supercharge your workout awareness   Things that were barely on the periphery of your consciousness in the past will come sharply into focus if your goal is to gather useful information. If, while you are practicing, your plan is to write about your experience, your attention will remain more focused —that's half the reason you were told to take notes in school.

Reinforce the concepts and applications you have a good handle on   Abstract concepts become concrete when you organize your thoughts in a way that allows you to communicate them to others. Making yourself use complete sentences and well-constructed paragraphs will force you to connect loose ends in your thinking and awareness.

Expose gaps in your knowledge   When you try to use complete sentences to express something that you think you understand, it is easier to spot the potholes in your road to aquatic nirvana. Concepts that you don't truly understand will tend to become questions as you try to verbalize your thoughts. Write the questions down and then find the answers—perhaps by practicing more, observing others, reading, watching videos, or cornering a coach. You learn faster if the answers are responses to questions you have formulated on your own.

Get your mind right, and then get wet   Before hitting the water, reread what you've already given great thought to. From the very first stroke, you'll be better prepared for and more focused on your workout.

Leverage your time   When you learn something valuable during a workout, a competition, or a conversation with a coach or another swimmer, write it down. Then read and reread your diary regularly. It is easier to use your diary to help you recall a hard-learned lesson than it is to relearn that same lesson by repeating your past mistakes in the pool. A small investment of time can save you from riding the learning rollercoaster again and again.

If you keep a diary correctly, the payoff will be well worth the time and effort. The following are hints to help you get the most from your diary:

- Get a medium-sized notebook. If it has pockets, you can store articles that relate to what you are writing about. Include several different-colored pens with waterproof ink—and perhaps a highlighter pen.

- Store all this in a heavy-duty, zippered kitchen storage bag or similar waterproof container. I know that you don't *plan* on getting it wet, but it happens. Properly kept, your diary will be an irreplaceable asset. A plastic bag is cheap insurance in an inherently wet environment.

- Express your thoughts completely and include plenty of questions (and blank spaces for answers). Write in such a way that someone who is less knowledgeable about swimming would be able to read your work and get an idea of what you are doing.

- Write from a variety of perspectives (one day writing in the first person, another day in the third person). This allows you to examine your swimming in ways that are not possible otherwise.

- Keeping your diary electronically offers some advantages (backup, text search, communicating with others). A tech-savvy swimmer might make diary entries on her computer and sync them to a PDA so that she can reread them in the locker room or at the pool's edge just before hopping in.

- Consider having another swimmer or coach read your entries and make comments—blogging, perhaps?

- Plan your schedule to ensure that you have enough time to reread prior entries before you hit the water and to write down your thoughts as soon after your practice as possible.

- Have a waterproof notebook handy at the end of the pool during your practices so that you can jot down notes and the occasional "Aha!" that you can elaborate on later.

- Don't do it wrong. (Hint: There is no wrong way to keep a swimming diary, other than not keeping one at all.)

T-Swim Test Performances

Set (circle one):   T-20   T-30

Equipment (circle all that apply):

None   Snorkel   Fins   SBFins   Other: _____

Date	Distance swum	Finish time	Cruise pace per 100 (look up)	Average SPL	HRM average or IHR

From E. Hines, 2008, *Fitness Swimming, 2nd ed.* (Champaign, IL: Human Kinetics).

Swimming Golf (SGolf) Performances

Equipment (circle all that apply):

None   Snorkel   Other: _____

Date	Distance	Finish time	Total seconds	Total stroke count	SGolf score	IHR	ASGolf score

SGolf score = total strokes + total seconds

Advanced SGolf (ASGolf) score = SGolf score + IHR

From E. Hines, 2008, *Fitness Swimming, 2nd ed.* (Champaign, IL: Human Kinetics).

Lactate Endurance (LEnd) Test Set Performances

Set (circle one): 16 min. of 50s   18 min. of 75s   20 min. of 100s   24 min. of 200s
                   :02 Range   :03 Range   :04 Range   :06 Range

Equipment (circle all that apply):   None   Snorkel   Fins   SBFins   Other: _____

Date	Number of repeats	Repeat interval	Fastest swim time	Next fastest swim time	Slowest swim time	Weighted average swim time	Calculated range	Average SPL	Highest heart rate (HHR)

Weighted average swim time = (fastest + next fastest + slowest)/3
Calculated range = slowest − fastest

From E. Hines, 2008, Fitness Swimming, 2nd ed. (Champaign, IL: Human Kinetics).

Lactate Tolerance (LTol) Test Set Performances

Set (circle one): 8 × 50   6 × 50   4 × 75   4 × 100   3 × 150   3 × 200
on 3:00   on 4:00   on 6:00   on 6:00   on 12:00   on 12:00

Equipment (circle all that apply):   Snorkel   Fins   SBFins   Other: _____

Date	Fastest swim time	Next fastest swim time	Slowest swim time	Weighted average swim time	Calculated range	Average SPL	Highest heart rate (HHR)

Weighted average swim time = (fastest + next fastest + slowest)/3
Calculated range = slowest – fastest

From E. Hines, 2008, *Fitness Swimming, 2nd ed.* (Champaign, IL: Human Kinetics).

APPENDIX A

T-20 CRUISE PACE PER 100 CHART						
Dist	**20:00**	**20:10**	**20:20**	**20:30**	**20:40**	**20:50**
500	4:00	4:02	4:04	4:06	4:08	4:10
550	3:38	3:40	3:42	3:44	3:45	3:47
600	3:20	3:22	3:23	3:25	3:27	3:28
650	3:05	3:06	3:08	3:09	3:11	3:12
700	2:51	2:53	2:54	2:56	2:57	2:59
750	2:40	2:41	2:43	2:44	2:45	2:47
800	2:30	2:31	2:33	2:34	2:35	2:36
850	2:21	2:22	2:24	2:25	2:26	2:27
900	2:13	2:14	2:16	2:17	2:18	2:19
950	2:06	2:07	2:08	2:09	2:11	2:12
1000	2:00	2:01	2:02	2:03	2:04	2:05
1050	1:54.3	1:55.2	1:56.2	1:57.1	1:58.1	1:59.0
1100	1:49.1	1:50.0	1:50.9	1:51.8	1:52.7	1:53.6
1150	1:44.3	1:45.2	1:46.1	1:47.0	1:47.8	1:48.7
1200	1:40.0	1:40.8	1:41.7	1:42.5	1:43.3	1:44.2
1250	1:36.0	1:36.8	1:37.6	1:38.4	1:39.2	1:40.0
1300	1:32.3	1:33.1	1:33.8	1:34.6	1:35.4	1:36.2
1350	1:28.9	1:29.6	1:30.4	1:31.1	1:31.9	1:32.6
1400	1:25.7	1:26.4	1:27.1	1:27.9	1:28.6	1:29.3
1450	1:22.8	1:23.4	1:24.1	1:24.8	1:25.5	1:26.2
1500	1:20.0	1:20.7	1:21.3	1:22.0	1:22.7	1:23.3
1550	1:17.4	1:18.1	1:18.7	1:19.4	1:20.0	1:20.6
1600	1:15.0	1:15.6	1:16.3	1:16.9	1:17.5	1:18.1
1650	1:12.7	1:13.3	1:13.9	1:14.5	1:15.2	1:15.8
1700	1:10.6	1:11.2	1:11.8	1:12.4	1:12.9	1:13.5
1750	1:08.6	1:09.1	1:09.7	1:10.3	1:10.9	1:11.4
1800	1:06.7	1:07.2	1:07.8	1:08.3	1:08.9	1:09.4
1850	1:04.9	1:05.4	1:05.9	1:06.5	1:07.0	1:07.6
1900	1:03.2	1:03.7	1:04.2	1:04.7	1:05.3	1:05.8
1950	1:01.5	1:02.1	1:02.6	1:03.1	1:03.6	1:04.1
2000	1:00.0	1:00.5	1:01.0	1:01.5	1:02.0	1:02.5

Instructions: In the distance column, find the distance you completed in your T-20 swim. Look across both pages of that line to the column closest to your T-20 swim finish time. Read and record your cruise pace per 100.

				T-20 CRUISE PACE PER 100 CHART			
Dist	**21:00**	**21:10**	**21:20**	**21:30**	**21:40**	**21:50**	**22:00**
500	4:12	4:14	4:16	4:18	4:20	4:22	4:24
550	3:49	3:51	3:53	3:55	3:56	3:58	4:00
600	3:30	3:32	3:33	3:35	3:37	3:38	3:40
650	3:14	3:15	3:17	3:18	3:20	3:22	3:23
700	3:00	3:01	3:03	3:04	3:06	3:07	3:09
750	2:48	2:49	2:51	2:52	2:53	2:55	2:56
800	2:38	2:39	2:40	2:41	2:42	2:44	2:45
850	2:28	2:29	2:31	2:32	2:33	2:34	2:35
900	2:20	2:21	2:22	2:23	2:24	2:26	2:27
950	2:13	2:14	2:15	2:16	2:17	2:18	2:19
1000	2:06	2:07	2:08	2:09	2:10	2:11	2:12
1050	2:00	2:01	2:02	2:03	2:04	2:05	2:06
1100	1:54.5	1:55.5	1:56.4	1:57.3	1:58.2	1:59.1	2:00
1150	1:49.6	1:50.4	1:51.3	1:52.2	1:53.0	1:53.9	1:54.8
1200	1:45.0	1:45.8	1:46.7	1:47.5	1:48.3	1:49.2	1:50.0
1250	1:40.8	1:41.6	1:42.4	1:43.2	1:44.0	1:44.8	1:45.6
1300	1:36.9	1:37.7	1:38.5	1:39.2	1:40.0	1:40.8	1:41.5
1350	1:33.3	1:34.1	1:34.8	1:35.6	1:36.3	1:37.0	1:37.8
1400	1:30.0	1:30.7	1:31.4	1:32.1	1:32.9	1:33.6	1:34.3
1450	1:26.9	1:27.6	1:28.3	1:29.0	1:29.7	1:30.3	1:31.0
1500	1:24.0	1:24.7	1:25.3	1:26.0	1:26.7	1:27.3	1:28.0
1550	1:21.3	1:21.9	1:22.6	1:23.2	1:23.9	1:24.5	1:25.2
1600	1:18.8	1:19.4	1:20.0	1:20.6	1:21.2	1:21.9	1:22.5
1650	1:16.4	1:17.0	1:17.6	1:18.2	1:18.8	1:19.4	1:20.0
1700	1:14.1	1:14.7	1:15.3	1:15.9	1:16.5	1:17.1	1:17.6
1750	1:12.0	1:12.6	1:13.1	1:13.7	1:14.3	1:14.9	1:15.4
1800	1:10.0	1:10.6	1:11.1	1:11.7	1:12.2	1:12.8	1:13.3
1850	1:08.1	1:08.6	1:09.2	1:09.7	1:10.3	1:10.8	1:11.4
1900	1:06.3	1:06.8	1:07.4	1:07.9	1:08.4	1:08.9	1:09.5
1950	1:04.6	1:05.1	1:05.6	1:06.2	1:06.7	1:07.2	1:07.7
2000	1:03.0	1:03.5	1:04.0	1:04.5	1:05.0	1:05.5	1:06.0

From E. Hines, 2008, *Fitness Swimming, 2nd ed.* (Champaign, IL: Human Kinetics).

APPENDIX B

Dist	30:00	30:10	30:20	30:30	30:40	30:50
750	4:00	4:01	4:03	4:04	4:05	4:07
800	3:45	3:46	3:48	3:49	3:50	3:51
850	3:32	3:33	3:34	3:35	3:36	3:38
900	3:20	3:21	3:22	3:23	3:24	3:26
950	3:09	3:11	3:12	3:13	3:14	3:15
1000	3:00	3:01	3:02	3:03	3:04	3:05
1050	2:51	2:52	2:53	2:54	2:55	2:56
1100	2:44	2:45	2:45	2:46	2:47	2:48
1150	2:37	2:37	2:38	2:39	2:40	2:41
1200	2:30	2:31	2:32	2:33	2:33	2:34
1250	2:24	2:25	2:26	2:26	2:27	2:28
1300	2:18	2:19	2:20	2:21	2:22	2:22
1350	2:13	2:14	2:15	2:16	2:16	2:17
1400	2:09	2:09	2:10	2:11	2:11	2:12
1450	2:04	2:05	2:06	2:06	2:07	2:08
1500	2:00	2:01	2:01	2:02	2:03	2:03
1550	1:56.1	1:56.8	1:57.4	1:58.1	1:58.7	1:59.4
1600	1:52.5	1:53.1	1:53.8	1:54.4	1:55.0	1:55.6
1650	1:49.1	1:49.7	1:50.3	1:50.9	1:51.5	1:52.1
1700	1:45.9	1:46.5	1:47.1	1:47.6	1:48.2	1:48.8
1750	1:42.9	1:43.4	1:44.0	1:44.6	1:45.1	1:45.7
1800	1:40.0	1:40.6	1:41.1	1:41.7	1:42.2	1:42.8
1850	1:37.3	1:37.8	1:38.4	1:38.9	1:39.5	1:40.0
1900	1:34.7	1:35.3	1:35.8	1:36.3	1:36.8	1:37.4
1950	1:32.3	1:32.8	1:33.3	1:33.8	1:34.4	1:34.9
2000	1:30.0	1:30.5	1:31.0	1:31.5	1:32.0	1:32.5
2050	1:27.8	1:28.3	1:28.8	1:29.3	1:29.8	1:30.2
2100	1:25.7	1:26.2	1:26.7	1:27.1	1:27.6	1:28.1
2150	1:23.7	1:24.2	1:24.7	1:25.1	1:25.6	1:26.0
2200	1:21.8	1:22.3	1:22.7	1:23.2	1:23.6	1:24.1
2250	1:20.0	1:20.4	1:20.9	1:21.3	1:21.8	1:22.2
2300	1:18.3	1:18.7	1:19.1	1:19.6	1:20.0	1:20.4
2350	1:16.6	1:17.0	1:17.4	1:17.9	1:18.3	1:18.7
2400	1:15.0	1:15.4	1:15.8	1:16.3	1:16.7	1:17.1
2450	1:13.5	1:13.9	1:14.3	1:14.7	1:15.1	1:15.5
2500	1:12.0	1:12.4	1:12.8	1:13.2	1:13.6	1:14.0
2550	1:10.6	1:11.0	1:11.4	1:11.8	1:12.2	1:12.5
2600	1:09.2	1:09.6	1:10.0	1:10.4	1:10.8	1:11.2
2650	1:07.9	1:08.3	1:08.7	1:09.1	1:09.4	1:09.8
2700	1:06.7	1:07.0	1:07.4	1:07.8	1:08.1	1:08.5
2750	1:05.5	1:05.8	1:06.2	1:06.5	1:06.9	1:07.3
2800	1:04.3	1:04.6	1:05.0	1:05.4	1:05.7	1:06.1
2850	1:03.2	1:03.5	1:03.9	1:04.2	1:04.6	1:04.9
2900	1:02.1	1:02.4	1:02.8	1:03.1	1:03.4	1:03.8
2950	1:01.0	1:01.4	1:01.7	1:02.0	1:02.4	1:02.7
3000	1:00.0	1:00.3	1:00.7	1:01.0	1:01.3	1:01.7

T-30 CRUISE PACE PER 100 CHART

Instructions: In the distance column, find the distance you completed in your T-30 swim. Look across both pages of that line to the column closest to your T-30 swim finish time. Read and record your cruise pace per 100.

T-30 CRUISE PACE PER 100 CHART							
Dist	31:00	31:10	31:20	31:30	31:40	31:50	32:00
750	4:08	4:09	4:11	4:12	4:13	4:15	4:16
800	3:53	3:54	3:55	3:56	3:58	3:59	4:00
850	3:39	3:40	3:41	3:42	3:44	3:45	3:46
900	3:27	3:28	3:29	3:30	3:31	3:32	3:33
950	3:16	3:17	3:18	3:19	3:20	3:21	3:22
1000	3:06	3:07	3:08	3:09	3:10	3:11	3:12
1050	2:57	2:58	2:59	3:00	3:01	3:02	3:03
1100	2:49	2:50	2:51	2:52	2:53	2:54	2:55
1150	2:42	2:43	2:43	2:44	2:45	2:46	2:47
1200	2:35	2:36	2:37	2:38	2:38	2:39	2:40
1250	2:29	2:30	2:30	2:31	2:32	2:33	2:34
1300	2:23	2:24	2:25	2:25	2:26	2:27	2:28
1350	2:18	2:19	2:19	2:20	2:21	2:21	2:22
1400	2:13	2:14	2:14	2:15	2:16	2:16	2:17
1450	2:08	2:09	2:10	2:10	2:11	2:12	2:12
1500	2:04	2:05	2:05	2:06	2:07	2:07	2:08
1550	2:00	2:01	2:01	2:02	2:03	2:03	2:04
1600	1:56.3	1:56.9	1:57.5	1:58.1	1:58.8	1:59.4	2:00
1650	1:52.7	1:53.3	1:53.9	1:54.5	1:55.2	1:55.8	1:56.4
1700	1:49.4	1:50.0	1:50.6	1:51.2	1:51.8	1:52.4	1:52.9
1750	1:46.3	1:46.9	1:47.4	1:48.0	1:48.6	1:49.1	1:49.7
1800	1:43.3	1:43.9	1:44.4	1:45.0	1:45.6	1:46.1	1:46.7
1850	1:40.5	1:41.1	1:41.6	1:42.2	1:42.7	1:43.2	1:43.8
1900	1:37.9	1:38.4	1:38.9	1:39.5	1:40.0	1:40.5	1:41.1
1950	1:35.4	1:35.9	1:36.4	1:36.9	1:37.4	1:37.9	1:38.5
2000	1:33.0	1:33.5	1:34.0	1:34.5	1:35.0	1:35.5	1:36.0
2050	1:30.7	1:31.2	1:31.7	1:32.2	1:32.7	1:33.2	1:33.7
2100	1:28.6	1:29.0	1:29.5	1:30.0	1:30.5	1:31.0	1:31.4
2150	1:26.5	1:27.0	1:27.4	1:27.9	1:28.4	1:28.8	1:29.3
2200	1:24.5	1:25.0	1:25.5	1:25.9	1:26.4	1:26.8	1:27.3
2250	1:22.7	1:23.1	1:23.6	1:24.0	1:24.4	1:24.9	1:25.3
2300	1:20.9	1:21.3	1:21.7	1:22.2	1:22.6	1:23.0	1:23.5
2350	1:19.1	1:19.6	1:20.0	1:20.4	1:20.9	1:21.3	1:21.7
2400	1:17.5	1:17.9	1:18.3	1:18.8	1:19.2	1:19.6	1:20.0
2450	1:15.9	1:16.3	1:16.7	1:17.1	1:17.6	1:18.0	1:18.4
2500	1:14.4	1:14.8	1:15.2	1:15.6	1:16.0	1:16.4	1:16.8
2550	1:12.9	1:13.3	1:13.7	1:14.1	1:14.5	1:14.9	1:15.3
2600	1:11.5	1:11.9	1:12.3	1:12.7	1:13.1	1:13.5	1:13.8
2650	1:10.2	1:10.6	1:10.9	1:11.3	1:11.7	1:12.1	1:12.5
2700	1:08.9	1:09.3	1:09.6	1:10.0	1:10.4	1:10.7	1:11.1
2750	1:07.6	1:08.0	1:08.4	1:08.7	1:09.1	1:09.5	1:09.8
2800	1:06.4	1:06.8	1:07.1	1:07.5	1:07.9	1:08.2	1:08.6
2850	1:05.3	1:05.6	1:06.0	1:06.3	1:06.7	1:07.0	1:07.4
2900	1:04.1	1:04.5	1:04.8	1:05.2	1:05.5	1:05.9	1:06.2
2950	1:03.1	1:03.4	1:03.7	1:04.1	1:04.4	1:04.7	1:05.1
3000	1:02.0	1:02.3	1:02.7	1:03.0	1:03.3	1:03.7	1:04.0

From E. Hines, 2008, *Fitness Swimming, 2nd ed.* (Champaign, IL: Human Kinetics).

APPENDIX C

			CRUISE TIMES CHART								
25	50	75	Cruise pace per 100	150	200	250	300	350	400	450	500
1:00.0	2:00.0	3:00.0	**4:00**	6:00	8:00	10:00	12:00	14:00	16:00	18:00	20:00
1:00.0	1:59.5	2:59.0	**3:59**	5:59	7:58	9:58	11:57	13:57	15:56	17:56	19:55
:59.5	1:59.0	2:58.5	**3:58**	5:57	7:56	9:55	11:54	13:53	15:52	17:51	19:50
:59.0	1:58.5	2:58.0	**3:57**	5:56	7:54	9:53	11:51	13:50	15:48	17:47	19:45
:59.0	1:58.0	2:57.0	**3:56**	5:54	7:52	9:50	11:48	13:46	15:44	17:42	19:40
:59.0	1:57.5	2:56.0	**3:55**	5:53	7:50	9:48	11:45	13:43	15:40	17:38	19:35
:58.5	1:57.0	2:55.5	**3:54**	5:51	7:48	9:45	11:42	13:39	15:36	17:33	19:30
:58.0	1:56.5	2:55.0	**3:53**	5:50	7:46	9:43	11:39	13:36	15:32	17:29	19:25
:58.0	1:56.0	2:54.0	**3:52**	5:48	7:44	9:40	11:36	13:32	15:28	17:24	19:20
:58.0	1:55.5	2:53.0	**3:51**	5:47	7:42	9:38	11:33	13:29	15:24	17:20	19:15
:57.5	1:55.0	2:52.5	**3:50**	5:45	7:40	9:35	11:30	13:25	15:20	17:15	19:10
:57.0	1:54.5	2:52.0	**3:49**	5:44	7:38	9:33	11:27	13:22	15:16	17:11	19:05
:57.0	1:54.0	2:51.0	**3:48**	5:42	7:36	9:30	11:24	13:18	15:12	17:06	19:00
:57.0	1:53.5	2:50.0	**3:47**	5:41	7:34	9:28	11:21	13:15	15:08	17:02	18:55
:56.5	1:53.0	2:49.5	**3:46**	5:39	7:32	9:25	11:18	13:11	15:04	16:57	18:50
:56.0	1:52.5	2:49.0	**3:45**	5:38	7:30	9:23	11:15	13:08	15:00	16:53	18:45
:56.0	1:52.0	2:48.0	**3:44**	5:36	7:28	9:20	11:12	13:04	14:56	16:48	18:40
:56.0	1:51.5	2:47.0	**3:43**	5:35	7:26	9:18	11:09	13:01	14:52	16:44	18:35
:55.5	1:51.0	2:46.5	**3:42**	5:33	7:24	9:15	11:06	12:57	14:48	16:39	18:30
:55.0	1:50.5	2:46.0	**3:41**	5:32	7:22	9:13	11:03	12:54	14:44	16:35	18:25
:55.0	1:50.0	2:45.0	**3:40**	5:30	7:20	9:10	11:00	12:50	14:40	16:30	18:20
:55.0	1:49.5	2:44.0	**3:39**	5:29	7:18	9:08	10:57	12:47	14:36	16:26	18:15
:54.5	1:49.0	2:43.5	**3:38**	5:27	7:16	9:05	10:54	12:43	14:32	16:21	18:10
:54.0	1:48.5	2:43.0	**3:37**	5:26	7:14	9:03	10:51	12:40	14:28	16:17	18:05
:54.0	1:48.0	2:42.0	**3:36**	5:24	7:12	9:00	10:48	12:36	14:24	16:12	18:00
:54.0	1:47.5	2:41.0	**3:35**	5:23	7:10	8:58	10:45	12:33	14:20	16:08	17:55
:53.5	1:47.0	2:40.5	**3:34**	5:21	7:08	8:55	10:42	12:29	14:16	16:03	17:50
:53.0	1:46.5	2:40.0	**3:33**	5:20	7:06	8:53	10:39	12:26	14:12	15:59	17:45
:53.0	1:46.0	2:39.0	**3:32**	5:18	7:04	8:50	10:36	12:22	14:08	15:54	17:40
:53.0	1:45.5	2:38.0	**3:31**	5:17	7:02	8:48	10:33	12:19	14:04	15:50	17:35
:52.5	1:45.0	2:37.5	**3:30**	5:15	7:00	8:45	10:30	12:15	14:00	15:45	17:30
:52.0	1:44.5	2:37.0	**3:29**	5:14	6:58	8:43	10:27	12:12	13:56	15:41	17:25
:52.0	1:44.0	2:36.0	**3:28**	5:12	6:56	8:40	10:24	12:08	13:52	15:36	17:20
:52.0	1:43.5	2:35.0	**3:27**	5:11	6:54	8:38	10:21	12:05	13:48	15:32	17:15
:51.5	1:43.0	2:34.5	**3:26**	5:09	6:52	8:35	10:18	12:01	13:44	15:27	17:10
:51.0	1:42.5	2:34.0	**3:25**	5:08	6:50	8:33	10:15	11:58	13:40	15:23	17:05
:51.0	1:42.0	2:33.0	**3:24**	5:06	6:48	8:30	10:12	11:54	13:36	15:18	17:00
:51.0	1:41.5	2:32.0	**3:23**	5:05	6:46	8:28	10:09	11:51	13:32	15:14	16:55
:50.5	1:41.0	2:31.5	**3:22**	5:03	6:44	8:25	10:06	11:47	13:28	15:09	16:50
:50.0	1:40.5	2:31.0	**3:21**	5:02	6:42	8:23	10:03	11:44	13:24	15:05	16:45
:50.0	1:40.0	2:30.0	**3:20**	5:00	6:40	8:20	10:00	11:40	13:20	15:00	16:40
:50.0	1:39.5	2:29.0	**3:19**	4:59	6:38	8:18	9:57	11:37	13:16	14:56	16:35
:49.5	1:39.0	2:28.5	**3:18**	4:57	6:36	8:15	9:54	11:33	13:12	14:51	16:30
:49.0	1:38.5	2:28.0	**3:17**	4:56	6:34	8:13	9:51	11:30	13:08	14:47	16:25

Instructions: Use the cruise pace per 100 you recorded from one of the T-swim cruise pace charts. Look down the bolded cruise pace per 100 column and find the entry closest to your recorded cruise pace. Look across that line of the page and write down the distance and cruise time for each column across that line.

							CRUISE TIMES CHART					
25	50	75	Cruise pace per 100	150	200	250	300	350	400	450	500
:49.0	1:38.0	2:27.0	**3:16**	4:54	6:32	8:10	9:48	11:26	13:04	14:42	16:20
:49.0	1:37.5	2:26.0	**3:15**	4:53	6:30	8:08	9:45	11:23	13:00	14:38	16:15
:48.5	1:37.0	2:25.5	**3:14**	4:51	6:28	8:05	9:42	11:19	12:56	14:33	16:10
:48.0	1:36.5	2:25.0	**3:13**	4:50	6:26	8:03	9:39	11:16	12:52	14:29	16:05
:48.0	1:36.0	2:24.0	**3:12**	4:48	6:24	8:00	9:36	11:12	12:48	14:24	16:00
:48.0	1:35.5	2:23.0	**3:11**	4:47	6:22	7:58	9:33	11:09	12:44	14:20	15:55
:47.5	1:35.0	2:22.5	**3:10**	4:45	6:20	7:55	9:30	11:05	12:40	14:15	15:50
:47.0	1:34.5	2:22.0	**3:09**	4:44	6:18	7:53	9:27	11:02	12:36	14:11	15:45
:47.0	1:34.0	2:21.0	**3:08**	4:42	6:16	7:50	9:24	10:58	12:32	14:06	15:40
:47.0	1:33.5	2:20.0	**3:07**	4:41	6:14	7:48	9:21	10:55	12:28	14:02	15:35
:46.5	1:33.0	2:19.5	**3:06**	4:39	6:12	7:45	9:18	10:51	12:24	13:57	15:30
:46.0	1:32.5	2:19.0	**3:05**	4:38	6:10	7:43	9:15	10:48	12:20	13:53	15:25
:46.0	1:32.0	2:18.0	**3:04**	4:36	6:08	7:40	9:12	10:44	12:16	13:48	15:20
:46.0	1:31.5	2:17.0	**3:03**	4:35	6:06	7:38	9:09	10:41	12:12	13:44	15:15
:45.5	1:31.0	2:16.5	**3:02**	4:33	6:04	7:35	9:06	10:37	12:08	13:39	15:10
:45.0	1:30.5	2:16.0	**3:01**	4:32	6:02	7:33	9:03	10:34	12:04	13:35	15:05
:45.0	1:30.0	2:15.0	**3:00**	4:30	6:00	7:30	9:00	10:30	12:00	13:30	15:00
:45.0	1:29.5	2:14.0	**2:59**	4:29	5:58	7:28	8:57	10:27	11:56	13:26	14:55
:44.5	1:29.0	2:13.5	**2:58**	4:27	5:56	7:25	8:54	10:23	11:52	13:21	14:50
:44.0	1:28.5	2:13.0	**2:57**	4:26	5:54	7:23	8:51	10:20	11:48	13:17	14:45
:44.0	1:28.0	2:12.0	**2:56**	4:24	5:52	7:20	8:48	10:16	11:44	13:12	14:40
:44.0	1:27.5	2:11.0	**2:55**	4:23	5:50	7:18	8:45	10:13	11:40	13:08	14:35
:43.5	1:27.0	2:10.5	**2:54**	4:21	5:48	7:15	8:42	10:09	11:36	13:03	14:30
:43.0	1:26.5	2:10.0	**2:53**	4:20	5:46	7:13	8:39	10:06	11:32	12:59	14:25
:43.0	1:26.0	2:09.0	**2:52**	4:18	5:44	7:10	8:36	10:02	11:28	12:54	14:20
:43.0	1:25.5	2:08.0	**2:51**	4:17	5:42	7:08	8:33	9:59	11:24	12:50	14:15
:42.5	1:25.0	2:07.5	**2:50**	4:15	5:40	7:05	8:30	9:55	11:20	12:45	14:10
:42.0	1:24.5	2:07.0	**2:49**	4:14	5:38	7:03	8:27	9:52	11:16	12:41	14:05
:42.0	1:24.0	2:06.0	**2:48**	4:12	5:36	7:00	8:24	9:48	11:12	12:36	14:00
:42.0	1:23.5	2:05.0	**2:47**	4:11	5:34	6:58	8:21	9:45	11:08	12:32	13:55
:41.5	1:23.0	2:04.5	**2:46**	4:09	5:32	6:55	8:18	9:41	11:04	12:27	13:50
:41.0	1:22.5	2:04.0	**2:45**	4:08	5:30	6:53	8:15	9:38	11:00	12:23	13:45
:41.0	1:22.0	2:03.0	**2:44**	4:06	5:28	6:50	8:12	9:34	10:56	12:18	13:40
:41.0	1:21.5	2:02.0	**2:43**	4:05	5:26	6:48	8:09	9:31	10:52	12:14	13:35
:40.5	1:21.0	2:01.5	**2:42**	4:03	5:24	6:45	8:06	9:27	10:48	12:09	13:30
:40.0	1:20.5	2:01.0	**2:41**	4:02	5:22	6:43	8:03	9:24	10:44	12:05	13:25
:40.0	1:20.0	2:00.0	**2:40**	4:00	5:20	6:40	8:00	9:20	10:40	12:00	13:20
:40.0	1:19.5	1:59.0	**2:39**	3:59	5:18	6:38	7:57	9:17	10:36	11:56	13:15
:39.5	1:19.0	1:58.5	**2:38**	3:57	5:16	6:35	7:54	9:13	10:32	11:51	13:10
:39.0	1:18.5	1:58.0	**2:37**	3:56	5:14	6:33	7:51	9:10	10:28	11:47	13:05
:39.0	1:18.0	1:57.0	**2:36**	3:54	5:12	6:30	7:48	9:06	10:24	11:42	13:00
:39.0	1:17.5	1:56.0	**2:35**	3:53	5:10	6:28	7:45	9:03	10:20	11:38	12:55
:38.5	1:17.0	1:55.5	**2:34**	3:51	5:08	6:25	7:42	8:59	10:16	11:33	12:50

(continued)

CRUISE TIMES CHART

25	50	75	Cruise pace per 100	150	200	250	300	350	400	450	500
:38.0	1:16.5	1:55.0	**2:33**	3:50	5:06	6:23	7:39	8:56	10:12	11:29	12:45
:38.0	1:16.0	1:54.0	**2:32**	3:48	5:04	6:20	7:36	8:52	10:08	11:24	12:40
:38.0	1:15.5	1:53.0	**2:31**	3:47	5:02	6:18	7:33	8:49	10:04	11:20	12:35
:37.5	1:15.0	1:52.5	**2:30**	3:45	5:00	6:15	7:30	8:45	10:00	11:15	12:30
:37.0	1:14.5	1:52.0	**2:29**	3:44	4:58	6:13	7:27	8:42	9:56	11:11	12:25
:37.0	1:14.0	1:51.0	**2:28**	3:42	4:56	6:10	7:24	8:38	9:52	11:06	12:20
:37.0	1:13.5	1:50.0	**2:27**	3:41	4:54	6:08	7:21	8:35	9:48	11:02	12:15
:36.5	1:13.0	1:49.5	**2:26**	3:39	4:52	6:05	7:18	8:31	9:44	10:57	12:10
:36.0	1:12.5	1:49.0	**2:25**	3:38	4:50	6:03	7:15	8:28	9:40	10:53	12:05
:36.0	1:12.0	1:48.0	**2:24**	3:36	4:48	6:00	7:12	8:24	9:36	10:48	12:00
:36.0	1:11.5	1:47.0	**2:23**	3:35	4:46	5:58	7:09	8:21	9:32	10:44	11:55
:35.5	1:11.0	1:46.5	**2:22**	3:33	4:44	5:55	7:06	8:17	9:28	10:39	11:50
:35.0	1:10.5	1:46.0	**2:21**	3:32	4:42	5:53	7:03	8:14	9:24	10:35	11:45
:35.0	1:10.0	1:45.0	**2:20**	3:30	4:40	5:50	7:00	8:10	9:20	10:30	11:40
:35.0	1:09.5	1:44.0	**2:19**	3:29	4:38	5:48	6:57	8:07	9:16	10:26	11:35
:34.5	1:09.0	1:43.5	**2:18**	3:27	4:36	5:45	6:54	8:03	9:12	10:21	11:30
:34.0	1:08.5	1:43.0	**2:17**	3:26	4:34	5:43	6:51	7:60	9:08	10:17	11:25
:34.0	1:08.0	1:42.0	**2:16**	3:24	4:32	5:40	6:48	7:56	9:04	10:12	11:20
:34.0	1:07.5	1:41.0	**2:15**	3:23	4:30	5:38	6:45	7:53	9:00	10:08	11:15
:33.5	1:07.0	1:40.5	**2:14**	3:21	4:28	5:35	6:42	7:49	8:56	10:03	11:10
:33.0	1:06.5	1:40.0	**2:13**	3:20	4:26	5:33	6:39	7:46	8:52	9:59	11:05
:33.0	1:06.0	1:39.0	**2:12**	3:18	4:24	5:30	6:36	7:42	8:48	9:54	11:00
:33.0	1:05.5	1:38.0	**2:11**	3:17	4:22	5:28	6:33	7:39	8:44	9:50	10:55
:32.5	1:05.0	1:37.5	**2:10**	3:15	4:20	5:25	6:30	7:35	8:40	9:45	10:50
:32.0	1:04.5	1:37.0	**2:09**	3:14	4:18	5:23	6:27	7:32	8:36	9:41	10:45
:32.0	1:04.0	1:36.0	**2:08**	3:12	4:16	5:20	6:24	7:28	8:32	9:36	10:40
:32.0	1:03.5	1:35.0	**2:07**	3:11	4:14	5:18	6:21	7:25	8:28	9:32	10:35
:31.5	1:03.0	1:34.5	**2:06**	3:09	4:12	5:15	6:18	7:21	8:24	9:27	10:30
:31.0	1:02.5	1:34.0	**2:05**	3:08	4:10	5:13	6:15	7:18	8:20	9:23	10:25
:31.0	1:02.0	1:33.0	**2:04**	3:06	4:08	5:10	6:12	7:14	8:16	9:18	10:20
:31.0	1:01.5	1:32.0	**2:03**	3:05	4:06	5:08	6:09	7:11	8:12	9:14	10:15
:30.5	1:01.0	1:31.5	**2:02**	3:03	4:04	5:05	6:06	7:07	8:08	9:09	10:10
:30.0	1:00.5	1:31.0	**2:01**	3:02	4:02	5:03	6:03	7:04	8:04	9:05	10:05
:30.0	1:00.0	1:30.0	**2:00**	3:00	4:00	5:00	6:00	7:00	8:00	9:00	10:00
:30.0	:59.5	1:29.0	**1:59**	2:59	3:58	4:58	5:57	6:57	7:56	8:56	9:55
:29.5	:59.0	1:28.5	**1:58**	2:57	3:56	4:55	5:54	6:53	7:52	8:51	9:50
:29.0	:58.5	1:28.0	**1:57**	2:56	3:54	4:53	5:51	6:50	7:48	8:47	9:45
:29.0	:58.0	1:27.0	**1:56**	2:54	3:52	4:50	5:48	6:46	7:44	8:42	9:40
:29.0	:57.5	1:26.0	**1:55**	2:53	3:50	4:48	5:45	6:43	7:40	8:38	9:35
:28.5	:57.0	1:25.5	**1:54**	2:51	3:48	4:45	5:42	6:39	7:36	8:33	9:30
:28.0	:56.5	1:25.0	**1:53**	2:50	3:46	4:43	5:39	6:36	7:32	8:29	9:25
:28.0	:56.0	1:24.0	**1:52**	2:48	3:44	4:40	5:36	6:32	7:28	8:24	9:20
:28.0	:55.5	1:23.0	**1:51**	2:47	3:42	4:38	5:33	6:29	7:24	8:20	9:15
:27.5	:55.0	1:22.5	**1:50**	2:45	3:40	4:35	5:30	6:25	7:20	8:15	9:10
:27.0	:54.5	1:22.0	**1:49**	2:44	3:38	4:33	5:27	6:22	7:16	8:11	9:05
:27.0	:54.0	1:21.0	**1:48**	2:42	3:36	4:30	5:24	6:18	7:12	8:06	9:00
:27.0	:53.5	1:20.0	**1:47**	2:41	3:34	4:28	5:21	6:15	7:08	8:02	8:55
:26.5	:53.0	1:19.5	**1:46**	2:39	3:32	4:25	5:18	6:11	7:04	7:57	8:50

CRUISE TIMES CHART

25	50	75	Cruise pace per 100	150	200	250	300	350	400	450	500
:26.0	:52.5	1:19.0	**1:45**	2:38	3:30	4:23	5:15	6:08	7:00	7:53	8:45
:26.0	:52.0	1:18.0	**1:44**	2:36	3:28	4:20	5:12	6:04	6:56	7:48	8:40
:26.0	:51.5	1:17.0	**1:43**	2:35	3:26	4:18	5:09	6:01	6:52	7:44	8:35
:25.5	:51.0	1:16.5	**1:42**	2:33	3:24	4:15	5:06	5:57	6:48	7:39	8:30
:25.0	:50.5	1:16.0	**1:41**	2:32	3:22	4:13	5:03	5:54	6:44	7:35	8:25
:25.0	:50.0	1:15.0	**1:40**	2:30	3:20	4:10	5:00	5:50	6:40	7:30	8:20
:25.0	:49.5	1:14.0	**1:39**	2:29	3:18	4:08	4:57	5:47	6:36	7:26	8:15
:24.5	:49.0	1:13.5	**1:38**	2:27	3:16	4:05	4:54	5:43	6:32	7:21	8:10
:24.0	:48.5	1:13.0	**1:37**	2:26	3:14	4:03	4:51	5:40	6:28	7:17	8:05
:24.0	:48.0	1:12.0	**1:36**	2:24	3:12	4:00	4:48	5:36	6:24	7:12	8:00
:24.0	:47.5	1:11.0	**1:35**	2:23	3:10	3:58	4:45	5:33	6:20	7:08	7:55
:23.5	:47.0	1:10.5	**1:34**	2:21	3:08	3:55	4:42	5:29	6:16	7:03	7:50
:23.0	:46.5	1:10.0	**1:33**	2:20	3:06	3:53	4:39	5:26	6:12	6:59	7:45
:23.0	:46.0	1:09.0	**1:32**	2:18	3:04	3:50	4:36	5:22	6:08	6:54	7:40
:23.0	:45.5	1:08.0	**1:31**	2:17	3:02	3:48	4:33	5:19	6:04	6:50	7:35
:22.5	:45.0	1:07.5	**1:30**	2:15	3:00	3:45	4:30	5:15	6:00	6:45	7:30
:22.0	:44.5	1:07.0	**1:29**	2:14	2:58	3:43	4:27	5:12	5:56	6:41	7:25
:22.0	:44.0	1:06.0	**1:28**	2:12	2:56	3:40	4:24	5:08	5:52	6:36	7:20
:22.0	:43.5	1:05.0	**1:27**	2:11	2:54	3:38	4:21	5:05	5:48	6:32	7:15
:21.5	:43.0	1:04.5	**1:26**	2:09	2:52	3:35	4:18	5:01	5:44	6:27	7:10
:21.0	:42.5	1:04.0	**1:25**	2:08	2:50	3:33	4:15	4:58	5:40	6:23	7:05
:21.0	:42.0	1:03.0	**1:24**	2:06	2:48	3:30	4:12	4:54	5:36	6:18	7:00
:21.0	:41.5	1:02.0	**1:23**	2:05	2:46	3:28	4:09	4:51	5:32	6:14	6:55
:20.5	:41.0	1:01.5	**1:22**	2:03	2:44	3:25	4:06	4:47	5:28	6:09	6:50
:20.0	:40.5	1:01.0	**1:21**	2:02	2:42	3:23	4:03	4:44	5:24	6:05	6:45
:20.0	:40.0	1:00.0	**1:20**	2:00	2:40	3:20	4:00	4:40	5:20	6:00	6:40
:20.0	:39.5	:59.0	**1:19**	1:59	2:38	3:18	3:57	4:37	5:16	5:56	6:35
:19.5	:39.0	:58.5	**1:18**	1:57	2:36	3:15	3:54	4:33	5:12	5:51	6:30
:19.0	:38.5	:58.0	**1:17**	1:56	2:34	3:13	3:51	4:30	5:08	5:47	6:25
:19.0	:38.0	:57.0	**1:16**	1:54	2:32	3:10	3:48	4:26	5:04	5:42	6:20
:19.0	:37.5	:56.0	**1:15**	1:53	2:30	3:08	3:45	4:23	5:00	5:38	6:15
:18.5	:37.0	:55.5	**1:14**	1:51	2:28	3:05	3:42	4:19	4:56	5:33	6:10
:18.0	:36.5	:55.0	**1:13**	1:50	2:26	3:03	3:39	4:16	4:52	5:29	6:05
:18.0	:36.0	:54.0	**1:12**	1:48	2:24	3:00	3:36	4:12	4:48	5:24	6:00
:18.0	:35.5	:53.0	**1:11**	1:47	2:22	2:58	3:33	4:09	4:44	5:20	5:55
:17.5	:35.0	:52.5	**1:10**	1:45	2:20	2:55	3:30	4:05	4:40	5:15	5:50
:17.0	:34.5	:52.0	**1:09**	1:44	2:18	2:53	3:27	4:02	4:36	5:11	5:45
:17.0	:34.0	:51.0	**1:08**	1:42	2:16	2:50	3:24	3:58	4:32	5:06	5:40
:17.0	:33.5	:50.0	**1:07**	1:41	2:14	2:48	3:21	3:55	4:28	5:02	5:35
:16.5	:33.0	:49.5	**1:06**	1:39	2:12	2:45	3:18	3:51	4:24	4:57	5:30
:16.0	:32.5	:49.0	**1:05**	1:38	2:10	2:43	3:15	3:48	4:20	4:53	5:25
:16.0	:32.0	:48.0	**1:04**	1:36	2:08	2:40	3:12	3:44	4:16	4:48	5:20
:16.0	:31.5	:47.0	**1:03**	1:35	2:06	2:38	3:09	3:41	4:12	4:44	5:15
:15.5	:31.0	:46.5	**1:02**	1:33	2:04	2:35	3:06	3:37	4:08	4:39	5:10
:15.0	:30.5	:46.0	**1:01**	1:32	2:02	2:33	3:03	3:34	4:04	4:35	5:05
:15.0	:30.0	:45.0	**1:00**	1:30	2:00	2:30	3:00	3:30	4:00	4:30	5:00

From E. Hines, 2008, *Fitness Swimming, 2nd ed.* (Champaign, IL: Human Kinetics).

APPENDIX D

CRUISE INTERVAL CHART						
Cruise pace per 100	50	75	100	150	200	250
4:00	2:10-57	3:15-55	4:15-56	6:25-55	8:30-57	10:30-54
3:58	2:10-55	3:15-53	4:15-53	6:20-52	8:30-52	10:30-49
3:56	2:10-54	3:10-53	4:15-51	6:20-48	8:30-48	10:20-44
3:54	2:10-52	3:10-51	4:10-50	6:15-46	8:20-44	10:20-39
3:52	2:05-54	3:10-49	4:10-47	6:10-43	8:20-40	10:10-34
3:50	2:05-52	3:05-49	4:05-46	6:10-40	8:10-35	10:10-29
3:48	2:05-50	3:05-47	4:05-43	6:05-37	8:10-30	10:00-24
3:46	2:05-49	3:05-45	4:05-41	6:00-34	8:10-26	10:00-19
3:44	2:00-50	3:00-45	4:00-40	6:00-31	8:00-23	9:50-17
3:42	2:00-49	3:00-43	4:00-37	5:55-28	8:00-18	9:50-11
3:40	2:00-47	3:00-40	3:55-35	5:50-26	7:50-15	9:40-07
3:38	2:00-45	2:55-40	3:55-32	5:50-22	7:50-10	9:40-01
3:36	2:00-44	2:55-37	3:50-32	5:45-19	7:50-06	9:30-57
3:34	1:55-45	2:55-34	3:50-29	5:45-16	7:40-03	9:30-51
3:32	1:55-43	2:50-35	3:50-25	5:40-13	7:40-58	9:20-47
3:30	1:55-41	2:50-33	3:45-25	5:35-11	7:30-55	9:20-41
3:28	1:55-39	2:50-30	3:45-22	5:35-07	7:30-50	9:10-37
3:26	1:55-37	2:45-31	3:40-22	5:30-04	7:30-46	9:10-31
3:24	1:50-40	2:45-29	3:40-19	5:25-02	7:20-43	9:00-27
3:22	1:50-38	2:45-26	3:35-18	5:25-58	7:20-38	9:00-21
3:20	1:50-36	2:40-27	3:35-15	5:20-56	7:05-36	8:50-17
3:18	1:50-34	2:40-25	3:35-12	5:15-53	7:00-32	8:50-11
3:16	1:50-32	2:40-22	3:30-12	5:15-49	7:00-27	8:40-07
3:14	1:45-35	2:40-19	3:30-09	5:10-47	6:55-23	8:40-01
3:12	1:45-33	2:35-20	3:25-08	5:10-43	6:50-20	8:30-57
3:10	1:45-31	2:35-18	3:25-05	5:05-41	6:45-16	8:30-51
3:08	1:45-29	2:35-15	3:25-02	5:00-38	6:40-12	8:20-47
3:06	1:40-31	2:30-16	3:20-02	5:00-34	6:35-07	8:20-41
3:04	1:40-30	2:30-14	3:20-59	4:55-31	6:35-02	8:10-35
3:02	1:40-28	2:30-11	3:15-58	4:50-28	6:30-58	8:10-29
3:00	1:40-26	2:25-12	3:15-55	4:50-25	6:25-55	8:00-25
2:58	1:40-24	2:25-10	3:10-55	4:45-22	6:20-51	8:00-19
2:56	1:35-26	2:25-07	3:10-52	4:40-20	6:15-47	7:50-15
2:54	1:35-25	2:20-08	3:10-49	4:40-16	6:10-43	7:50-09
2:52	1:35-23	2:20-05	3:05-48	4:35-13	6:05-39	7:40-05

Instructions: Use the cruise pace per 100 you recorded from one of the T-swim cruise pace charts. Look in the bolded cruise pace per 100 column and find the entry closest to your recorded cruise pace. Look across both pages and write down the distance and cruise intervals for each column across that line.

CRUISE INTERVAL CHART					
Cruise pace per 100	300	350	400	450	500
4:00	12:45-52	14:45-51	16:45-50	18:45-49	20:45-48
3:58	12:30-46	14:30-44	16:30-42	18:30-40	20:30-38
3:56	12:30-40	14:30-37	16:30-34	18:30-31	20:30-31
3:54	12:30-34	14:15-30	16:15-26	18:15-22	20:15-18
3:52	12:10-29	14:15-23	16:15-18	18:00-13	20:00-08
3:50	12:00-23	14:15-16	16:00-10	18:00-04	20:00-01
3:48	12:00-17	14:00-10	16:00-02	17:45-55	19:45-48
3:46	11:50-11	14:00-03	15:45-54	17:45-46	19:30-38
3:44	11:50-05	13:45-56	15:45-47	17:30-37	19:30-31
3:42	11:40-59	13:45-49	15:30-39	17:15-29	19:15-18
3:40	11:30-53	13:30-42	15:30-31	17:15-20	19:00-09
3:38	11:30-47	13:30-35	15:15-23	17:00-11	19:00-01
3:36	11:20-41	13:15-28	15:00-15	17:00-02	18:45-49
3:34	11:20-35	13:15-21	15:00-07	16:45-53	18:30-39
3:32	11:10-29	13:00-14	14:45-59	16:30-44	18:30-31
3:30	11:00-23	13:00-07	14:45-51	16:30-35	18:15-19
3:28	11:00-17	12:45-00	14:30-43	16:15-26	18:00-09
3:26	10:50-11	12:45-53	14:30-35	16:15-17	18:00-01
3:24	10:50-05	12:30-46	14:15-27	16:00-08	17:45-49
3:22	10:40-59	12:30-39	14:15-19	15:45-59	17:30-39
3:20	10:30-54	12:10-33	14:00-12	15:45-51	17:30-31
3:18	10:30-48	12:10-26	14:00-04	15:30-42	17:15-20
3:16	10:20-42	12:00-19	13:45-56	15:30-33	17:00-10
3:14	10:20-36	11:50-12	13:45-48	15:15-24	17:00-01
3:12	10:10-30	11:50-05	13:30-40	15:00-15	16:45-50
3:10	10:00-24	11:40-58	13:30-32	15:00-06	16:30-40
3:08	10:00-18	11:30-51	13:15-24	14:45-57	16:30-31
3:06	9:50-14	11:30-44	13:00-16	14:45-48	16:15-20
3:04	9:50-08	11:20-37	13:00-08	14:30-39	16:00-10
3:02	9:40-02	11:10-30	12:45-00	14:15-30	16:00-01
3:00	9:30-57	11:00-23	12:45-52	14:15-21	15:45-51
2:58	9:30-50	11:00-16	12:30-44	14:00-12	15:30-41
2:56	9:20-44	10:50-09	12:30-36	14:00-04	15:30-31
2:54	9:20-38	10:40-02	12:10-29	13:45-55	15:15-21
2:52	9:10-32	10:40-55	12:00-21	13:30-46	15:00-11

(continued)

CRUISE INTERVAL CHART						
Cruise pace per 100	50	75	100	150	200	250
2:50	1:35-21	2:20-03	3:05-45	4:35-10	6:05-35	7:40-59
2:48	1:35-19	2:15-04	3:00-45	4:30-07	6:00-31	7:30-55
2:46	1:30-21	2:15-01	3:00-42	4:25-05	5:55-27	7:30-49
2:44	1:30-20	2:15-59	2:55-40	4:25-01	5:50-23	7:20-45
2:42	1:30-18	2:10-00	2:55-37	4:20-58	5:45-19	7:20-39
2:40	1:30-16	2:10-57	2:55-33	4:15-56	5:40-16	7:05-36
2:38	1:30-14	2:10-55	2:50-34	4:15-52	5:35-12	7:00-31
2:36	1:25-16	2:10-52	2:50-30	4:10-50	5:35-07	6:55-26
2:34	1:25-15	2:05-53	2:45-30	4:05-47	5:30-03	6:50-21
2:32	1:25-13	2:05-50	2:45-27	4:05-43	5:25-59	6:45-16
2:30	1:25-11	2:05-48	2:40-27	4:00-41	5:20-56	6:40-11
2:28	1:20-13	2:00-49	2:40-24	4:00-37	5:15-52	6:35-05
2:26	1:20-11	2:00-46	2:40-20	3:55-34	5:10-48	6:30-00
2:24	1:20-10	2:00-44	2:35-20	3:50-32	5:10-43	6:25-55
2:22	1:20-08	1:55-44	2:35-17	3:50-27	5:05-39	6:20-50
2:20	1:20-06	1:55-41	2:30-17	3:45-25	5:00-36	6:15-45
2:18	1:15-08	1:55-38	2:30-14	3:45-20	4:55-31	6:10-40
2:16	1:15-06	1:50-40	2:30-10	3:40-19	4:50-27	6:05-35
2:14	1:15-05	1:50-37	2:25-10	3:35-17	4:45-23	6:00-30
2:12	1:15-03	1:50-34	2:25-07	3:35-12	4:40-20	5:50-26
2:10	1:15-01	1:45-35	2:20-07	3:30-10	4:40-15	5:45-21
2:08	1:10-03	1:45-33	2:20-04	3:25-08	4:35-11	5:40-16
2:06	1:10-01	1:45-30	2:15-04	3:25-04	4:30-07	5:35-11
2:04	1:10-00	1:40-31	2:15-00	3:20-02	4:25-03	5:30-06
2:02	1:10-58	1:40-29	2:15-57	3:15-00	4:20-00	5:25-01
2:00	1:05-00	1:40-26	2:10-57	3:15-55	4:15-56	5:20-56
1:59	1:05-59	1:40-24	2:10-55	3:15-53	4:15-53	5:20-53
1:58	1:05-58	1:40-23	2:10-54	3:10-53	4:15-51	5:15-51
1:57	1:05-57	1:35-26	2:10-52	3:10-51	4:10-50	5:15-48
1:56	1:05-56	1:35-25	2:05-54	3:10-49	4:10-47	5:10-46
1:55	1:05-55	1:35-23	2:05-52	3:05-49	4:05-46	5:05-44
1:54	1:05-55	1:35-22	2:05-50	3:05-47	4:05-43	5:05-41
1:53	1:05-54	1:35-20	2:05-49	3:05-45	4:05-41	5:00-39
1:52	1:05-53	1:35-19	2:00-50	3:00-45	4:00-40	5:00-36
1:51	1:05-52	1:30-22	2:00-49	3:00-43	4:00-37	4:55-33
1:50	1:00-55	1:30-20	2:00-47	3:00-40	3:55-35	4:55-30
1:49	1:00-54	1:30-19	2:00-45	2:55-40	3:55-32	4:50-28
1:48	1:00-53	1:30-18	2:00-44	2:55-37	3:50-32	4:50-25
1:47	1:00-52	1:30-16	1:55-45	2:55-34	3:50-29	4:45-23
1:46	1:00-51	1:30-15	1:55-43	2:50-35	3:50-25	4:45-20
1:45	1:00-50	1:25-18	1:55-41	2:50-33	3:45-25	4:40-18
1:44	1:00-50	1:25-16	1:55-39	2:50-30	3:45-22	4:40-15
1:43	1:00-49	1:25-15	1:55-37	2:45-31	3:40-22	4:35-13

Cruise pace per 100	300	350	400	450	500
CRUISE INTERVAL CHART					
2:50	9:00-27	10:30-49	11:50-13	13:30-37	15:00-01
2:48	9:00-20	10:20-42	11:50-05	13:15-28	14:45-51
2:46	8:50-14	10:20-35	11:40-57	13:15-19	14:30-41
2:44	8:50-08	10:10-28	11:30-49	13:00-10	14:30-31
2:42	8:40-02	10:00-21	11:20-41	12:45-01	14:15-21
2:40	8:30-57	9:50-17	11:10-33	12:45-52	14:00-12
2:38	8:30-50	9:50-09	11:10-25	12:30-43	14:00-02
2:36	8:20-44	9:40-02	11:00-17	12:30-34	13:45-52
2:34	8:20-38	9:30-55	10:50-09	12:10-26	13:30-42
2:32	8:10-30	9:30-48	10:40-01	12:00-17	13:30-32
2:30	8:00-25	9:20-41	10:30-54	11:50-08	13:15-22
2:28	8:00-18	9:10-34	10:30-46	11:40-59	13:00-12
2:26	7:50-13	9:10-27	10:20-38	11:30-50	13:00-02
2:24	7:50-06	9:00-20	10:10-30	11:20-41	12:45-52
2:22	7:40-00	8:50-13	10:00-22	11:10-32	12:30-42
2:20	7:30-55	8:40-07	9:50-17	11:00-23	12:10-33
2:18	7:30-48	8:40-59	9:50-08	11:00-14	12:00-23
2:16	7:20-43	8:30-52	9:40-00	10:50-05	11:50-13
2:14	7:20-36	8:20-45	9:30-52	10:40-56	11:40-03
2:12	7:00-32	8:20-38	9:20-44	10:30-48	11:30-53
2:10	6:55-26	8:10-29	9:10-37	10:20-39	11:20-43
2:08	6:50-20	8:00-23	9:10-28	10:10-30	11:10-33
2:06	6:45-13	8:00-15	9:00-20	10:00-21	11:00-23
2:04	6:35-07	7:50-08	8:50-12	9:50-14	10:50-13
2:02	6:30-01	7:40-02	8:40-04	9:40-05	10:40-03
2:00	6:25-55	7:30-55	8:30-57	9:30-57	10:30-54
1:59	6:20-52	7:30-51	8:30-52	9:30-52	10:30-49
1:58	6:20-48	7:30-47	8:30-48	9:30-47	10:20-44
1:57	6:15-46	7:20-44	8:20-44	9:20-43	10:20-39
1:56	6:10-43	7:20-40	8:20-40	9:20-38	10:10-34
1:55	6:10-40	7:20-36	8:10-35	9:10-34	10:10-29
1:54	6:05-37	7:05-35	8:10-30	9:10-29	10:00-24
1:53	6:00-34	7:00-31	8:10-26	9:00-25	10:00-19
1:52	6:00-31	7:00-27	8:00-23	9:00-20	9:50-17
1:51	5:55-28	6:55-24	8:00-18	8:50-16	9:50-11
1:50	5:50-26	6:50-21	7:50-15	8:50-11	9:40-07
1:49	5:50-22	6:45-17	7:50-10	8:50-06	9:40-01
1:48	5:45-19	6:45-13	7:50-06	8:40-02	9:30-57
1:47	5:45-16	6:40-10	7:40-03	8:40-57	9:30-51
1:46	5:40-13	6:35-06	7:40-58	8:30-53	9:20-47
1:45	5:35-11	6:30-03	7:30-55	8:30-48	9:20-41
1:44	5:35-07	6:30-58	7:30-50	8:20-44	9:10-37
1:43	5:30-04	6:25-55	7:30-46	8:20-39	9:10-31

(continued)

CRUISE INTERVAL CHART						
Cruise pace per 100	50	75	100	150	200	250
1:42	1:00-48	1:25-14	1:50-40	2:45-29	3:40-19	4:35-10
1:41	1:00-47	1:25-12	1:50-38	2:45-26	3:35-18	4:30-08
1:40		1:25-11	1:50-36	2:40-27	3:35-15	4:25-06
1:39		1:25-09	1:50-34	2:40-25	3:35-12	4:25-03
1:38		1:20-12	1:50-32	2:40-22	3:30-12	4:20-01
1:37		1:20-11	1:45-35	2:40-19	3:30-09	4:20-58
1:36		1:20-10	1:45-33	2:35-20	3:25-08	4:15-56
1:35		1:20-08	1:45-31	2:35-18	3:25-05	4:15-53
1:34		1:20-07	1:45-29	2:35-15	3:25-02	4:10-51
1:33		1:20-05	1:40-31	2:30-16	3:20-02	4:10-48
1:32		1:15-08	1:40-30	2:30-14	3:20-59	4:05-46
1:31		1:15-07	1:40-28	2:30-11	3:15-58	4:05-43
1:30		1:15-05	1:40-26	2:25-12	3:15-55	4:00-41
1:29		1:15-04	1:40-24	2:25-10	3:10-55	4:00-38
1:28		1:15-03	1:35-26	2:25-07	3:10-52	3:55-35
1:27		1:15-01	1:35-25	2:20-08	3:10-49	3:55-31
1:26		1:15-00	1:35-23	2:20-05	3:05-48	3:50-30
1:25		1:10-03	1:35-21	2:20-03	3:05-45	3:50-26
1:24		1:10-01	1:35-19	2:15-04	3:00-45	3:45-25
1:23		1:10-00	1:30-21	2:15-01	3:00-42	3:45-21
1:22		1:10-59	1:30-20	2:15-59	2:55-40	3:40-20
1:21		1:10-57	1:30-18	2:10-00	2:55-37	3:40-16
1:20		1:05-00	1:30-16	2:10-57	2:55-33	3:35-15
1:19		1:05-58	1:30-14	2:10-55	2:50-34	3:35-11
1:18		1:05-57	1:25-16	2:10-52	2:50-30	3:30-10
1:17		1:05-56	1:25-15	2:05-53	2:45-30	3:25-09
1:16		1:05-55	1:25-13	2:05-50	2:45-27	3:25-05
1:15		1:05-53	1:25-11	2:05-48	2:40-27	3:20-04
1:14		1:05-52	1:20-13	2:00-49	2:40-24	3:20-00
1:13		1:00-54	1:20-11	2:00-46	2:40-20	3:15-59
1:12		1:00-53	1:20-10	2:00-44	2:35-20	3:15-55
1:11		1:00-52	1:20-08	1:55-44	2:35-17	3:10-54
1:10		1:00-50	1:20-06	1:55-41	2:30-17	3:10-50
1:09		1:00-49	1:15-08	1:55-38	2:30-14	3:05-49
1:08		1:00-48	1:15-06	1:50-40	2:30-10	3:05-45
1:07		1:00-46	1:15-05	1:50-37	2:25-10	3:00-44
1:06			1:15-03	1:50-34	2:25-07	3:00-40
1:05			1:15-01	1:45-35	2:20-07	2:55-38
1:04			1:10-03	1:45-33	2:20-04	2:55-33
1:03			1:10-01	1:45-30	2:15-04	2:50-33
1:02			1:10-00	1:40-31	2:15-00	2:50-28
1:01			1:10-58	1:40-29	2:15-57	2:45-28
1:00			1:05-00	1:40-26	2:10-57	2:40-27

	CRUISE INTERVAL CHART				
Cruise pace per 100	300	350	400	450	500
1:42	5:25-02	6:20-52	7:20-43	8:10-34	9:00-27
1:41	5:25-58	6:15-49	7:20-38	8:10-29	9:00-21
1:40	5:20-56	6:15-45	7:05-36	8:00-25	8:50-17
1:39	5:15-53	6:10-41	7:00-32	8:00-20	8:50-11
1:38	5:15-49	6:05-38	7:00-27	8:00-15	8:40-07
1:37	5:10-47	6:00-35	6:55-23	7:50-11	8:40-01
1:36	5:10-43	6:00-31	6:50-20	7:50-06	8:30-57
1:35	5:05-41	5:55-28	6:45-16	7:40-02	8:30-51
1:34	5:00-38	5:50-24	6:40-12	7:40-57	8:20-47
1:33	5:00-34	5:50-20	6:35-07	7:30-53	8:20-41
1:32	4:55-31	5:45-17	6:35-02	7:30-48	8:10-35
1:31	4:50-28	5:40-14	6:30-58	7:20-44	8:10-29
1:30	4:50-25	5:35-11	6:25-55	7:20-39	8:00-25
1:29	4:45-22	5:35-06	6:20-51	7:20-34	8:00-19
1:28	4:40-20	5:30-03	6:15-47	7:00-32	7:50-15
1:27	4:40-16	5:25-00	6:10-43	6:55-27	7:50-09
1:26	4:35-13	5:20-57	6:05-39	6:55-22	7:40-05
1:25	4:35-10	5:20-53	6:05-35	6:50-18	7:40-59
1:24	4:30-07	5:15-49	6:00-31	6:45-13	7:30-55
1:23	4:25-05	5:10-46	5:55-27	6:40-09	7:30-49
1:22	4:25-01	5:05-43	5:50-23	6:35-03	7:20-45
1:21	4:20-58	5:05-39	5:45-19	6:30-59	7:20-39
1:20	4:15-56	5:00-36	5:40-16	6:25-55	7:05-36
1:19	4:15-52	4:55-31	5:35-12	6:20-50	7:00-31
1:18	4:10-50	4:50-28	5:35-07	6:15-46	6:55-26
1:17	4:05-47	4:50-24	5:30-03	6:10-41	6:50-21
1:16	4:05-43	4:45-21	5:25-59	6:05-37	6:45-16
1:15	4:00-41	4:40-18	5:20-56	6:00-33	6:40-11
1:14	4:00-37	4:35-15	5:15-52	5:55-28	6:35-05
1:13	3:55-34	4:35-10	5:10-48	5:50-24	6:30-00
1:12	3:50-32	4:30-07	5:10-43	5:45-19	6:25-55
1:11	3:50-27	4:25-04	5:05-39	5:40-15	6:20-50
1:10	3:45-25	4:20-01	5:00-36	5:35-11	6:15-45
1:09	3:45-20	4:20-56	4:55-31	5:30-06	6:10-40
1:08	3:40-19	4:15-53	4:50-27	5:25-02	6:05-35
1:07	3:35-17	4:10-50	4:45-23	5:20-57	6:00-30
1:06	3:35-12	4:05-47	4:40-20	5:15-53	5:50-26
1:05	3:30-10	4:05-43	4:40-15	5:15-48	5:45-21
1:04	3:25-08	4:00-40	4:35-11	5:10-43	5:40-16
1:03	3:25-04	3:55-36	4:30-07	5:05-39	5:35-11
1:02	3:20-02	3:55-30	4:25-03	5:00-34	5:30-06
1:01	3:15-00	3:50-28	4:20-00	4:55-29	5:25-01
1:00	3:15-55	3:45-25	4:15-56	4:50-25	5:20-56

From E. Hines, 2008, *Fitness Swimming, 2nd ed.* (Champaign, IL: Human Kinetics).

APPENDIX E

Focus Points

buoy pressure—Press your lungs toward the bottom of the pool. (page 34)

core-rotation tempo—Set swimming tempo with core rotation instead of with your arms. (page 154)

downhill swimming—Using buoy pressure to keep your hips and legs at the surface, which will make you feel like your whole body is tilted slightly downhill. (page 86)

downward angle arm extension—Extending the lead arm at a slightly-below-horizontal angle. (page 40, 61)

easy speed—Going fast, but making it feel and look easy rather than frantic. (page 166)

finish your strokes—Occasionally brush your thumb against your thigh to determine where your arm stroke finishes. (page 61)

forward lunge—Focus not on pulling one arm backward, but on feeling the other side of your body lunging forward as a result of core rotation. (page 139)

glove—Transferring an imaginary glove from hand to hand out in front of your body as you take strokes. (page 56)

hand and hip connection—Awareness and use of the internal muscular connection of the hand to the hip via the tension of your tight-line posture to power both the stroke and the entry. (page 119)

hand swapping—Keeping the extended arm in front of your body until the recovering, or entering, hand is ready to take its place. (page 86)

kayak paddling—Muscular tension that connects one hand across your back to the other hand and that transmits the action of the entering arm directly to the stroking arm, much like using a kayak paddle. (page 139)

kick from hips—Each kick should come predominantly from your hips, not from your knees. (page 103)

laser-beam rotation trigger—The recovering hand cuts through an imaginary laser beam that stretches across your lane at the front edge of your head, a few inches above the water's surface. Passing the imaginary laser beam triggers the next core rotation. (page 62)

marionette recovery—High elbow, low hand, forward-motion (not circuitous) recovery. (page 62)

neutral shoulder—Keeping the recovering elbow in front of the frontal body plane at all times. (page 62)

over-the-keg—Reaching over an imaginary keg as far out in front of the body as possible in order to make the catch at the beginning of your stroke. (page 61)

patches and cheeks—Keeping a patch of skin from one or both hips or from one or both butt cheeks exposed to the air at all times, especially when breathing. (page 56)

pierce (not push) down to extension—Entering arm pierces straight down to a fully extended position, as opposed to piercing forward then pushing down. (page 56)

red dot—Keeping an imaginary red dot in the center of the top of your head underwater and pointed at the end wall at all times. (page 44)

risky breathing—Keeping your head as deep as possible as you breathe—zero head-lift, zero torso-lift. (page 43)

shift and skate—Emulate a skater's surge of speed as he pushes off with one skate and shifts his weight into a glide on the other skate, which he holds until the next propulsive shift. (page 139)

side skating—Gliding on your side with your arm extended at a slightly downward angle while the recovering arm moves forward, past your head, to the laser-beam rotation-trigger point. (page 86)

sliding-board entry—Recapturing the potential energy of the high-elbow recovery to the kinetic energy of rotation and forward motion. (page 63)

snappy hips—Using your legs to drive the snappy rotations of your hips. (page 61)

stealth—Making as little noise as possible and disturbing the water as little as possible as you swim. (page 120)

stroke count—Count the strokes you take during each length. Count each hand as it enters the water, including the final hand entry at the end of the pool. (page 87)

tight line—Tall, tight, and straight posture vs. schlumpy posture. (page 31)

two-beat kick—Using one kick beat for each rotation and stroke instead of the three kicks per stroke that are used in six-beat kick timing. (page 120)

tube—An imaginary tube that your body and legs slide through as you swim. (page 102)

weightless arm—As you turn your head and breathe in, the lead arm should remain weightlessly extended. (page 120)

wide tracking—Each hand enters and extends directly in front of its own shoulder. The general lines of the strokes should be shoulder-width apart as well. (page 56)

Abbreviations, Acronyms, and Notations

alt—alternate repeats (or distances within a repeat) of two or more activities

avg—average

BOYLFS—breathe on your less favorite side

CInt—cruise interval

CPace—cruise pace

Dchoice—drill choice

Desc—descend, each one completed in less time than the previous one

Dmix—mix of drills

EZ—easy

good—side on which your skills are better

HR—heart rate

HHR—highest heart rate

IHR—immediate heart rate

LEnd—lactate endurance

lft—left

LOFO—last one, fast one

LTol—lactate tolerance

NS—negative split

OACI—on any comfortable interval

Opt—optional, as in *FinsOpt*

R—rest, as in :10R

RMin—minimum rest, as in :10RMin

RPE—rating of perceived exertion

rt—right

SBFins—short-blade fins

SGolf—swimming golf

SLSSS—super-low-and-slow stealth swimming

SLTHR—swimming lactate-threshold heart rate

SPL—strokes per length

TS—training snorkel

weak—side on which your skills are weaker

W/RInt—work/rest interval

List of Drills

Static Posture and Balance Drills (SPBDrills)

Dynamic Posture and Balance Drills (DPBDrills)

Stroke-Integration Drills (SIDrills)

Rotation-Connection Drills (RCDrills)

ABOUT THE AUTHOR

Emmett Hines is one of the top masters swimming coaches in the nation. He is one of only 13 coaches to hold the level 5 Masters certification, the American Swim Coaches Association's (ASCA) highest adult coaching certification. In 2002 he received the Masters Aquatic Coaches Association Lifetime Achievement Award. He also was honored as the U.S. Masters Swimming Coach of the Year in 1993. Hines has been coaching in some form since the age of 14. The director and head coach of H_2Ouston Swims, Hines has coached adult swimmers for more than 25 years—from beginners to those with Olympic pedigrees. He has conducted clinics across the country and internationally as a senior coach for Total Immersion Swim Camps, the world's most widely known and respected organization for adult swimming instruction.

Hines' articles have been featured in *Swim Magazine*, he writes a monthly column for *Runner Triathlete News*, and he has published over 200 articles in swimming and triathlon magazines and newsletters. He has spoken at the ASCA World Coaches Clinic and Pacific Coaches Clinic, two of the largest professional swim coaches' gatherings in the world. Swimmers under his guidance have won numerous team and individual national championship titles and set numerous national and world records. Hines has served as the assistant USMS editor for *Swim Magazine*, editor of the Masters Aquatic Coaches Association (MACA) newsletter, and editor of Gulf Masters Swim Committee (GMSC) newsletter.

Throughout all of his swim-related activities, Hines seeks to use his creativity and humor to expand the world of adult swimming while improving the knowledge and skill of swimmers and instructors alike.

His wife, Peggy, is a swim coach as well, and both of his boys are fish. Aside from swimming, the whole family is actively involved in competitive target archery.